SHAW
ON
MUSIC

EDITED BY

ERIC BENTLEY

APPLAUSE
NEW YORK • LONDON

Shaw On Music

Edited by Eric Bentley

Library of Congress Cataloging-in-Publication Data
Shaw, Bernard, 1856-1950.
     [Prose works. Selections.]
     Shaw on Music: a selection from the music criticism of
Bernard Shaw / made by Eric Bentley.
        p.   cm.
     ISBN 1-55783-149-1 (paper)
        1.   Music—England—London—History and   criticism.
     I. Bentley, Eric. 1916-   II. Title.
     ML286.8.L5S32   1995   95-5376
     780—dc20   CIP
                                  MN

APPLAUSE BOOKS

211 West 71st Street
New York, NY 10023
Phone (212) 496-7511
Fax: (212) 721-2856

406 Vale Road
Tonbridge Kent TN9 1XR
Phone 073 235-7755
Fax 073 207-7219

FOREWORD

Bernard Shaw served two terms as a regular music critic: 1888 to 1890 on *The Star* and 1890 to 1894 on *The World*. The pieces he wrote during the first term have been collected in *London Music in 1888–89 as Heard by Corno di Bassetto*, a single volume; those he wrote during the second in *Music in London 1890–94*, a set of three volumes. Shaw also wrote a short book on Wagner—*The Perfect Wagnerite* (1898)—and a scattering of articles distributed over the whole course of his long career.

To make a selection from this body of work is to face the problems of the anthologist in any large and rich field: since he cannot possibly please everybody, his surest hope of pleasing somebody is to begin by pleasing himself. In making this selection, I have pleased myself, and, if I cannot do more for readers of this volume, I can at least do them the courtesy of explaining *how* I have pleased myself, of stating what kind of thing I have chosen from Shaw's musical essays and what I have left alone.

Negative definition is always easier: I have not tried either to present a picture of musical London around 1890 or to give the fullest possible account of the mind and art of Bernard Shaw. Perhaps I have made a mistake? The journalism of Shaw is a mine for the musical and social historians, and one they have not yet exploited. The student of Shaw will find in this work of 1888–1894 much that prefigures the work of 1900 and 1920, while the Shaw enthusiast will find, among the music articles, some of the choicest examples of the master's wit and style.

But then the historian of England, musical or social, and the student of Shaw, professional or amateur, should read Shaw complete. If we are to cut down the music criticism to less than a quarter of its full bulk, we are doing so in the interests of—whom? My answer —not the only possible one, as I have admitted—is: the music lover. This is a book about music.

To make simply a book about music from the essays of so rich and many-sided a mind as Shaw's may seem an unduly puritanical procedure. Is not Shaw primarily something other than a music critic? And, in his music criticism, does he not forever digress onto every subject under the sun? He is; and he does. But, says W.H. Auden, he is also "probably the best music critic who ever lived." This is a large claim (I doubt that many people would agree to it); yet, so far as I know, it has (amazingly, perhaps) gone unchallenged.

The purpose of this book is to make the strongest possible case for Mr. Auden's thesis. Now any lawyer would agree that such a case could only be weakened by urging rival claims for Shaw: indeed it is probably because people admit that Shaw is a great playwright that they suppose he is not a great music critic. The fact that Shaw can "write on anything under the sun" is, as it were, *prima facie* evidence against what he writes on anything in particular.

I shall not insult the greatness of this music criticism by pleading for it. I limit myself to a single point. Shaw is also a great dramatic critic, and this *has* been conceded by all subsequent dramatic critics. I concur in the general judgment, yet, if I tried to compile a "book

on the drama" from Shaw's theatre articles, I should
find myself in a difficulty that does not face me with
the music articles. The dramatic pieces are all *arrière-
pensée*, the campaign oratory of a critic who wishes
to be elected Playwright. Now it is all very well to believe, as Shaw did, that all criticism is prejudiced, but,
with Shaw's drama criticism, the prejudice is more
important than anything else; much more than the essays
that go under that title, the theatre reviews are prefaces
to the plays of Shaw. This is a limitation, not a fault. My
point is that the music criticism is not limited in any
such way; for all Shaw's admissions of subjectivity, it
is as dispassionate as any critical writing can be. It is
entirely disinterested. It is inspired by pure joy at the
good, pure rage at the bad, in the art under observation. Pure is indeed the word for it. Following up Mr.
Auden's superlative with another, I would say that we
have here some of the purest criticism—of any art
whatsoever—in the language.

Why explain a man who always explained himself?
The point of this volume is not to add more words to
those that have already been written, but, on the contrary, by removing hundreds of thousands of words on
hundreds of topics, to leave ourselves with some one
hundred thousand words which are all, or very nearly
all, about music and musicians. I have assumed that
no one is going to exclaim: What a delicious oyster!
if all that is left is the pearl.

Eric Bentley

CONTENTS

Foreword by Eric Bentley

PART 1

The Point of View

PREFACE to *London Music in 1888–89*
as Heard by Corno di Bassetto   1

CRITICISM AND SUICIDE   32
DESTRUCTIVE FORCE   32
PERSONAL ANIMOSITY   34
TECHNICAL ANALYSIS   36
SIMPLY LISTEN   37
ELECTIONEERING   40
MY IMPOSTORSHIP   43
FUNERAL MARCH   46
RUSKIN ON MUSIC   48
MY STUFF AND DR STANFORD   56

PART 2

The Main Tradition

GLUCK'S ORFEO   62

MOZART

    Don Giovanni   67
    The Mozart Centenary, 1891   73
    Tuneful Little Trifles?   79
    His Gentleness   81
    Mozart and Beethoven   83

BEETHOVEN'S CENTENARY   83

ROSSINI CENTENARY, 1892   89

WEBER'S DER FREISCHÜTZ   93

BERLIOZ

    The Damnation of Faust   97
    The Trombone   103
    The Art of Composition   105

WAGNER

    Das Rheingold   105
    The Tone Poet   110
    Bayreuth   116

VERDI

    Falstaff   127
    A Word More about Verdi   133
    Spoof Opera   146

SCHÖNBERG AND ATONALITY   155

PART 3

Musical Questions

MORE ABOUT OPERA

    Acting in Opera   156
    Rigoletto   157
    Directing Opera   158

Cavalleria Rusticana   160
Dramatic Singing   162
A Bad Opera   164
Opera Burlesqued   169
Opera Impresario   173
The New Italian School   181

LIGHT ENTERTAINMENT

Sturgis and Sullivan   195
Gilbert and Offenbach   201
Gilbert and Solomon   203
Gilbert and Cellier   209
Gilbert, Sullivan & Others   213
Gilbert and Sullivan   214
Jane Annie   220
Music Hall   224
Christmas Pantomime   225
Bands   230
Comic Opera   233
Yvette Guilbert   239

MUSIC AND RELIGION

What Is Religious?   243
Handel's Messiah   245
The Messiah Again   247
Music in Church   252
Mendelssohn's Elijah   255
A Bad Oratorio   257

MISCELLANY

Richard III as Music   264
The Marseillaise   268
In the West Country   270
As Far as Greenwich   276
Diction   280
La Vie Parisienne   283
The Popular Dramatist   290
Incidental Music   292
Paderewski   299
A Recital Lecture   302
The Public   305

The Point
of View

PREFACE *to* London Music in 1888–89
as Heard by Corno di Bassetto

When my maiden novel, called Immaturity, was printed fifty years after it was written, I prefaced it with some account of the unhappy-go-lucky way in which I was brought up, ending with the nine years of shabby genteel destitution during which my attempts to gain a footing in literature were a complete and apparently hopeless failure.

I was rescued from this condition by William Archer, who transferred some of his book reviewing work to me, and pushed me into a post as picture critic which had been pushed on him, and for which he considered himself unqualified, as in fact he was. So, as reviewer for the old Pall Mall Gazette and picture critic for Edmund Yates's then fashionable weekly, The World, I carried on until I found an opening which I can explain only by describing the musical side of my childhood, to which I made only a passing allusion in my Immaturity preface, but which was of cardinal importance in my education.

In 1888, I being then 32 and already a noted critic and political agitator, the Star newspaper was founded under the editorship of the late T. P. O'Connor (nicknamed Tay Pay by Yates), who had for his very much more competent assistant the late H. W.

Massingham. Tay Pay survived until 1936; but his mind never advanced beyond the year 1865, though his Fenian sympathies and his hearty detestation of the English nation disguised that defect from him. Massingham induced him to invite me to join the political staff of his paper; but as I had already, fourteen years before Lenin, read Karl Marx, and was preaching Socialism at every street corner or other available forum in London and the provinces, the effect of my articles on Tay Pay may be imagined. He refused to print them, and told me that, man alive, it would be five hundred years before such stuff would become practical political journalism. He was too goodnatured to sack me; and I did not want to throw away my job; so I got him out of his difficulty by asking him to let me have two columns a week for a feuilleton on music. He was glad to get rid of my politics on these terms; but he stipulated that—musical criticism being known to him only as unreadable and unintelligible jargon—I should, for God's sake, not write about Bach in B Minor. I was quite alive to that danger: in fact I had made my proposal because I believed I could make musical criticism readable even by the deaf. Besides, my terms were moderate: two guineas a week.

I was strong on the need for signed criticism written in the first person instead of the journalistic "we"; but as I then had no name worth signing, and G. B. S. meant nothing to the public, I had to invent a fantastic personality with something like a foreign title. I thought of Count di Luna (a character in Verdi's Trovatore), but finally changed it for Corno di Bassetto, as it sounded like a foreign title, and nobody knew what a corno di bassetto was.

As a matter of fact the corno di bassetto is not a foreigner with a title but a musical instrument called in English the basset horn. It is a wretched instrument, now completely snuffed out for general use by the bass clarinet. It would be forgotten and unplayed if it were not that Mozart has scored for it in his Requiem, evidently because its peculiar watery melancholy, and the total absence of any richness or passion in its tone, is just the thing for a funeral. Mendelssohn wrote some chamber music for it, presumably to oblige somebody who played it; and it is kept alive by these works and by our Mr Whall. If I had ever heard a note of it in 1888 I should not have selected it for a character which I intended to be sparkling. The devil himself could not make a basset horn sparkle.

For two years I sparkled every week in The Star under this ridiculous name, and in a manner so absolutely unlike the conventional musical criticism of the time that all the journalists believed that the affair was a huge joke, the point of which was that I knew nothing whatever about music. How it had come about that I was one of the few critics of that time who really knew their business I can explain only by picking up the thread of autobiography which I dropped in my scrappy prefix to Immaturity. For the sake of those who have not read the Immaturity preface, or have forgotten it, I shall have to repeat here some of my father's history, but only so far as is necessary to explain the situation of my mother.

Technically speaking I should say she was the worst mother conceivable, always, however, within the limits of the fact that she was incapable of unkindness to any child, animal, or flower, or indeed to any person or thing whatsoever. But if such a thing as a maternity welfare centre had been established or even imagined in Ireland in her time, and she had been induced to visit it, every precept of it would have been laughably strange to her. Though she had been severely educated up to the highest standard for Irish "carriage ladies" of her time, she was much more like a Trobriand islander as described by Mr Malinowski than like a modern Cambridge lady graduate in respect of accepting all the habits, good or bad, of the Irish society in which she was brought up as part of an uncontrollable order of nature. She went her own way with so complete a disregard and even unconsciousness of convention and scandal and prejudice that it was impossible to doubt her good faith and innocence; but it never occurred to her that other people, especially children, needed guidance or training, or that it mattered in the least what they ate and drank or what they did as long as they were not actively mischievous. She accepted me as a natural and customary phenomenon, and took it for granted that I should go on occurring in that way. In short, living to her was not an art: it was something that happened. But there were unkind parts of it that could be avoided; and among these were the constraints and tyrannies, the scoldings and browbeatings and punishments she had suffered in her childhood as the method of her education. In her righteous reaction against it she reached a negative attitude in which, having no substitute to propose, she carried domestic anarchy as far as in the nature of things it can be carried.

She had been tyrannously taught French enough to recite one or two of La Fontaine's fables; to play the piano the wrong way; to harmonize by rule from Logier's Thoroughbass; to sit up straight and speak and dress and behave like a lady, and an Irish lady at that. She knew nothing of the value of money nor of housekeeping nor of hygiene nor of anything that could be left to servants or governesses or parents or solicitors or apothecaries or any other member of the retinue, indoor and outdoor, of a country house. She had great expectations from a humpbacked little aunt, a fairylike creature with a will of iron, who had brought up her motherless niece with a firm determination to make her a paragon of good breeding, to achieve a distinguished marriage for her, and to leave her all her money as a dowry.

Manufacturing destinies for other people is a dangerous game. Its results are usually as unexpected as those of a first-rate European war. When my mother came to marriageable age her long widowed father married again. The brother of his late wife, to whom he was considerably in debt, disapproved so strongly that on learning the date of the approaching ceremony from my mother he had the bridegroom arrested on his way to church. My grandfather naturally resented this manoeuvre, and in his wrath could not be persuaded that his daughter was not my granduncle's accomplice in it. Visits to relatives in Dublin provided a temporary refuge for her; and the affair would have blown over but for the intervention of my father.

My father was a very ineligible suitor for a paragon with great expectations. His family pretensions were enormous; but they were founded on many generations of younger sons, and were purely psychological. He had managed to acquire a gentlemanly post in the law courts. This post had been abolished and its holder pensioned. By selling the pension he was enabled to start in business as a wholesaler in the corn trade (retail trade was beneath his family dignity) of which he knew nothing. He accentuated this deficiency by becoming the partner of a Mr Clibborn, who had served an apprenticeship to the cloth trade. Their combined ignorances kept the business going, mainly by its own inertia, until they and it died. Many years after this event I paid a visit of curiosity to Jervis St Dublin; and there, on one of the pillars of a small portico, I found the ancient inscription "Clibborn & Shaw" still decipherable, as it were on the tombs of the Pharaohs. I cannot believe that this business yielded my father at any time more than three or four hundred a year; and it got less as time went on, as that partic-

ular kind of business was dying a slow death throughout the latter half of the nineteenth century.

My father was in principle an ardent teetotaller. Nobody ever felt the disgrace and misery and endless
mischief of drunkenness as he did: he impressed it so
deeply on me in my earliest years that I have been a
teetotaller ever since. Unfortunately his conviction in
this matter was founded on personal experience. He
was the victim of a drink neurosis which cropped up
in his family from time to time: a miserable affliction,
quite unconvivial, and accompanied by torments of remorse and shame.

My father was past forty, and no doubt had san-
guine illusions as to the future of his newly acquired
business when he fell in love with my mother and was
emboldened by her expectations and his business
hopes to propose to her just at the moment when marriage seemed her only way of escape from an angry
father and a stepmother. Immediately all her relatives,
who had tolerated this middle-aged gentleman as a
perfectly safe acquaintance with an agreeable vein of
humor, denounced him as a notorious drunkard. My
mother, suspicious of this sudden change of front, put
the question directly to my father. His eloquence and
sincerity convinced her that he was, as he claimed to
be, and as he was in principle, a bigoted teetotaller.
She married him; and her disappointed and infuriated
aunt disinherited her, not foreseeing that the consequences of the marriage would include so remarkable
a phenomenon as myself.

When my mother was disillusioned, and found out
what living on a few hundreds a year with three children meant, even in a country where a general servant
could be obtained for eight pounds a year, her condition must have been about as unhappy and her pros-
pects as apparently hopeless as her aunt could have
desired even in her most vindictive moments.

But there was one trump in her hand. She was fond of music, and had a mezzo-soprano voice of remarkable purity of tone. In the next street to ours, Harrington Street, where the houses were bigger and more fashionable than in our little by-street, there was a teacher of singing, lamed by an accident in childhood which had left one of his legs shorter than the other, but a man of mesmeric vitality and force. He was a bachelor living with his brother, whom he supported and adored, and a terrible old woman who was his servant of all work. His name was George John Vandaleur Lee, known in Dublin as Mr G. J. Lee. Singing lessons were cheap in Dublin; and my mother went to Lee to learn how to sing properly. He trained her voice to such purpose that she became indispensable to him as an amateur prima donna. For he was a most magnetic conductor and an indefatigable organizer of concerts, and later on of operas, with such amateur talent, vocal and orchestral, as he could discover and train in Dublin, which, as far as public professional music was concerned, was, outside the churches, practically a vacuum.

Lee soon found his way into our house, first by giving my mother lessons there, and then by using our drawing-room for rehearsals. I can only guess that the inadequacies of old Ellen in the Harrington Street house, and perhaps the incompatibilities of the brother, outweighed the comparative smallness of our house in Synge Street. My mother soon became not only prima donna and chorus leader but general musical factotum in the whirlpool of Lee's activity. Her grounding in Logier's Thoroughbass enabled her to take boundless liberties with composers. When authentic band parts were missing she thought nothing of making up an orchestral accompaniment of her own from the pianoforte score. Lee, as far as I know, had never seen a full orchestral score in his life: he con-

ducted from a first violin part or from the vocal score,
and had not, I think, any decided notion of orchestration as an idiosyncratic and characteristic part of a
composer's work. He had no scholarship according to
modern ideas; but he could do what Wagner said is the
whole duty of a conductor: he could give the right
time to the band; and he could pull it out of its amateur difficulties in emergencies by sheer mesmerism.
Though he could not, or at any rate within my hearing
never did sing a note, his taste in singing was classically perfect. In his search for the secret of *bel canto*
he had gone to all the teachers within his reach. They
told him that there was a voice in the head, a voice
in the throat, and a voice in the chest. He dissected
birds, and, with the connivance of medical friends, human subjects, in his search for these three organs. He
then told the teachers authoritatively that the three
voices were fabulous, and that the voice was produced
by a single instrument called the larynx. They replied
that musical art had nothing to do with anatomy, and
that for a musician to practise dissection was un-
heard-of and disgusting. But as, tested by results, their
efforts to teach their pupils to screech like locomotive
whistles not only outraged his ear but wrecked the
voices and often the health of their victims, their practice was as unacceptable to him as their theory.

Thus Lee became the enemy of every teacher of
singing in Dublin; and they reciprocated heartily. In
this negative attitude he was left until, at the opera,
he heard an Italian baritone named Badeali, who at
the age of 80, when he first discovered these islands,
had a perfectly preserved voice, and, to Lee's taste, a
perfectly produced one. Lee, thanks to his dissections,
listened with a clear knowledge of what a larynx is
really like. The other vocal organs and their action
were obvious and conscious. Guided by this knowledge, and by his fine ear, his fastidious taste, and his

instinct, he found out what Badeali was doing when he was singing. The other teachers were interested in Badeali only because one of his accomplishments was to drink a glass of wine and sing a sustained note at the same time. Finally Lee equipped himself with a teaching method which became a religion for him: the only religion, I may add, he ever professed. And my mother, as his pupil, learnt and embraced this musical faith, and rejected all other creeds as uninteresting superstitions. And it did not fail her; for she lived to be Badeali's age and kept her voice without a scrape on it until the end.

I have to dwell on The Method, as we called it in the family, because my mother's association with Lee, and the *ménage à trois* in which it resulted, would be unpleasantly misunderstood without this clue to it. For after the death of Lee's brother, which affected him to the verge of suicide, we left our respective houses and went to live in the same house, number one Hatch Street, which was half in Lower Leeson Street. The arrangement was economical; for we could not afford to live in a fashionable house, and Lee could not afford to give lessons in an unfashionable one, though, being a bachelor, he needed only a music room and a bedroom. We also shared a cottage in Dalkey, high up on Torca Hill, with all Dublin Bay from Dalkey Island to Howth visible from the garden, and all Killiney Bay with the Wicklow mountains in the background from the hall door. Lee bought this cottage and presented it to my mother, though she never had any legal claim to it and did not benefit by its sale later on. It was not conveniently situated for rehearsals or lessons; but there were musical neighbors who allowed me to some extent to run in and out of their houses when there was music going on.

The *ménage à trois*, alternating between Hatch St and Dalkey, worked in its ramshackle way quite

smoothly until I was fifteen or thereabouts, when Lee
went to London and our family broke up into fragments that never got pieced together again.

In telling the story so far, I have had to reconstruct
the part of it which occurred before I came into it and
began, as my nurse put it, to take notice. I can remember the ante-Lee period in Synge St when my father,
as sole chief of the household, read family prayers and
formally admitted that we had done those things
which we ought not to have done and left undone
those things which we ought to have done, which was
certainly true as far as I was personally concerned.
He added that there was no health in us; and this also
was true enough about myself; for Dr Newland, our
apothecary, was in almost continual attendance to ad-
minister cathartics; and when I had a sore throat I
used to hold out for sixpence before submitting to a
mustard plaster round my neck. We children (I had
two sisters older than myself and no brothers) were
abandoned entirely to the servants, who, with the exception of Nurse Williams, who was a good and honest
woman, were utterly unfit to be trusted with the
charge of three cats, much less three children. I had
my meals in the kitchen, mostly of stewed beef, which
I loathed, badly cooked potatoes, sound or diseased as
the case might be, and much too much tea out of
brown delft teapots left to "draw" on the hob until it
was pure tannin. Sugar I stole. I was never hungry,
because my father, often insufficiently fed in his childhood, had such a horror of child hunger that he insisted on unlimited bread and butter being always
within our reach. When I was troublesome a servant
thumped me on the head until one day, greatly daring, I rebelled, and, on finding her collapse abjectly,
became thenceforth uncontrollable. I hated the servants and liked my mother because, on the one or two
rare and delightful occasions when she buttered my

bread for me, she buttered it thickly instead of merely wiping a knife on it. Her almost complete neglect of me had the advantage that I could idolize her to the utmost pitch of my imagination and had no sordid or disillusioning contacts with her. It was a privilege to be taken for a walk or a visit with her, or on an excursion.

My ordinary exercise whilst I was still too young to be allowed out by myself was to be taken out by a servant, who was supposed to air me on the banks of the canal or round the fashionable squares where the atmosphere was esteemed salubrious and the surroundings gentlemanly. Actually she took me into the slums to visit her private friends, who dwelt in squalid tenements. When she met a generous male acquaintance who insisted on treating her she took me into the public house bars, where I was regaled with lemonade and gingerbeer; but I did not enjoy these treats, because my father's eloquence on the evil of drink had given me an impression that a public house was a wicked place into which I should not have been taken. Thus were laid the foundations of my lifelong hatred of poverty, and the devotion of all my public life to the task of exterminating the poor and rendering their resurrection for ever impossible.

Note, by the way, that I should have been much more decently brought up if my parents had been too poor to afford servants.

As to early education I can remember our daily governess, Miss Hill, a needy lady who seemed to me much older than she can really have been. She puzzled me with her attempts to teach me to read; for I can remember no time at which a page of print was not intelligible to me, and can only suppose that I was born literate. She tried to give me and my two sisters a taste for poetry by reciting "Stop; for thy tread is on an empire's dust" at us, and only succeeded, poor lady, in awakening our sense of derisive humor. She punished me by little strokes with her fingers that would not have discomposed a fly, and even persuaded me that I ought to cry and feel disgraced on such occasions. She gave us judgment books and taught us to feel jubilant when after her departure we could rush to the kitchen crying "No marks today" and to hang back ashamed when this claim could not be substantiated. She taught me to add, subtract, and multiply, but could not teach me division, because she kept saying two into four, three into six, and so forth without ever explaining what the word "into" meant in this connection. This was explained to me on my first day at school; and I solemnly declare that it was the only thing I ever learnt at school. However, I must not complain; for my immurement in that damnable boy prison effected its real purpose of preventing my being a nuisance to my mother at home for at least half the day.

The only other teaching I had was from my clerical Uncle William George (surnamed Carroll) who, being married to one of my many maternal aunts (my father had no end of brothers and sisters), had two boys of his own to educate, and took me on with them for awhile in the early mornings to such purpose that when his lessons were ended by my being sent to school, I knew more Latin grammar than any other boy in the First Latin Junior, to which I was relegated. After a few years in that establishment I had forgotten most of it, and, as aforesaid, learnt nothing; for there was only the thinnest pretence of teaching anything but Latin and Greek, if asking a boy once a day in an overcrowded class the Latin for a man or a horse or what not, can be called teaching him Latin. I was far too busy educating myself out of school by reading every book I could lay hands on, and clambering all over Killiney hill looking at the endless pictures nature painted for me, meanwhile keeping my mind busy by telling myself all sorts of stories, to puzzle about my vocabulary lesson, as the punishments were as futile as the teaching. At the end of my schooling I knew nothing of what the school professed to teach; but I was a highly educated boy all the same. I could sing and whistle from end to end leading works by Handel, Haydn, Mozart, Beethoven, Rossini, Bellini, Donizetti and Verdi. I was saturated with English literature, from Shakespear and Bunyan to Byron and Dickens. And I was so susceptible to natural beauty that, having had some glimpse of the Dalkey scenery on an excursion, I still remember the moment when my mother told me that we were going to live there as the happiest of my life.

And all this I owed to the meteoric impact of Lee, with his music, his method, his impetuous enterprise and his magnetism, upon the little Shaw household where a thoroughly disgusted and disillusioned woman was suffering from a hopelessly disappointing husband and three uninteresting children grown too old to be petted like the animals and birds she was so fond of, to say nothing of the humiliating inadequacy of my father's income. We never felt any affection for Lee; for he was too excessively unlike us, too completely a phenomenon, to rouse any primitive human feeling in us. When my mother introduced him to me, he played with me for the first and last time; but as his notion of play was to decorate my face with moustaches and whiskers in burnt cork in spite of the most furious resistance I could put up, our encounter was not a success; and the defensive attitude in which it left me lasted, though without the least bitterness, until the decay of his energies and the growth of mine put us on more than equal terms. He never read anything except Tyndall on Sound, which he kept in his bedroom for years. He complained that an edition of Shakespear

which I lent him was incomplete because it did not
contain The School for Scandal, which for some reason
he wanted to read; and when I talked of Carlyle he
understood me to mean the Viceroy of that name who
had graciously attended his concerts in the Antient
Concert Rooms. Although he supplanted my father as
the dominant factor in the household, and appropiated
all the activity and interest of my mother, he was so
completely absorbed in his musical affairs that there
was no friction and hardly any intimate personal contacts between the two men: certainly no unpleasantness. At first his ideas astonished us. He said that
people should sleep with their windows open. The daring of this appealed to me; and I have done so ever
since. He ate brown bread instead of white: a startling
eccentricity. He had no faith in doctors, and when my
mother had a serious illness took her case in hand unhesitatingly and at the end of a week or so gave my
trembling father leave to call in a leading Dublin doctor, who simply said "My work is done" and took his
hat. As to the apothecary and his squills, he could not
exist in Lee's atmosphere; and I was never attended
by a doctor again until I caught the smallpox in the
epidemic of 1881. He took no interest in pictures or in
any art but his own; and even in music his interest was
limited to vocal music: I did not know that such things
as string quartets or symphonies existed until I began,
at sixteen, to investigate music for myself. Beethoven's
sonatas and the classical operatic overtures were all I
knew of what Wagner called absolute music. I should
be tempted to say that none of us knew of the existence
of Bach were it not that my mother sang My Heart
Ever Faithful, the banjo like obbligato of which
amused me very irreverently.

Lee was like all artists whose knowledge is solely a
working knowledge: there were holes in his culture
which I had to fill up for myself. Fortunately his richer

pupils sometimes presented him with expensive illustrated books. He never opened them; but I did. He was so destitute of any literary bent that when he published a book entitled *The Voice,* it was written for him by a scamp of a derelict doctor whom he entertained for that purpose, just as in later years his prospectuses and press articles were written by me. He never visited the Dublin National Gallery, one of the finest collections of its size in Europe, with the usual full set of casts from what was called the antique, meaning ancient Greek sculpture. It was by prowling in this gallery that I learnt to recognize the work of the old masters at sight. I learnt French history from the novels of Dumas *père,* and English history from Shakespear and Walter Scott. Good boys were meanwhile learning lessons out of schoolbooks and receiving marks at examinations: a process which left them pious barbarians whilst I was acquiring an equipment which enabled me not only to pose as Corno di Bassetto when the chance arrived, but to add the criticism of pictures to the various strings I had to my bow as a feuilletonist.

Meanwhile nobody ever dreamt of teaching me anything. At fifteen, when the family broke up, I could neither play nor read a note of music. Whether you choose to put it that I was condemned to be a critic or saved from being an executant, the fact remains that when the house became musicless, I was forced to teach myself how to play written music on the piano from a book with a diagram of the keyboard in it or else be starved of music.

Not that I wanted to be a professional musician. My ambition was to be a great painter like Michael Angelo (one of my heroes); but my attempts to obtain instruction in his art at the School of Design presided over by the South Kensington Department of Science and Art only prevented me from learning anything except how to earn five shilling grants for the masters (payment by results) by filling up ridiculous examination papers in practical geometry and what they called freehand drawing.

With competent instruction I daresay I could have become a painter and draughtsman of sorts; but the School of Design convinced me that I was a hopeless failure in that direction on no better ground than that I found I could not draw like Michael Angelo or paint like Titian at the first attempt without knowing how. But teaching, of art and everything else, was and still is so little understood by our professional instructors (mostly themselves failures) that only the readymade geniuses make good; and even they are as often as not the worse for their academic contacts.

As an alternative to being a Michael Angelo I had dreams of being a Badeali. (Note, by the way, that of literature I had no dreams at all, any more than a duck has of swimming.) What that led to was not fully explained until Matthias Alexander, in search, like Lee, of a sound vocal method, invented his technique of self-control.

I had sung like a bird all through my childhood; but when my voice broke I at once fell into the error unmasked by Alexander of trying to gain my end before I had studied the means. In my attempts to reproduce the frenzies of the Count di Luna, the sardonic accents of Gounod's Mephistopheles, the noble charm of Don Giovanni, and the supernatural menace of the Commendatore, not to mention all the women's parts and the tenor parts as well (for all parts, high or low, male or female, had to be sung or shrieked or whistled or growled somehow) I thought of nothing but the dramatic characters; and in attacking them I set my jaws and my glottis as if I had to crack walnuts with them. I might have ruined my voice if I had not imitated good singers instead of bad ones; but even so the results were wretched. When I rejoined my mother in

London and she found that I had taught myself to play accompaniments and to amuse myself with operas and oratorios as other youths read novels and smoke cigarets, she warned me that my voice would be spoiled if I went on like that. Thereupon I insisted on being shewn the proper way to sing. The instructive result was that when, following my mother's directions, I left my jaw completely loose, and my tongue flat instead of convulsively rolling it up; when I operated my diaphragm so as to breathe instead of "blowing"; when I tried to round up my pharynx and soft palate and found it like trying to wag my ears, I found that for the first time in my life I could not produce an audible note. It seemed that I had no voice. But I believed in Lee's plan and knew that my own was wrong. I insisted on being taught how to use my voice as if I had one; and in the end the unused and involuntary pharyngeal muscles became active and voluntary, and I developed an uninteresting baritone voice of no exceptional range which I have ever since used for my private satisfaction and exercise without damaging either it or myself in the process.

Here I must digress for a moment to point a moral. Years after I learnt how to sing without spoiling my voice and wrecking my general health, a musician-reciter (Matthias Alexander aforesaid) found himself disabled by the complaint known as clergyman's sore throat. Having the true scientific spirit and industry, he set himself to discover what it was that he was really doing to disable himself in this fashion by his efforts to produce the opposite result. In the end he found this out, and a great deal more as well. He established not only the beginnings of a far reaching science of the apparently involuntary movements we call reflexes, but a technique of correction and selfcontrol which forms a substantial addition to our very slender resources in personal education.

Meanwhile a Russian doctor named Pavlov devoted himself to the investigation of the same subject by practising the horrible voodoo into which professional medical research had lapsed in the nineteenth century. For quarter of a century he tormented and mutilated dogs most abominably, and finally wrote a ponderous treatise on reflexes in which he claimed to have established on a scientific basis the fact that a dog's mouth will water at the sound of a dinner bell when it is trained to associate that sound with a meal, and that dogs, if tormented, thwarted, baffled, and incommoded continuously, will suffer nervous breakdown and be miserably ruined for the rest of their lives. He was also able to describe what happens to a dog when half its brains are cut out.

What his book and its shamefully respectful reception by professional biologists does demonstrate is that the opening of the scientific professions to persons qualified for them neither by general capacity nor philosophic moral training plunges professional Science, as it has so often plunged professional Religion and Jurisprudence, into an abyss of stupidity and cruelty from which nothing but the outraged humanity of the laity can rescue it.

In the department of biology especially, the professors, mostly brought up as Fundamentalists, are informed that the book of Genesis is not a scientific document, and that the tribal idol whom Noah conciliated by the smell of roast meat is not God and never had any objective existence. They absurdly infer that the pursuit of scientific knowledge: that is, of all knowledge, is exempt from moral obligations, and consequently that they are privileged as scientists to commit the most revolting cruelties when they are engaged in research.

Their next step in this crazy logic is that no research is scientific unless it involves such cruelties. With all the infinite possibilities of legitimate and kindly research open to anyone with enough industry and ingenuity to discover innocent methods of exploration, they set up a boycott of brains and a ritual of sacrifice of dogs and guinea pigs which impresses the superstitious public as all such rituals do. Thereby they learn many things that no decent person ought to know; for it must not be forgotten that human advancement consists not only of adding to the store of human knowledge and experience but eliminating much that is burdensome and brutish. Our forefathers had the knowledge and experience gained by seeing heretics burnt at the stake and harlots whipped through the streets at the cart's tail. Mankind is better without such knowledge and experience.

If Pavlov had been a poacher he would have been imprisoned for his cruelty and despised for his moral imbecility. But as Director of the Physiological Department of the Institute of Experimental Medicine at St Petersburg, and Professor of the Medical Academy, he was virtually forced to mutilate and torment dogs instead of discovering the methods by which humane unofficial investigators were meanwhile finding out all that he was looking for.

The reaction against this voodoo is gathering momentum; but still our rich philanthropic industrialists lavish millions on the endowment of research without taking the most obvious precautions against malversation of their gifts for the benefit of dog stealers, guinea pig breeders, laboratory builders and plumbers, and a routine of cruel folly and scoundrelism that perverts and wastes all the scientific enthusiasm that might otherwise have by this time reduced our death and disease rates to their natural minimum. I am sorry to have to describe so many highly respected gentlemen quite deliberately as fools and scoundrels; but the only definition of scoundrelism known to me is anarchism in

morals; and I cannot admit that the hackneyed pleas
of the dynamiter and the assassin in politics become
valid in the laboratory and the hospital, or that the
man who thinks they do is made any less a fool by
calling him a professor of physiology.

And all this because in 1860 the men who thought
they wanted to substitute scientific knowledge for superstition really wanted only to abolish God and marry
their deceased wives' sisters!

I should add that there is no reason to suppose that
Pavlov was by nature a bad man. He bore a strong ex-
ternal resemblance to myself, and was wellmeaning,
intelligent, and devoted to science. It was his academic environment that corrupted, stultified, and ster-
ilized him. If only he had been taught to sing by my
mother no dog need ever have collapsed in terror at
his approach; and he might have shared the laurels of
Alexander.

And now I must return to my story. Lee's end was
more tragic than Pavlov's. I do not know at what moment he began to deteriorate. He was a sober and moderate liver in all respects; and he was never ill until he
treated himself to a tour in Italy and caught malaria
there. He fought through it without a doctor on cold
water, and returned apparently well; but whenever he
worked too hard it came back and prostrated him for
a day or two. Finally his ambition undid him. Dublin
in those days seemed a hopeless place for an artist; for
no success counted except a London success. The sum-
mit of a provincial conductor's destiny was to preside at
a local musical festival modelled on the Three Choirs
or Handel Festivals. Lee declared that he would organize and conduct a Dublin Festival with his own
chorus and with all the famous leading singers from the
Italian opera in London. This he did in connection with
an Exhibition in Dublin. My mother, of course, led the
chorus. At a rehearsal the contralto, Madame de Meric

Lablache, took exception to something and refused to sing. Lee shrugged his shoulders and asked my mother to carry on, which she did to such purpose that Madame Lablache took care not to give her another such chance. At the Festivals Lee reached the Dublin limit of eminence. Nothing remained but London. He was assured that London meant a very modest beginning all over again, and perhaps something of an established position after fifteen years or so. Lee said that he would take a house in Park Lane, then the most exclusive and expensive thoroughfare in the west end, sacred to peers and millionaires, and—stupendous on the scale of Irish finance—make his pupils pay him a guinea a lesson. And this he actually did with a success that held out quite brilliantly for several seasons and then destroyed him. For whereas he had succeeded in Dublin by the sheer superiority of his method and talent and character, training his pupils honestly for a couple of years to sing beautifully and classically, he found that the London ladies who took him up so gushingly would have none of his beauty and classicism, and would listen to nothing less than a promise to make them sing "like Patti" in twelve lessons. It was that or starve.

He submitted perforce; but he was no longer the same man, the man to whom all circumstances seemed to give way, and who made his own musical world and reigned in it. He had even to change his name and his aspect. G. J. Lee, with the black whiskers and the clean shaven resolute lip and chin, became Vandaleur Lee, whiskerless, but with a waxed and pointed moustache and an obsequious attitude. It suddenly became evident that he was an elderly man, and, to those who had known him in Dublin, a humbug. Performances of Marchetti's Ruy Blas with my sister as the Queen of Spain, and later on of Sullivan's Patience and scraps of Faust and Il Trovatore were achieved; but musical

society in London at last got tired of the damaged
Svengali who could manufacture Pattis for twelve guineas; and the guineas ceased to come in. Still, as there
were no night clubs in those days, it was possible to let
a house in Park Lane for the night to groups of merry-
makers; and Lee was holding out there without pupils
when he asked me to draft a circular for him announcing that he could cure clergyman's sore throat. He was
still at Park Lane when he dropped dead in the act of
undressing himself, dying as he had lived, without a
doctor. The postmortem and inquest revealed the fact
that his brain was diseased and had been so for a long
time. I was glad to learn that his decay was pathologi-
cal as well as ecological, and that the old efficient and
honest Lee had been real after all. But I took to heart
the lesson in the value of London fashionable successes.
To this day I look to the provincial and the amateur
for honesty and genuine fecundity in art.

Meanwhile, what had happened to the *ménage à
trois?* and how did I turn up in Park Lane playing accompaniments and getting glimpses of that artstruck
side of fashionable society which takes refuge in music
from the routine of politics and sport which occupies
the main Philistine body?

Well, when Lee got his foot in at a country house in
Shropshire whither he had been invited to conduct
some private performances, he sold the Dalkey cottage
and concluded his tenancy of Hatch Street. This left
us in a house which we could afford less than ever; for
my father's moribund business was by now considerably deader than it had been at the date of my birth.
My younger sister was dying of consumption caught
from reckless contacts at a time when neither consumption nor pneumonia were regarded as catching.
All that could be done was to recommend a change of
climate. My elder sister had a beautiful voice. In the
last of Lee's Dublin adventures in amateur opera she

had appeared as Amina in Bellini's La Sonnambula, on which occasion the tenor lost his place and his head, and Lucy obligingly sang most of his part as well as her own. Unfortunately her musical endowment was so complete that it cost her no effort to sing or play anything she had once heard, or to read any music at sight. She simply could not associate the idea of real work with music; and as in any case she had never received any sort of training, her very facility prevented her from becoming a serious artist, though, as she could sing difficult music without breaking her voice, she got through a considerable share of public singing in her time.

Now neither my mother nor any of us knew how much more is needed for an opera singer than a voice and natural musicianship. It seemed to us that as, after a rehearsal or two, she could walk on to the stage, wave her arms about in the absurd manner then in vogue in opera, and sing not only her own part but everybody else's as well, she was quite qualified to take the place of Christine Nilsson or Adelina Patti if only she could get a proper introduction. And clearly Lee, now in the first flush of his success in Park Lane, would easily be able to secure this for her.

There was another resource. My now elderly mother believed that she could renounce her amateur status and make a living in London by teaching singing. Had she not the infallible Method to impart? So she realized a little of the scrap of settled property of which her long deceased aunt had not been able to deprive her; sold the Hatch Street furniture; settled my father and myself in comfortable lodgings at 61 Harcourt St; and took my sisters to the Isle of Wight, where the younger one died. She then took a semi-detached villa in a *cul-de-sac* off the Fulham Road, and waited there for Lucy's plans and her own to materialize.

The result was almost a worse disillusion than her

marriage. That had been cured by Lee's music: besides, my father had at last realized his dream of being
a practising teetotaller, and was now as inoffensive an
old gentleman as any elderly wife could desire. It was
characteristic of the Shavian drink neurosis to vanish
suddenly in this way. But that Lee should be unfaithful! unfaithful to The Method! that he, the one genuine
teacher among so many quacks, should now stoop to
outquack them all and become a moustachioed charlatan with all the virtue gone out of him: this was the
end of all things; and she never forgave it. She was
not unkind: she tolerated Lee the charlatan as she had
tolerated Shaw the dipsomaniac because, as I guess,
her early motherless privation of affection and her
many disappointments in other people had thrown her
back on her own considerable internal resources and
developed her self-sufficiency and power of solitude to
an extent which kept her up under circumstances that
would have crushed or embittered any woman who
was the least bit of a clinger. She dropped Lee very
gently: at first he came and went at Victoria Grove,
Fulham Road; and she went and came at 13 Park Lane,
helping with the music there at his At Homes, and even
singing the part of Donna Anna for him (elderly prima
donnas were then tolerated as matters of course) at an
amateur performance of Don Giovanni. But my sister,
who had quarrelled with him as a child when he tried
to give her piano lessons, and had never liked him,
could not bear him at all in his new phase, and, when
she found that he could not really advance her pros-
pects of becoming a prima donna, broke with him
completely and made it difficult for him to continue his
visits. When he died we had not seen him for some
years; and my mother did not display the slightest
emotion at the news. He had been dead for her ever
since he had ceased to be an honest teacher of singing
and a mesmeric conductor.

Her plans for herself came almost to nothing for several years. She found that Englishwomen do not wish to be made to sing beautifully and classically: they want to sing erotically; and this my mother thought not only horrible but unladylike. Her love songs were those of Virginia Gabriel and Arthur Sullivan, all about bereaved lovers and ending with a hope for reunion in the next world. She could sing with perfect purity of tone and touching expression

Oh, Ruby, my darling, the small white hand
Which gathered the harebell was never my own.

But if you had been able to anticipate the grand march of human progress and poetic feeling by fifty years, and asked her to sing

You made me love you.
I didnt want to do it.
I didnt want to do it,

she would have asked a policeman to remove you to a third-class carriage.

Besides, though my mother was not consciously a snob, the divinity which hedged an Irish lady of her period was not acceptable to the British suburban parents, all snobs, who were within her reach. They liked to be treated with deference; and it never occurred to my mother that such people could entertain a pretension so monstrous in her case. Her practice with private pupils was negligible until she was asked to become musical instructress at the North London College. Her success was immediate; for not only did her classes leave the other schools nowhere musically, but the divinity aforesaid exactly suited her new rôle as schoolmistress. Other schools soon sought her services; and she remained in request until she insisted on retiring on the ground that her age made her public appearances ridiculous. By that time all the old money troubles were over and forgotten, as my financial po-

sition enabled me to make her perfectly comfortable in
that respect.

And now, what about myself, the incipient Corno di
Bassetto?

Well, when my mother sold the Hatch Street furniture, it never occurred to her to sell our piano, though
I could not play it, nor could my father. We did not
realize, nor did she, that she was never coming back,
and that, except for a few days when my father, taking
a little holiday for the first time in his life within my
experience, came to see us in London, she would never
meet him again. Family revolutions would seldom be
faced if they did not present themselves at first as temporary makeshifts. Accordingly, having lived since my
childhood in a house full of music, I suddenly found
myself in a house where there was no music, and could
be none unless I made it myself. I have recorded elsewhere how, having purchased one of Weale's Hand-
books which contained a diagram of the keyboard and
an explanation of musical notation, I began my self-
tuition, not with Czerny's five-finger exercises, but with
the overture to Don Giovanni, thinking rightly that I
had better start with something I knew well enough to
hear whether my fingers were on the right notes or not.
There were plenty of vocal scores of operas and oratorios in our lodging; and although I never acquired any
technical skill as a pianist, and cannot to this day play
a scale with any certainty of not foozling it, I acquired
what I wanted: the power to take a vocal score and
learn its contents as if I had heard it rehearsed by my
mother and her colleagues. I could manage arrangements of orchestral music much better than piano
music proper. At last I could play the old rum-tum accompaniments of those days well enough (knowing
how they *should* be played) to be more agreeable to
singers than many really competent pianists. I bought
more scores, among them one of Lohengrin, through

which I made the revolutionary discovery of Wagner. I bought arrangements of Beethoven's symphonies, and discovered the musical regions that lie outside opera and oratorio. Later on, I was forced to learn to play the classical symphonies and overtures in strict time by hammering the bass in piano duets with my sister in London. I played Bach's Inventions and his Art of the Fugue. I studied academic textbooks, and actually worked out exercises in harmony and counterpoint under supervision by an organist friend named Crament, avoiding consecutive fifths and octaves, and having not the faintest notion of what the result would sound like. I read pseudo-scientific treatises about the roots of chords which candidates for the degree of Mus.Doc. at the universities had to swallow, and learnt that Stainer's commonsense views would get you plucked at Oxford, and Ouseley's pedantries at Cambridge. I read Mozart's Succinct Thoroughbass (a scrap of paper with some helpful tips on it which he scrawled for his pupil Sussmaier); and this, many years later, Edward Elgar told me was the only document in existence of the smallest use to a student composer. It was, I grieve to say, of no use to me; but then I was not a young composer. It ended in my knowing much more about music than any of the great composers, an easy achievement for any critic, however barren. For awhile I must have become a little pedantic; for I remember being shocked, on looking up Lee's old vocal score of Don Giovanni, to find that he had cut out all the repetitions which Mozart had perpetrated as a matter of sonata form. I now see that Lee was a century before his time in this reform, and hope some day to hear a performance of Mozart's Idomeneo in which nothing is sung twice over.

When I look back on all the banging, whistling, roaring, and growling inflicted on nervous neighbors during this process of education, I am consumed with useless remorse. But what else could I have done? Today there is the wireless, which enables me to hear from all over Europe more good music in a week than I could then hear in ten years, if at all. When, after my five years office slavery, I joined my mother in London and lived with her for twenty years until my marriage, I used to drive her nearly crazy by my favorite selections from Wagner's Ring, which to her was "all recitative," and horribly discordant at that. She never complained at the time, but confessed it after we separated, and said that she had sometimes gone away to cry. If I had committed a murder I do not think it would trouble my conscience very much; but this I cannot bear to think of. If I had to live my life over again I should devote it to the establishment of some arrangement of headphones and microphones or the like whereby the noises made by musical maniacs should be audible to themselves only. In Germany it is against the law to play the piano with the window open. But of what use is that to the people in the house? It should be made felony to play a musical instrument in any other than a completely soundproof room. The same should apply to loud speakers on pain of confiscation.

Readers with a taste for autobiography must now take my Immaturity preface and dovetail it into this sketch to complete the picture. My business here is to account for my proposal to Tay Pay and my creation of Bassetto. From my earliest recorded sign of an interest in music when as a small child I encored my mother's singing of the page's song from the first act of Les Huguenots (note that I shared Herbert Spencer's liking for Meyerbeer) music has been an indispensable part of my life. Harley Granville-Barker was not far out when, at a rehearsal of one of my plays, he cried out "Ladies and gentlemen: will you please remember that this is Italian opera."

I reprint Bassetto's stuff shamefacedly after long hesitation with a reluctance which has been overcome only by my wife, who has found some amusement in reading it through, a drudgery which I could not bring myself to undertake. I know it was great fun when it was fresh, and that many people have a curious antiquarian taste (I have it myself) for old chronicles of dead musicians and actors. I must warn them, however, not to expect to find here the work of the finished critic who wrote my volumes entitled Music in London, 1890–94, and Our Theatres in the Nineties. I knew all that was necessary about music; but in criticism I was only a beginner. It is easy enough from the first to distinguish between what is pleasant or unpleasant, accurate or inaccurate in a performance; but when great artists have to be dealt with, only keenly analytical observation and comparison of them with artists who, however agreeable, are not great, can enable a critic to distinguish between what everybody can do and what only a very few can do, and to get his valuations right accordingly. All artsmen know what it is to be enthusiastically praised for something so easy that they are half ashamed of it, and to receive not a word of encouragement for their finest strokes.

I cannot deny that Bassetto was occasionally vulgar; but that does not matter if he makes you laugh. Vulgarity is a necessary part of a complete author's equipment; and the clown is sometimes the best part of the circus. The Star, then a hapenny newspaper, was not catering for a fastidious audience: it was addressed to the bicycle clubs and the polytechnics, not to the Royal Society of Literature or the Musical Association. I purposely vulgarized musical criticism, which was then refined and academic to the point of being unreadable and often nonsensical. Editors, being mostly ignorant of music, would submit to anything from their musical critics, not pretending to understand it. If I occasionally carried to the verge of ribaldry my reaction against

the pretentious twaddle and sometimes spiteful cli-
quishness they tolerated in their ignorance, think of me
as heading one of the pioneer columns of what was
then called The New Journalism; and you will wonder
at my politeness.

You may be puzzled, too, to find that the very music
I was brought up on: the pre-Wagner school of formal
melody in separate numbers which seemed laid out to
catch the encores that were then fashionable, was
treated by me with contemptuous levity as something
to be swept into the dustbin as soon as possible. The
explanation is that these works were standing in the
way of Wagner, who was then the furiously abused
coming man in London. Only his early works were
known or tolerated. Half a dozen bars of Tristan or The
Mastersingers made professional musicians put their
fingers in their ears. The Ride of the Valkyries was
played at the Promenade Concerts, and always encored, but only as an insanely rampagious curiosity.
The Daily Telegraph steadily preached Wagner down
as a discordant notoriety-hunting charlatan in six silk
dressing-gowns, who could not write a bar of melody,
and made an abominable noise with the orchestra. In
pantomime harlequinades the clown produced a trombone, played a bit of the pilgrims' march from Tannhäuser fortissimo as well as he could, and said "The
music of the future!" The wars of religion were not
more bloodthirsty than the discussions of the Wagnerites and the Anti-Wagnerites. I was, of course, a violent
Wagnerite; and I had the advantage of knowing the
music to which Wagner grew up, whereas many of the
most fanatical Wagnerites (Ashton Ellis, who translated the Master's prose works, was a conspicuous example) knew no other music than Wagner's, and believed that the music of Donizetti and Meyerbeer had
no dramatic quality whatever. "A few arpeggios" was

the description Ellis gave me of his notion of Les Huguenots. Nowadays the reaction is all the other way. Our young lions have no use for Wagner the Liberator. His harmonies, which once seemed monstrous cacophonies, are the commonplaces of the variety theatres. Audacious young critics disparage his grandeurs as tawdry. When the wireless strikes up the Tannhäuser overture I hasten to switch it off, though I can always listen with pleasure to Rossini's overture to William Tell, hackneyed to death in Bassetto's time. The funeral march from Die Götterdämmerung hardly keeps my attention, though Handel's march from Saul is greater than ever. Though I used to scarify the fools who said that Wagner's music was formless, I should not now think the worse of Wagner if, like Bach and Mozart, he had combined the most poignant dramatic expression with the most elaborate decorative design. It was necessary for him to smash the superstition that this was obligatory; to free dramatic melody from the tyranny of arabesques; and to give the orchestra symphonic work instead of rosalias and rum-tum; but now that this and all the other musical superstitions are in the dustbin, and the post-Wagnerian harmonic and contrapuntal anarchy is so complete that it is easier technically to compose another Parsifal than another Bach's Mass in B Minor or Don Giovanni I am no longer a combatant anarchist in music, not to mention that I have learnt that a successful revolution's first task is to shoot all revolutionists. This means that I am no longer Corno di Bassetto. He was pre- and pro-Wagner; unfamiliar with Brahms; and unaware that a young musician named Elgar was chuckling over his irreverent boutades. As to Cyril Scott, Bax, Ireland, Goossens, Bliss, Walton, Schönberg, Hindemith, or even Richard Strauss and Sibelius, their idioms would have been quite outside Bassetto's conception of music, though today they seem natural enough. Therefore I very greatly doubt whether poor old Bassetto is worth reading now. Still, you are not compelled to read him. Having read the preface you can shut the book and give it to your worst enemy as a birthday present.

MID-ATLANTIC,
Sunday, 2nd June 1935.

CRITICISM AND SUICIDE

I was loth to cast myself off the cliff; for I had just read Mr Walter Besant's sequel to Ibsen's Doll's House in the English Illustrated Magazine, and I felt that my suicide would be at once held up as the natural end of a reprobate who greatly prefers Ibsenism to Walter Besantism. Besides, it seemed to be rather Walter's place than mine to commit suicide after such a performance. Still, I felt so deadly dull that I should hardly have survived to tell the tale had not a desperate expedient to wile away the time occurred to me. Why not telegraph to London, I thought, *for some music to review?* Reviewing has one advantage over suicide. In suicide you take it out of yourself: in reviewing you take it out of other people. In my seaside temper that decided me. I sent to London at once; and the music came duly by parcels post.

3 January 1890

DESTRUCTIVE FORCE

Let me hasten to reassure those who have been terrified by certain striking examples of the destructive force of this column, and who are aghast at such power

being wielded by one man. Their fears are vain: I am
no more able to make or mar artistic enterprises at will
than the executioner has the power of life and death.
It is true that to all appearance a fourteen thousand
pound pantomime, which the critics declared the best
in London, collapsed at a touch of my pen. And the
imagination of the public has undoubtedly been
strongly seized by the spectacle of the much-written-
up Tosca at the height of its prosperity, withering, like
Klingsor's garden, at three lines in a postscript to my
weekly article. But there is no magic in the matter.
Though the east wind seems to kill the consumptive patient, he dies, not of the wind, but of phthisis. On the
strong-lunged man it blows in vain. La Tosca died of
disease, and not of criticism, which, indeed, did its best
to keep it alive.

For my part, I have struck too many blows at the
well-made play without immediate effect, to suppose
that it is my strength and not its own weakness that
has enabled me to double it up this time. When the
critics were full of the "construction" of plays, I stead-
fastly maintained that a work of art is a growth, and
not a construction. When the scribes and Sardous
turned out neat and showy cradles, the critics said,
"How exquisitely constructed!" I said, "Where's the
baby?" Of course, there never was any baby; and when
the cradles began to go out of fashion even the critics
began to find them as dowdy as last year's bonnets.
A *fantoccini* theatre, in which puppets play the parts
of men and women, is amusing; but the French theatre, in which men and women play the parts of puppets, is unendurable. Yet there was a time when some
persons wrote as if Adrienne Lecouvreur was a superior sort of tragedy, and Dora (alias Diplomacy) a
masterpiece of comedy. Even now their artificiality
passes for ingenuity. Just as a barrister in England gets
an immense reputation as a criminals' advocate when

a dozen of his clients have been hanged (the hanging being at once a proof and an advertisement of the importance of the cases), so when a dramatist has written five or six plays in which two hours of intrigues and telegrams are wasted in bringing about some situation which the audience would have accepted at once without any contrivance at all, he receives his diploma as a master of play construction!

7 March 1890

PERSONAL ANIMOSITY

Somebody has sent me a cutting from which I gather that a proposal to form a critics' club has reached the very elementary stage of being discussed in the papers in August. Now clearly a critic should not belong to a club at all. He should not know anybody: his hand should be against every man, and every man's hand against his. Artists insatiable by the richest and most frequent doses of praise; entrepreneurs greedy for advertisement; people without reputations who want to beg or buy them ready made; the rivals of the praised; the friends, relatives, partisans, and patrons of the damned: all these have their grudge against the unlucky Minos in the stalls, who is himself criticized in the most absurd fashion.

People have pointed out evidences of personal feeling in my notices as if they were accusing me of a misdemeanor, not knowing that a criticism written without personal feeling is not worth reading. It is the capacity for making good or bad art a personal matter that makes a man a critic. The artist who accounts for my disparagement by alleging personal animosity on my part is quite right: when people do less than their best, and do that less at once badly and self-complacently,

I hate them, loathe them, detest them, long to tear them limb from limb and strew them in gobbets about the stage or platform. (At the Opera, the temptation to go out and ask one of the sentinels for the loan of his Martini, with a round or two of ammunition, that I might rid the earth of an incompetent conductor or a conceited and careless artist, has come upon me so strongly that I have been withheld only by my fear that, being no marksman, I might hit the wrong person and incur the guilt of slaying a meritorious singer.)

In the same way, really fine artists inspire me with the warmest personal regard, which I gratify in writing my notices without the smallest reference to such monstrous conceits as justice, impartiality, and the rest of the ideals. When my critical mood is at its height, personal feeling is not the word: it is passion: the passion for artistic perfection—for the noblest beauty of sound, sight, and action—that rages in me. Let all young artists look to it, and pay no heed to the idiots who declare that criticism should be free from personal feeling. The true critic, I repeat, is the man who becomes your personal enemy on the sole provocation of a bad performance, and will only be appeased by good performances. Now this, though well for art and for the people, means that the critics are, from the social or clubable point of view, veritable fiends. They can only fit themselves for other people's clubs by allowing themselves to be corrupted by kindly feelings foreign to the purpose of art, unless, indeed, they join Philistine clubs, wherein neither the library nor the social economy of the place will suit their nocturnal, predatory habits. If they must have a club, let them have a pandemonium of their own, furnished with all the engines of literary vivisection. But its first and most sacred rule must be the exclusion of the criticized, except those few stalwarts who regularly and publicly turn upon and criticize their critics. (No critics' club would have any right to the name unless it included—but the printer warns me that I have reached the limit of my allotted space.)

3 *September 1890*

TECHNICAL ANALYSIS

Although I have not, at the moment of writing this, seen Cavalleria Rusticana, my refusal to buy the score has not left me in total ignorance of the work. Do not be alarmed, I am not going to perpetrate an "analysis." Those vivid emotions which the public derive from descriptions of "postludes brought to a close on the pedal of A, the cadence being retarded by four chords forming an arpeggio of a diminished seventh, each grade serving as tonic for a perfect chord," must be sought elsewhere than in these columns. It is perhaps natural that gentlemen who are incapable of criticism should fall back on parsing; but, for my own part, I find it better to hold my tongue when I have nothing to say. Yet I cannot help chuckling at the tricks they play on their innocent editors. An editor never does know anything about music, though his professions to that effect invariably belie his secret mind.

I have before me a journal in which the musical critic has induced the editor to allow him to launch into music type in order to give a suggestion of a certain "fanciful and suggestive orchestral design" in Cavalleria Rusticana. The quotation consists of a simple figuration of the common chord of G sharp minor, with "etc." after it. If a literary critic had offered this editor such a sample of the style of Shakespear as

"Now is the," etc.

he would probably have remonstrated. But he is perfectly happy with his chord of G sharp minor, which is ten times more absurd. And yet that editor devotes a column of his paper to criticizing me in the most disrespectful manner. Can he wonder that my sense of public duty does not permit me to remain silent on the subject of his utter incapacity within my special province?

The fact is, I have heard the music of Cavalleria Rusticana, and can certify that it is a youthfully vigorous piece of work, with abundant snatches of melody broken obstreperously off on one dramatic pretext or another. But, lively and promising as it is, it is not a whit more so than the freshest achievements of Mr Hamish MacCunn and Mr Cliffe. The people who say, on the strength of it, that Verdi has found a successor and Boito a competitor, would really say anything. Mascagni has shewn nothing of the originality or distinction which would entitle him to such a comparison. If he had, I am afraid I should now be defending him against a chorus of disparagement, instead of deprecating a repetition of the laudatory extravagances which so often compel me to take the ungracious attitude of demurring to the excesses of the criticism instead of the cordial one of pointing out what is good in the composition. Already I have read things about Cavalleria Rusticana which would require considerable qualification if they were applied to Die Meistersinger or Don Giovanni.

21 October 1891

SIMPLY LISTEN

That light-hearted body the Bach Choir has had what I may befittingly call another shy at the Mass in B Minor. When I last had occasion to criticize its singing,

I gathered that my remarks struck the more sensitive members as being in the last degree ungentlemanlike. This was due to a misunderstanding of the way in which a musical critic sets about his business when he has a choral performance in hand. He does not on such occasions prime himself with Spitta's biography of Bach, and, opening his mouth and shutting his ears, sit palpitating with reverent interest, culminating in a gasp of contrapuntal enthusiasm at each entry and answer of the fugue subject.

On the contrary, the first thing he does is to put Bach and Spitta and counterpoint and musical history out of the question, and simply listen to the body of sound that is being produced. And what clothes his judgments in terror is that he does not, like the ordinary man, remain unconscious of every sound except that which he is expecting to hear. He is alive not only to the music of the organ, but to the rattling and crashing caused by the beating of the partial tones and combination tones generated by the sounds actually played from in the score; and he is often led thereby to desire the sudden death of organists who use their stops heedlessly. He hears not only the modicum of vocal tone which the choristers are producing, but also the buzzing and wheezing and puffing and all sorts of uncouth sounds which ladies and gentlemen unknowingly bring forth in the agonies of holding on to a difficult part in a Bach chorus. And his criticism of the choir is primarily determined by the proportion of vocal tone to the mere noises.

To the amateur who has heroically wrestled with the bass or tenor part in the *Cum Sancto Spiritu* of the B Minor Mass, and succeeded in reaching the "Amen" simultaneously with the conductor, it probably seems, not musical criticism, but downright ruffianism to tell him publicly that instead of deserving well of his country he has been behaving more like a combination of a debilitated coalheaver with a suffocating grampus than a competent Bach chorister. But the more outraged he feels, the more necessary is it to persecute him remorselessly until he becomes humbly conscious that in the agonies of his preoccupation with his notes he may perhaps have slightly overlooked the need for keeping his tone sympathetic and telling, and his attack precise and firm. The conscientious critic will persecute him accordingly, not giving him those delicately turned and friendly hints which a fine artist catches at once, but rather correcting him with such salutary brutality as may be necessary to force him to amend his ways in spite of his natural tendency to question the existence of any room for improvement on his part.

When the critic has duly estimated the quality of the vocal material, he begins to take Bach into consideration. An untrained singer can no more sing Bach's florid choral parts than an untrained draughtsman can copy a drawing by Albrecht Dürer. The attempts of ordinary amateurs to make their way through a Bach chorus are no more to be taken as Bach's music than a child's attempt to copy one of Dürer's plumed helmets is to be taken as a reproduction of the original. The critic accordingly must proceed to consider whether the ladies and gentlemen before him are tracing the lines of the great Bach picture with certainty, mastery, and vigilantly sensitive artistic feeling, or whether they are scrawling them in impotent haste under the stick of the conductor.

In the first case, the master's design will come out in all its grandeur; and the critic will give himself up gratefully to pure enjoyment: in the second, he will sit in implacable scorn, asking how these people dare meddle with Bach when they are hardly fit to be trusted with The Chough and Crow. Need I add, that if they happen to have had the unbounded presumption to call themselves by the name of a great man,

he will entertain just so much extra contempt for them
as we feel for a bad circus clown who aggravates his
incompetence by calling himself The Shakespearean
Jester.

30 March 1892

ELECTIONEERING

It is only fair to the artists whom I have to criticize
in this hour of political battle to ask that a large allowance may be made for the deterioration of my character produced by electioneering. A fortnight ago I
still had, I will not say a conscience, but certain ves-
tiges of the moral habits formed in the days before I
became a critic. These have entirely disappeared; and,
as I now stand, I am capable of anything except a find-
able-out infringement of the Corrupt Practices Act. A
collation of the speeches I have delivered would destroy all faith in human nature. I have blessed in the
south and banned in the north with an unscrupulously
single-hearted devotion to the supreme end of getting
my man in which has wholly freed my intellect from
absolute conceptions of truth. I learnt long ago that
though there are several places from which the tourist
may enjoy a view of Primrose Hill, none of these can
be called *the* view of Primrose Hill. I now perceive
that the political situation is like Primrose Hill.
Wherever I have been I have found and fervently
uttered *a* true view of it; but as to *the* true view, believe me, there is no such thing. Place all the facts before me; and allow me to make an intelligent selection
(always with the object of getting my man in); and
the moral possibilities of the situation are exhausted.
And now I can almost hear some pillar of the great
church of Chadband saying, "Faugh! no more of this:

let us return to the purer atmosphere of art." But *is* the atmosphere of art any purer? One evening I find myself appealing to the loftiest feelings of a town where many of the inhabitants, when you canvass them, still keep up the primitive custom of shutting the door carefully, assuring you that they are "all right," and bluntly asking how much you are going to pay for their vote. The next evening I am at the Opera, with Wagner appealing to my loftiest sentiments. Perhaps Mr Chadband would call that a return to a purer atmosphere. But I know better. Speaking for myself alone, I am as much a politician at a first-night or a press-view as I am on the hustings.

When I was more among pictures than I am at present, certain reforms in painting which I desired were advocated by the Impressionist party, and resisted by the Academic party. Until those reforms had been effectually wrought I fought for the Impressionists—backed up men who could not draw a nose differently from an elbow against Leighton and Bouguereau—did everything I could to make the public conscious of the ugly unreality of studio-lit landscape and the inanity of second-hand classicism. Again, in dealing with the drama, I find that the forces which tend to make the theatre a more satisfactory resort for me are rallied for the moment, not round the so-called French realists, whom I should call simply anti-obscurantists, but around the Scandinavian realists; and accordingly I mount their platform, exhort England to carry their cause on to a glorious victory, and endeavor to surround their opponents with a subtle atmosphere of absurdity.

It is just the same in music. I am always electioneering. At the Opera I desire certain reforms; and, in order to get them, I make every notable performance an example of the want of them, knowing that in the long run these defects will seem as ridiculous as Monet has already made Bouguereau's backgrounds, or Ibsen the "poetical justice" of Tom Taylor. Never in my life have I penned an impartial criticism; and I hope I never may. As long as I have a want, I am necessarily partial to the fulfilment of that want, with a view to which I must strive with all my wit to infect everyone else with it. Thus there arises a deadly enmity between myself and the impresarios; for whereas their aim is to satisfy the public, often at huge risk and expense, I seize on their costliest efforts as the most conspicuous examples of the shortcomings which rob me of the fullest satisfaction of my artistic cravings.

They may feel this to be diabolically unfair to them whenever they have done the very utmost that existing circumstances allowed them; but that does not shake me, since I know that the critic who accepts existing circumstances loses from that moment all his dynamic quality. He stops the clock. His real business is to find fault; to ask for more; to knock his head against stone walls, in the full assurance that three or four good heads will batter down any wall that stands across the world's path. He is no dispenser of justice: reputations are to him only the fortresses of the opposing camps; and he helps to build or bombard them according to his side in the conflict. To be just to individuals—even if it were possible—would be to sacrifice the end to the means, which would be profoundly immoral.

One must, of course, know the facts, and that is where the critic's skill comes in; but a moral has to be drawn from the facts, and that is where his bias comes out. How many a poor bewildered artist, in the conflict of art movements, has found himself in the position of the harmless peasant who sees a shell bursting in his potato-patch because his little white house on the hill accidentally happens to help a field battery to find its range. Under such circumstances, a humane artillery officer can at least explain the position to the peasant.

Similarly, I feel bound to explain my position to those in whose gardens my shells occasionally burst. And the explanation is probably quite as satisfactory to the shattered victim in one case as in the other.

6 July 1892

MY IMPOSTORSHIP

A man cannot go on repeating what he has said a thousand times about the way the Monday Popular quartet played Haydn in G, No. 12 of Opus 756, or about Santley as Elijah. I turn in desperation to the musical journals, and my hopes rise as I see the words, "Ignorant Misstatement." But it is actually not G. B. S. this time; somebody else, I suppose, has made a remark sufficiently obvious to shake the foundation of make-believe on which "art" of the usual professional type is built. The tenants of that fashionable edifice are always protesting that I am an impudent pretender to musical authority, betraying my ignorance, in spite of my diabolical cunning, in every second sentence. And I do not mind confessing that I do not know half as much as you would suppose from my articles; but in the kingdom of the deaf the one-eared is king.

The other evening I was looking into a shop-window in Oxford Street, when a gentleman accosted me modestly, and, after flattering me with great taste and modesty into an entire willingness to make his acquaintance, began with evident misgiving and hesitation, but with no less evident curiosity, to approach the subject of these columns. At last he came to his point with a rush by desperately risking the question, "Excuse me, Mr G. B. S., but *do* you know anything about music? The fact is, I am not capable of forming an opinion myself; but Dr Blank says you dont, and—er—Dr Blank is such a great authority that one hardly knows what to think." Now this question put me into a difficulty, because I had already learnt by experience that the reason my writings on music and musicians are so highly appreciated is, that they are supposed by many of my greatest admirers to be a huge joke, the point of which lies in the fact that I am totally ignorant of music, and that my character of critic is an exquisitely ingenious piece of acting, undertaken to gratify my love of mystification and paradox.

From this point of view every one of my articles appears as a fine stroke of comedy, occasionally broadening into a harlequinade, in which I am the clown, and Dr Blank the policeman. At first I did not realize this, and could not understand the air of utter disillusion and loss of interest in me that would come over people in whose houses I incautiously betrayed some scrap of amateurish enlightenment. But the naïve exclamation, "Oh! you *do* know something about it, then," at last became familiar to me; and I now take particular care not to expose my knowledge. When people hand me a sheet of instrumental music, and ask my opinion of it, I carefully hold it upside down, and pretend to study it in that position with the eye of an expert. When they invite me to try their new grand piano, I attempt to open it at the wrong end; and when the young lady of the house informs me that she is practising the 'cello, I innocently ask her whether the mouthpiece did not cut her lips dreadfully at first. This line of conduct gives enormous satisfaction, in which I share to a rather greater extent than is generally supposed. But, after all, the people whom I take in thus are only amateurs.

To place my impostorship beyond question I require to be certified as such by authorities like our Bachelors and Doctors of music—gentlemen who can write a Nunc Dimittis in five real parts, and know the difference between a tonal fugue and a real one, and can tell you how old Monteverdi was on his thirtieth birthday, and have views as to the true root of the discord of the seventh on the supertonic, and devoutly believe that *si contra fa diabolus est.* But I have only to present myself to them in the character of a man who has been through these dreary games without ever discovering the remotest vital connection between them and the art of music—a state of mind so inconceivable by them —to make them exclaim:

Preposterous ass! that never read so far
To know the cause why music was ordained,

and give me the desired testimonials at once. And so I manage to scrape along without falling under suspicion of being an honest man.

However, since mystification is not likely to advance us in the long run, may I suggest that there must be something wrong in the professional tests which have been successively applied to Handel, to Mozart, to Beethoven, to Wagner, and last, though not least, to me, with the result in every case of our condemnation as ignoramuses and charlatans. Why is it that when Dr Blank writes about music nobody but a professional musician can understand him; whereas the man-in-the-street, if fond of art and capable of music, can understand the writings of Mendelssohn, Wagner, Liszt, Berlioz, or any of the composers?

Why, again, is it that my colleague, W. A., for instance, in criticizing Mr Henry Arthur Jones's play the other day, did not *parse* all the leading sentences in it? I will not be so merciless as to answer these questions now, though I know the solution, and am capable of giving it if provoked beyond endurance. Let it suffice for the moment that writing is a very difficult art, criticism a very difficult process, and music not easily to be distinguished, without special critical training, from the scientific, technical, and professional conditions of its performance, composition, and teaching. And if the critic is to please the congregation, who want to read only about the music, it is plain that he must appear quite beside the point to the organ-blower, who wants to read about his bellows, which he can prove to be the true source of all the harmony.

15 February 1893

FUNERAL MARCH

The fact is, I am not always fortunate enough to arrive at these specially solemn concerts in the frame of mind proper to the occasion. The funeral march in the Eroica symphony, for instance, is extremely impressive to a man susceptible to the funereal emotions. Unluckily, my early training in this respect was not what it should have been. To begin with, I was born with an unreasonably large stock of relations, who have increased and multiplied ever since. My aunts and uncles were legion, and my cousins as the sands of the sea without number. Consequently, even a low death-rate meant, in the course of mere natural decay, a tolerably steady supply of funerals for a by no means affectionate but exceedingly clannish family to go to. Add to this that the town we lived in, being divided in religious opinion, buried its dead in two great cemeteries, each of which was held by the opposite faction to be the antechamber of perdition, and by its own patrons to be the gate of paradise. These two cemeteries lay a mile or two outside the town; and this circumstance, insignificant as it appears, had a marked effect on the funerals, because a considerable portion of the journey to the tomb, especially when the deceased had lived in the suburbs, was made along country roads. Now the sorest bereavement does not cause men to forget wholly that time is money. Hence, though we used to proceed slowly and sadly enough through the streets or terraces at the early stages of our progress, when we got into the open a change came over the spirit in which the coachmen drove. Encouraging words were addressed to the horses; whips were flicked; a jerk all along the line warned us to slip our arms through the broad elbow-straps of the mourning-coaches, which were balanced on longitudinal poles by enormous and totally inelastic springs; and then the funeral began in earnest. Many a clinking run have I had through that bit of country at the heels of some deceased uncle who had himself many a time enjoyed the same sport. But in the immediate neighborhood of the cemetery the houses recommenced; and at that point our grief returned upon us with overwhelming force: we were able barely to crawl along to the great iron gates where a demoniacal black pony was waiting with a sort of primitive gun-carriage and a pall to convey our burden up the avenue to the mortuary chapel, looking as if he might be expected at every step to snort fire, spread a pair of gigantic bat's wings, and vanish, coffin and all, in thunder and brimstone. Such were the scenes which have disqualified me for life from feeling the march in the Eroica symphony as others do. It is that fatal episode where the oboe carries the march into the major key and the whole composition brightens and steps out, so to speak, that ruins me. The moment it begins, I instinctively look beside me for an elbow-strap; and the voices of the orchestra are lost in those of three men, all holding on tight as we jolt and swing madly to and fro, the youngest, a cousin, telling me a romantic tale of an encounter with the Lord Lieutenant's beautiful consort in the hunting-field (an entirely imaginary incident); the eldest, an uncle, giving my father an interminable account of an old verge watch which cost five shillings and kept perfect time for forty years subsequently; and my father speculating as to how far the deceased was cut short by his wife's temper, how far by alcohol, and how far by what might be called natural causes. When the sudden and somewhat unprepared relapse of the movement into the minor key takes place, then I imagine that we have come to the houses again. Finally I wake up completely, and realize that for the last page or two of the score I have not been listening critically to a note of the performance. I do not defend my conduct, present or past: I merely describe it so that my infirmities may be duly taken into account in weighing my critical verdicts. Boyhood takes its fun where it finds it, without looking beneath the surface; and, since society chose to dispose of its dead with a grotesque pageant out of which farcical incidents sprang naturally and inevitably at every turn, it is not to be wondered at that funerals made me laugh when I was a boy nearly as much as they disgust me now that I am older, and have had glimpses from behind the scenes of the horrors of what a sentimental public likes to hear described as "God's acre."

14 February 1894

RUSKIN ON MUSIC

I have been indulging in five shillings' worth of Ruskin on Music, in a volume just published by Mr George Allen. As it happened, the first sentence I lighted on when I opened the book was "the oratorio, withering the life of religion into dead bones on the Syren sands." Immediately I woke up; for the fact that modern oratorio is mostly a combination of frivolity and sensuality with hypocrisy and the most oppressive dullness is still sufficiently a trade secret to make its discovery by an outsider interesting. A few pages off I found Mr

Ruskin describing the singing he heard south of the Alps. Usually the Englishman in Italy, carefully primed beforehand with literary raptures concerning a nation of born musicians speaking the most vocal language in the world, is sufficiently careful of his own credit as a man of taste to discover a Giuglini in every gondolier and St Cecilia's lute in every accordion.

Mr Ruskin innovated so far as to use his own judgment; and here is the result: "Of bestial howling, and entirely frantic vomiting up of damned souls through their still carnal throats, I have heard more than, please God, I will ever endure the hearing of again, in one of His summers." I take the liberty of squeezing Mr Ruskin's hand in mute sympathy with the spirit of this passage. In Italy, where the chance of being picked up off the streets and brought out as *primo tenore* at the Opera occupies the same space in the imagination of the men as the chance of selecting a Derby winner does in England, you cannot get away from the ignoble bawling which Mr Ruskin describes so forcibly—and yet not too forcibly, or forcibly enough; for language will not hold the full pretentiousness and cupidity of the thing, let alone the unpleasantness of the noise it makes.

It is at once the strength and weakness of Mr Ruskin in dealing with music that he is in love with it. There is always a certain comedy in the contrast between people as they appear transfigured in the eyes of those who love them, and as they appear to those who are under no such inspiration—or, for the matter of that, as they appear to themselves. And the tragi-comedy of the love of men and women for one another is reproduced in their love for art.

Mr Ruskin is head and ears in love with Music; and so am I; but I am married to her, so to speak, as a professional critic, whereas he is still a wooer, and has the illusions of imperfect knowledge as well as the illuminations of perfect love. Listen to this, for example: "True music is the natural expression of a lofty passion for a right cause. In proportion to the kingliness and force of any personality, the expression either of its joy or suffering becomes measured, chastened, calm, and capable of interpretation only by the majesty of ordered, beautiful, and worded sound. Exactly in proportion to the degree in which we become narrow in the cause and conception of our passions, incontinent in the utterance of them, feeble of perseverance in them, sullied or shameful in the indulgence of them, their expression by musical means becomes broken, mean, fatuitous, and at last impossible: the measured waves of heaven will not lend themselves to the expression of ultimate vice: it must be for ever sunk in discordance or silence."

I entirely agree with Mr Ruskin in this; but it will not hold water, for all that. "The measured waves of heaven" are not so particular as he thinks. Music will express any emotion, base or lofty. She is absolutely unmoral: we find her in Verdi's last work heightening to the utmost the expression of Falstaff's carnal gloating over a cup of sack, just as willingly as she heightened the expression of "a lofty passion for a right cause" for Beethoven in the Ninth Symphony. She mocked and prostituted the Orpheus legend for Offenbach just as keenly and effectively as she ennobled it for Gluck. Mr Ruskin himself has given an instance of this—a signally wrong instance, by the way; but let that pass for a moment:

"And yonder musician, who used the greatest power which (in the art he knew) the Father of Spirits ever yet breathed into the clay of this world; who used it, I say, to follow and fit with perfect sound the words of the Zauberflöte and of Don Giovanni—foolishest and most monstrous of conceivable human words and subjects of thought—for the future amusement of his race!

No such spectacle of unconscious (and in that unconsciousness all the more fearful) moral degradation of the highest faculty to the lowest purpose can be found in history."

This is a capital instance of Mr Ruskin's besetting sin—virtuous indignation. If these two operas are examples of "foolishest and most monstrous" words fitted and followed with perfect sound—that is, with true music—what becomes of the definition which limits true music to "the natural expression of a lofty passion for a right cause"? Clearly, that will not do.

And now may I beg Mr Ruskin to mend his illustration, if not his argument? The generation which could see nothing in Die Zauberflöte but a silly extravaganza was one which Mr Ruskin certainly belonged to in point of time; and he has for once sunk to the average level of its thought in this shallow criticism of the work which Mozart deliberately devoted to the expression of his moral sympathies. Everything that is true and vital in his worship of music would be shattered if it were a fact—happily it is not—that the music of Sarastro came from a silly and trivial mood. If I were to assure Mr Ruskin that Bellini's Madonna with St Ursula, in Venice, was originally knocked off as a sign for a tavern by the painter, Mr Ruskin would simply refuse to entertain the story, no matter what the evidence might be, knowing that the thing was eternally impossible. Since he sees no such impossibility in the case of Die Zauberflöte, I must conclude that he does not know the masterpieces of music as he knows those of painting.

As to Don Giovanni, otherwise The Dissolute One Punished, the only immoral feature of it is its supernatural retributive morality. Gentlemen who break through the ordinary categories of good and evil, and come out at the other side singing *Finch' han dal vino* and *Là ci darem,* do not, as a matter of fact, get called on by statues, and taken straight down through the floor to eternal torments; and to pretend that they do is to shirk the social problem they present. Nor is it yet by any means an established fact that the world owes more to its Don Ottavios than to its Don Juans. It is, of course, impossible to make a serious stand on a libretto which is such an odd mixture of the old Punch tradition with the highly emancipated modern philosophy of Molière; but whether you apply Mr Ruskin's hasty criticism to Punch and Judy or to Le Festin de Pierre, you will, I think, see that it is fundamentally nothing but an explosion of pious horror of the best Denmark Hill brand. The hard fact is that Don Giovanni is eminent in virtue of its uncommon share of wisdom, beauty, and humor; and if any theory of morals leads to the conclusion that it is foolish and monstrous, so much the worse for the theory.

I must, further, remonstrate with Mr Ruskin about his advice to the girls of England. First, like a veritable serpent in the garden, he tempts the young English lady, already predisposed to self-righteousness, with the following wicked words: "From the beginning consider all your accomplishments as means of assistance to others." This is Denmark Hill with a vengeance. But the artist in Mr Ruskin is always getting the better of Denmark Hill; and on the very next page he says, "Think only of accuracy; never of effect or expression."

Now, will anyone kindly tell me how a young lady is to consider all her accomplishments "as means of assistance to others"—that is, to think of nothing but effect and expression, and consequently to cultivate self-consciousness and its attendant personal susceptibility up to the highest point—and at the same time not to think of effect or expression at all, but only of accuracy. Speaking as a rival sage—as one who, in musical matters at least, considers himself fitted to play

Codlin to Mr Ruskin's Short—I earnestly advise the
young ladies of England, whether enrolled in the
Guild of St George or not, to cultivate music solely for
the love and need of it, and to do it in all humility
of spirit, never forgetting that they are most likely inflicting all-but-unbearable annoyance on every musician within earshot, instead of rendering "assistance to
others."

The greatest assistance the average young lady musician can render to others is to stop. Mind, I speak
of life as it is. Some day, perhaps, when it is like a
page out of Wilhelm Meister or Sesame and Lilies,
when the piano is dead and our maidens go up into
the mountains to practise their first exercises on the
harp, Mr Ruskin's exhortations as to the sinfulness of
doing anything merely because you like it may gain
some sort of plausibility. At present they will not wash.

"It is, I believe," says Mr Ruskin, "as certain that in
the last twenty years we have learnt to better understand good music, and to love it more, as that in the
same time our knowledge and love of pictures have
not increased. The reason is easily found. Our music
has been chosen for us by masters; and our pictures
have been chosen by ourselves."

Alas! how easy it is to find a reason for the thing
that is not! Not that there is not here, as usual, a hundred times more insight in Mr Ruskin's mistake than
in most other men's accuracies. It is quite true that
the favorite works at our good concerts are of a much
higher class than the favorite works at the Royal
Academy, and that the difference is due to the fact
that Beethoven and Wagner are still in a position to
dictate to the public what is good for them. But the
public is not really conscious of that part of Beethoven's work which raises it above the level of popular
painting. It finds a great deal of Beethoven incom-
prehensible, and therefore dull, putting up with it only

because the alternative is either no music at all or something a good deal duller. But will it put up with it when vulgar musicians have completely mastered the trade of producing symphonies and operas containing all the cheap, popular, obvious, carnal luxuries of the Beethovenian music, without its troublesome nobilities, depths, and spiritual grandeurs?

I doubt it. Wagner accused Meyerbeer of following the great masters as a starling follows the plough, picking up the titbits which their force unearthed, and serving them up to Paris unmixed with nobler matter. That process, which has been going on in music for less than a century, has been going on in painting for three or four hundred years, so that our contemporary popular painters have rid themselves far more completely of what was greatest in the great masters of Florence, Rome, and Venice, than our contemporary composers of what was greatest in Mozart, Beethoven, and Wagner; but the process is going on all the same under the influence of popular demand; and we shall soon have the field held by vulgar music as much as by vulgar painting, as is right and proper in a country with a vulgar population.

I need hardly add that Mr Ruskin himself, true to his method of never collating his utterances, but taking his inspiration as it comes, so that on every possible subject he says the right thing and the wrong thing with equal eloquence within the same ten minutes, does not really believe any such nonsense as that people can be kept on high ground by having their music chosen for them by masters. For instance:

"You cannot paint or sing yourselves into being good men. You must be good men before you can either paint or sing; and then the color and the sound will complete all in you that is best."

Neither can people appreciate good music, whether chosen for them by masters or not, except to the extent to which they are "good" themselves. You can chain a terrier to Richter's desk, and force it to listen to all the symphonies of Beethoven, without changing its opinion one jot as to the relative delights of rathunting and classical music; and the same thing is true in its degree of mankind. The real point is, that most of us, far from being chained to the desk, never get the chance of finding out whether we can appreciate great music or not.

Mr Ruskin is probably right in anticipating that a change in the tone of public feeling would be produced "if, having been accustomed only to hear black Christy's, blind fiddlers, and hoarse beggars scrape and howl about their streets, the people were permitted daily audience of faithful and gentle orchestral rendering of the work of the highest classical masters."

Here I must leave an infinitely suggestive and provocative book, the publication of which no musical critic can very well ignore. To finish, I will give, without comment, one more quotation as a sample of what Mr Ruskin's musical criticism would, perhaps, have been like if he had taken to my branch of the trade instead of to his own:

"Grisi and Malibran sang at least one-third slower than any modern cantatrice; and Patti, the last time I heard her, massacred Zerlina's part in *Là ci darem*, as if the audience and she had but the one object of getting Mozart's air done with as soon as possible. . . . Afterwards I was brought to the point of trying to learn to sing, in which, though never even getting so far as to read with ease, I nevertheless, between my fine rhythmic ear and true-lover's sentiment, got to understand some principles of musical art, which I shall perhaps be able to enforce, with benefit on the musical public mind, even today."

MY STUFF AND DR STANFORD

Dr Villiers Stanford has been favoring us with his
views on Some Aspects of Musical Criticism in England in the shape of a magazine article. I am very
strongly tempted to quote it here at full length; for it
is the best article I ever saw on the subject, unex-
ceptionally judicious and accurate, and much better
written than most musical criticisms are. I shall at least
quote his exposition of his main point, as I cannot
paraphrase it to any advantage:

"A new opera, which has been, perhaps, the work
of years, and the outcome of the daily thought and
labor of composer and librettist, is produced on a Monday night; and by 2 A.M. on Tuesday morning a critic,
who has just made his first acquaintance with the composition, is expected to have completed a full and just
chronicle of its merits and faults, its workmanship and
its effect, fit to be put into print, and intended to in-
struct the public before breakfast as to what attitude
they should be prepared to take when they find themselves in the audience. I say, as one who is, from much
experience in the musician's craft, perhaps exceptionally quick in seizing the points of a new work at first
hearing, that to expect the best possible criticism, or
indeed criticism of any lasting value at all under such
circumstances is grotesque; and the insistence upon
such hot haste production is a hardship to the writer,
an injury to the producer, and a mischief to the public."

True as this is, and deeply as I am touched by the
tribute here implied, and elsewhere explicitly rendered, to the superiority of those weekly articles of
which my own may be taken as examples, I am not
sure that the opinion elaborated in a week is always so

much more valuable than the impression made in a moment. The only musical compositions which will bear thinking of for more than half an hour are those which require an intimate acquaintance of at least ten years for their critical mastery. As to the weekly article being any more "just" than the daily one, I do not see how that can be sustained for a moment. Let us try to vivify our ideas on the subject by getting away from the abstraction "criticism" to the reality from which it is abstracted: that is, the living, breathing, erring, human, nameable and addressable individual who writes criticism.

To avoid getting into trouble I shall not cite any musical critics. The dramatic and parliamentary ones will serve my turn as well. Two of the best dramatic critics in London, Mr Clement Scott and Mr Walkley, write both weekly essays and two-o'clock-in-the-morning notices of new plays. Both write the immediate notice as impressionists. Mr Scott writes his deferred notice also as an impressionist, rubbing in his first impression, and as often as not spoiling it. Mr Walkley is an acute analyst; and in his case the gain in intellectual elaboration in the deferred notice is immense. But has anyone ever observed any gain in either case in the matter of justice? I certainly never have.

Take another case in point. I have for years urged upon editors the necessity of sending a fine critic into the House of Commons to write notices of the sittings of the House exactly as they send a critic to the Opera. The result of giving such a critic a brief for Lord Rosebery against Lord Salisbury is as absurd as it would be to give me a brief for Calvé as against Melba, or my colleague W. A. a brief for Mr Irving as against Mr Tree. Of late years the custom of prefacing the verbatim reports of the sittings of the House by a descriptive report has been developing parliamentary criticism on my lines.

For example, Mr Massingham, a typical parliamentary critic of the new kind, will, in criticizing a debate, praise the performances of Mr Balfour and Mr John Burns, and slate Sir William Harcourt and Mr Chamberlain, or vice versa, as if there were no such thing as party politics in the world. This sounds impartial; but does anybody find Mr Massingham "just"; or is it likely that he would be any the juster if his extraordinary small-hour performances were replaced by weekly ones? The fact is, justice is not the critic's business; and there is no more dishonest and insufferable affectation in criticism than that impersonal, abstract, judicially authoritative air which, since it is so easy to assume, and so well adapted to rapid phrase stringing, is directly encouraged by the haste which Dr Stanford deprecates.

In Dr Stanford's article which is a masterpiece in the way of tact, no individual critic now alive and working on the English press is talked either of or at. Instead, we have "the critic," "the musical correspondent," and so on. Now "the critic" is a very fine character. One can quite believe that if only the noble creature is given time to consider his utterances, he will hold the scales balanced to a hair's breadth. But just substitute for "the critic" the initials G. B. S. Instantly the realities of the case leap to light; and you see without any argument that the lapse of a few days beween the performance and the notice, far from obliterating the writer's partialities and prejudices, his personal likes and dislikes, his bias, his temperament, his local traditions, his nationality—in a word, himself, only enables him to express them the more insidiously when he wishes to conceal their influence.

No man sensitive enough to be worth his salt as a critic could for years wield a pen which, from the nature of his occupation, is scratching somebody's nerves at every stroke, without becoming conscious of how monstrously indefensible the superhuman attitude of impartiality is for him. If the countless injustices which I have done in these columns had been perpetrated in that attitude I should deserve hanging. I therefore add to Dr Stanford's plea for the more considerate utterance of the weekly feuilleton, a further plea for sincerity of expression, not only of the critic's opinion, but of the mood in which that opinion was formed.

We cannot get away from the critic's tempers, his impatiences, his sorenesses, his friendships, his spite, his enthusiasms (amatory and other), nay, his very politics and religion if they are touched by what he criticizes. They are all there hard at work; and it should be his point of honor—as it is certainly his interest if he wishes to avoid being dull—not to attempt to conceal them or to offer their product as the dispassionate dictum of infallible omniscience. If the public were to receive such a self exhibition by coldly saying, "We dont want to know the sort of person you are: we want to know whether such a work or artist or performance is good or bad," then the critic could unanswerably retort, "How on earth can you tell how much my opinion on that point is worth unless you know the sort of person I am?" As a matter of fact the public never does meet a good critic with any such rebuff. The critic who cannot interest the public in his real self has mistaken his trade: that is all.

Dr Stanford touches a painful point when he speaks of "the danger that editors who happen themselves to be ignorant of music, should engage the services of writers almost equally ignorant merely because they possess the gift of literary style." Here, for almost the only moment in his article, Dr Stanford speaks without inside knowledge of journalism. Editors, by some law of Nature which still baffles science, are *always* ignorant of music, and consequently always abjectly superstitious on the subject. Instead of looking the more keenly to the critic's other qualifications because they cannot judge of his musical ones, they regard him with an awe which makes them incapable of exercising any judgment at all about him.

Find me an editor who can tell at a glance whether a review, a leading article, a London letter, or a news paragraph is the work of a skilled hand or not, and who has even some power of recognizing what is money's worth and what is not in the way of a criticism of the Royal Academy or the last new play; and I, by simply writing that "the second subject, a graceful and flowing theme contrasting happily with the rugged vigor of its predecessor, appears unexpectedly in the key of the dominant," will reduce that able editor to a condition so abject that he will let me inundate his columns with pompous platitude, with the dullest plagiarisms from analytic programs, with shameless puffery, with bad grammar, bad logic, wrong dates, wrong names, with every conceivable blunder and misdemeanor that a journalist can commit, provided I do it in the capacity of his musical critic.

Not that my stuff will not bore and worry him as much as it will bore and worry other people; but what with his reluctance to risk a dispute with me on a subject he does not understand, and his habit of considering music as a department of lunacy, practised and read about by people who are not normally sane and healthy human beings, he will find it easiest to "suppose it is all right" and to console himself with the reflection that it does not matter anyhow. Dr Stanford says, "If editors appoint an incompetent person, public opinion is pretty sure, sooner or later, to find out and expose the ignoramus." This expectation is so entirely and desperately unwarranted by experience, that I may take it that Dr Stanford only offers it rather than leave the difficulty without at least a pretence of a solution.

But why not form a Vigilance Committee of musicians for the exposure of incompetent critics? The other day, as we all remember, five eminent musicians published a protest against a certain musical critic. Being new to their work, they did not do it well; and the critic got the best of it; but I sincerely hope the five will not be discouraged. After a few trials, a Vigilance Committee would learn to attack cautiously and effectively, and to avoid the professional weakness of exaggerating the importance of those blunders as to historic facts and musical technicalities which sometimes give a ludicrous air to really shrewd and essentially sound criticism.

Musical criticisms, like sermons, are of low average quality simply because they are never discussed or contradicted; and I should rejoice were such a committee to be formed, especially if Dr Stanford were to be chairman, and would undertake the drafting of such public protests as it might be deemed advisable to issue.

13 June 1894

The

Main Tradition

Is Gluck, the conqueror of Paris, at last going to con-
quer London? I hope so; for the man was a great master, one for whom we are hardly ready even yet.
Hitherto our plan of sweeping together a sackful of
opera-singers from Milan, Vienna, Montevideo, Chi-
cago, Clapham, China, and Peru, and emptying them
on to the Covent Garden stage to tumble through
Trovatore or Traviata as best they can, has not succeeded with Gluck. This Orfeo, for instance! Anyone
can see before the curtain is half-a-minute up that it
grew by the introduction of vocal music, not into
chaos, but into an elaborate existing organization of
ballet. The opening chorus, S' in questo bosco, sounds
nobly to people who are looking at groups of figures
in poetic motion or eloquent pose, at draperies falling
in graceful lines and flowing in harmonious colors, and
at scenery binding the whole into a complete and
single picture.

Under such circumstances, our old friend Monsei-
gneur of the Œil de Bœuf, when he had a taste that
way, no doubt enjoyed himself. But when we, to wit,
Smith and Jones, with our suburban traditions, going
to the Opera full of that sense of unaccustomed adven-
ture which the fine arts give us, are dumbfounded by
the spectacle of our old original choristers appealing

with every feature and limb against the unreasonableness of asking them to look like classical shepherds and shepherdesses—when their desperate Theocritean weeds have the promiscuity of Rag Fair without its picturesqueness—when even Katti Lanner's young ladies move awkwardly and uncertainly, put out of step by these long-drawn elegiac strains—when the scene suggests Wimbledon on a cold day, and Euridice's tomb is something between a Druidic cromlech and a milestone, bearing the name of the deceased in the tallest advertising stencil—then it must be confessed that *S' in questo bosco* affects its new acquaintances far from cheerfully.

These drawbacks were in full force at Covent Garden last Wednesday; but Orfeo triumphed in spite of them. Gluck and Giulia Ravogli were too many even for the shabby sofa, apparently borrowed from a decayed seaside lodging, which was shamelessly placed in the middle of the stage, just outside the mouth of Hades, for Euridice to die conveniently on. It was the stage-manager's last insult; and when it failed, he collected all his forces behind the scenes and set them talking at the top of their voices, so as to drown the singing and distract the attention of the audience. What a thing it is to live in the richest capital in the world, and yet have to take your grand opera, at its largest and most expensive theatre, with the makeshifts and absurdities of the barn and the booth! And to add to the exasperation of it, you are kept waiting longer between the acts for the dumping down of this miserable sofa on the bare boards than would be required for the setting of the most elaborate stage-picture at the Lyceum or Drury Lane.

I am not sure that Gluck is not in a better way to be understood now than he has been any time since the French Revolution. Listening to the strains in the Elysian Fields the other night, I could not help feeling

that music had strayed far away from them, and only
regained them the other day when Wagner wrote the
Good Friday music in Parsifal. No musical experience
in the journey between these two havens of rest seems
better than either. The Zauberflöte and the Ninth
Symphony have a discomforting consciousness of virtue, an uphill effort of aspiration, about them; but in
the Elysian Fields, in the Good Friday meadows, virtue and effort are transcended: there is no need to be
good or to strive upward any more: one has arrived,
and all those accursed hygienics of the soul are done
with and forgotten. Not that they were without a prig-
gish ecstasy of their own: I am far from denying that.
Virtue, like vice, has its attractions. It was well worth
while to slip through the Elysian hedge into the domain of Klingsor, and be shewn the enchantments of
his magic gardens by Weber, plunged into his struggles
and hopes by Beethoven, introduced to polite society
in his castle drawing room by Mendelssohn, besides being led by Mozart through many unforgettable episodes of comedy and romance—episodes producing no
bitter reaction like that which was apt to follow the
scenes of tragic passion or rapturous sentimentality
which Meyerbeer, Verdi, and Gounod managed so well
for Klingsor. I do not forget these for a moment; and
yet I am glad to be in the Elysian Fields again. And it
is because I have also been in the Good Friday meadows that I can now see, more clearly than anyone could
before Parsifal, how exactly Gluck was the Wagner of
his day—a thing that would have been violently dis-
puted by Berlioz, who was, nevertheless, almost as
good a critic as I. Listen to Orfeo, and you hear that
perfect union of the poem and the music—that growth
of every musical form, melodic interval, harmonic pro-
gression, and orchestral tone out of some feeling or purpose belonging to the drama—which you have only
heard before in the cantatas of Bach and the music

dramas of Wagner. Instead of the mere opera-making musician, tied to his poem as to a stake, and breaking loose whenever it gives him an excuse for a soldiers' chorus, or a waltz, or a crashing finale, we have the poet-musician who has no lower use for music than the expression of poetry.

Though it is easy to see all this in Orfeo during such numbers as *Che farò?* it might not have been so apparent last Wednesday in the ballet-music, although that never loses its poetic character, but for Giulia Ravogli, about whom I now confess myself infatuated. It is no longer anything to me that her diction is not always so pure as Salvini's, that her roulade is inferior in certainty and spontaneity to Signor Foli's, that the dress in which I first saw her as Amneris ought to have had ever so many yards more stuff in the train, that she would not put on the grey eyebrows and wrinkles of Azucena, and even that she is capable of coming out of a stage faint to bow to the applause it evokes. Ah, that heart-searching pantomime, saturated with feeling beyond all possibility of shortcoming in grace, as Orfeo came into those Elysian Fields, and stole from shade to shade, trying to identify by his sense of touch the one whom he was forbidden to seek with his eyes! Flagrant ballet-girls all those shades were; but it did not matter: Giulia awakened in us the power by which a child sees a living being in its rag doll. Even the *première danseuse* was transfigured to a possible Euridice as Giulia's hand, trembling with a restrained caress, passed over her eyes! And then the entry into Hades, the passionate pleading with the Furies, and, later on, the eloquence of the famous aria in the last act! I was hardly surprised, though I was alarmed, to see a gentleman in a stage-box, with frenzy in his eye, seize a substantial-looking bouquet and hurl it straight at her head, which would probably have been removed from her shoulders had not the missile fallen some yards short of its mark. Her success was immense. Nobody noticed that there were only two other solo-singers in the whole opera, both less than nothing beside her. She—and Gluck—sufficed. In the singer, as in the composer, we saw a perfectly original artistic impulse naïvely finding its way to the heart of the most artificial and complex of art forms.

Of the performance generally I have little to say. I intended to remonstrate about the Meyerbeerian cadenza which sounded so incongruously at the end of the first act; but I leave the remonstrance unspoken: Giulia shall do what she pleases, even if her next whim be to receive Eros in the first act with a strophe of *L'Amour, ce dieu profane*. But I submit as a matter for Bevignani's consideration—whilst acknowledging the care and thoroughness with which he has rehearsed the work—that the chorus *Che mai dell' Erebo* is hopeless at Covent Garden as an andante. His motley forces are utterly incapable of the Titanic tread with which this giant measure should march—"ben marcato," each crotchet a bar in itself. Under the circumstances it would be better to take it at exactly the same speed, and with the same strength and precision of accent, as the first movement of the Eroica Symphony. At this rate the groups of three sforzandos for the basses would sound like three gruff, fierce barks from the three-headed dog at the gate of hell (which is what Gluck intended), whereas at present they only suggest that Orpheus is a stout sluggish gentleman, giving his boots three careful scrapes outside the door *pour se décrotter*.

12 November 1890

MOZART

Don Giovanni

Ever since I was a boy I have been in search of a satisfactory performance of Don Giovanni; and I have at last come to see that Mozart's turn will hardly be in my time. I have had no lack of opportunities and disappointments; for the Don is never left long on the shelf, since it is so far unlike the masterpieces of Wagner, Berlioz, and Bach, that it cannot be done at all without arduous preparation. Any opera singer can pick up the notes and tumble through the concerted pieces with one eye on the conductor: any band can scrape through the orchestral parts at sight. Last year and the year before, it was tried in this fashion for a night at Covent Garden, with D'Andrade as Don Juan, and anybody who came handy in the other parts. This year it has been recognized that trifling with Mozart can be carried too far even for the credit of the Royal Italian Opera.

At the performance last Thursday, the first three acts of the four (twice too many) into which the work is divided at Covent Garden shewed signs of rehearsal. Even the last had not been altogether neglected. In the orchestra especially the improvement was marked. Not that anything very wonderful was accomplished in this department: the vigorous passages were handled in the usual timid, conventional way; and the statue music, still as impressive as it was before Wagner and Berlioz were born, was muddled through like a vote of thanks at the end of a very belated public meeting. But the overture was at least attentively played; and in some of the quieter and simpler numbers the exhalations of the magical atmosphere of the

Mozartian orchestra were much less scanty and foggy
than last year, when I could not, without risk of being
laughed at, have assured a novice that in the subtle-
ties of dramatic instrumentation Mozart was the greatest master of them all. The cast was neither a very bad
nor a very good one. Its weakest point was the
Leporello of Isnardon. Lacking the necessary weight
in the middle of his voice, as well as the personal force
demanded by the character, he was quite unable to
lead the final section of the great sextet, *Mille torbidi
pensieri,* which, thus deprived of its stage significance,
became a rather senseless piece of "absolute music."
Again, in *O statua gentilissima,* he hardly seized a
point from beginning to end.

Now if an artist has neither voice enough nor musical perception enough to interpret forcibly and intelli-
gently such an obvious and simple dramatic transition
as that which follows the incident of the statue nodding
acceptance of the invitation to supper, he is not fit to
meddle with Mozart. Isnardon certainly makes a considerable show of acting throughout the opera; but as
he is only trying to be facetious—abstractly facetious,
if I may say so—without the slightest feeling for his
part, the effect is irritating and irrelevant. Such pieces
of business as his pointing the words, *Voi sapete quel
che fa,* by nudging Elvira with his elbow at the end
of *Madamina,* almost make one's blood boil. Poor old
Sganarelle-Leporelle, with all his failings, was no Yel-
low-plush: he would not have presumed upon a familiarity of that character with Donna Elvira, even if she
had been a much meeker and less distinguished person
than Molière made her. There is one man in Mr
Harris's company whose clear artistic duty it is to play
Leporello; and he, unfortunately, is an arrant *fainéant,*
whose identity I charitably hide under the designation
of Brother Edouard, which, I need hardly add, is not
that under which he appears in the bills. In Leporello

he would have one of the greatest parts ever written, exactly suited to his range, and full of points which his musical intelligence would seize instinctively without unaccustomed mental exertion. And now that I have begun sketching a new cast, I may as well complete it. *Dalla sua pace* is not an easy song to sing; but if Jean de Reszke were to do it justice, the memory thereof would abide when all his Gounod successes were lapsed and lost.

With Giulia Ravogli as Zerlina, and the rest of the parts allotted much as at present, a tremendous house would be drawn. Nevertheless the tremendous house would be bored and kept late for its trains unless the representation were brought up to date by the following measures. Take a pot of paste, a scissors and some tissue paper, and start on the recitativo secco by entirely expunging the first two dialogues after the duel and before *Ah, chi mi dice mai.* Reduce all the rest to such sentences as are barely necessary to preserve the continuity of the action. Play the opera in two acts only. And use the time thus gained to restore not only the Don's song, *Metà di voi,* which Faure used to sing, but, above all, the last three movements of the second finale, thereby putting an end for ever to the sensational vulgarity of bringing down the curtain on the red fire and the ghost and the trapdoor. There are other suppressed pages of the score to be reconsidered—a capital song which gets Leporello off the stage after the sextet, a curiously old-fashioned tragic air, almost Handelian, for Elvira between *Là ci darem* and the quartet, and a comic duet for Zerlina and Leporello, one of the later Vienna interpolations, which, however, is a very dispensable piece of buffoonery.

To return to the actual Don Giovanni of Thursday last, I need say no more of Miss de Lussan, who does not grow more interesting as her voice loses freshness and sustaining power and her manner becomes perter and trickier, than that she is one of those Zerlinas who end *Batti, batti,* on the upper octave of the note written, as a sort of apology for having been unable to do anything else with the song. The effect of this suburban grace can be realized by anyone who will take the trouble to whistle Pop Goes the Weasel with the last note displaced an octave.

I am sorry to add that alterations of Mozart's text were the order of the evening, every one of the singers lacking Mozart's exquisite sense of form and artistic dignity. Maurel, though he stopped short of reviving the traditional atrocity of going up to F sharp in the serenade, did worse things by dragging an F natural into the end of *Finch' han dal vino,* and two unpardonable G's into the finale of the first ballroom scene, just before the final stretto, thereby anticipating and destroying the climax *Odi il tuon* from the sopranos. Madame Tavary still clings to that desolating run up and down the scale with which she contrives to make the conclusion of *Non mi dir* ridiculous; and Montariol, unable to evade *Il mio tesoro* by omitting it like *Dalla sua pace,* did strange things with it in his desperation. His Ottavio was altogether a melancholy performance, as he was put out of countenance from the beginning by being clothed in a seedy misfit which made him look lamentably down on his luck. Mr Harris would not dream of allowing such a costume to be seen on his stage in a modern opera; and I must really urge upon him that there are limits to the application even of the principle that anything is good enough for Mozart.

Maurel's Don Giovanni, though immeasurably better than any we have seen of late years, is not to be compared to his Rigoletto, his Iago, or, in short, to any of his melodramatic parts. Don Juan may be as handsome, as irresistible, as adroit, as unscrupulous, as brave as you please; but the one thing that is not to be tolerated is that he should consciously parade these qualities as

if they were elaborate accomplishments instead of his
natural parts. And this is exactly where Maurel failed.
He gave us a description of Don Juan rather than an
impersonation of him. The confident smile, the heroic
gesture, the splendid dress, even the intentionally se-
ductive vocal inflexion which made such a success of
Là ci darem in spite of Miss de Lussan's coquettish
inanity, were all more or less artificial. A Don Juan
who is continually aiming at being Don Juan may excite our admiration by the skill with which he does
it; but he cannot convince us that he is the real man. I
remember seeing Jean de Reszke play the part when
he had less than a tenth of Maurel's present skill and
experience; and yet I think Mozart would have found
the younger man the more sympathetic interpreter.

It seems ungrateful to find fault with an artist who
rescues a great rôle from the hands of such ignoble
exponents as the common or Covent Garden Dons who
swagger feebly through it like emancipated billiard-
markers; but it would hardly be a compliment to
Maurel to praise him for so cheap a superiority. And,
indeed, there is no fault-finding in the matter. It is a
question of temperament. When all is said, the fundamental impossibility remains that Maurel's artistic vein
is not Mozartian. One or two points of detail may be
mentioned. He was best in the love-making scenes and
worst in those with Leporello, whom he treated with
a familiarity which was rather that of Robert Macaire
with Jacques Strop than of a gentleman with his valet.
The scene of the exposure in the ballroom he played
rather callously. Nothing in the score is clearer than
that Don Juan is discomfited, confused, and at a loss
from the moment in which they denounce him until,
seeing that there is nothing for it but to fight his way
out, he ceases to utter hasty exclamations of dismay,
and recovers himself at the words *Ma non manca in
me coraggio.* Maurel dehumanized and melodrama-

tized the scene by missing this entirely, and maintaining a defiant and self-possessed bearing throughout.

And again, on the entry of the statue, which Don Juan, however stable his nerve may be imagined to have been, can hardly have witnessed without at least a dash of surprise and curiosity, Maurel behaved very much as if his uncle had dropped in unexpectedly in the middle of a bachelor's supper-party. The result was that the scene went for nothing, though it is beyond all comparison the most wonderful of the wonders of dramatic music. But if the audience is ever to be cured of the habit of treating it as a sort of voluntary to play them out, it must be very carefully studied by the artist playing Don Juan, upon whose pantomime the whole action of the scene depends, since the statue can only stand with a stony air of weighing several tons, whilst the orchestra makes him as awful as the conductor will allow it. Since Maurel let this scene slip completely through his fingers, I do not see how he can be classed with the great Don Juans (if there ever were any great ones). The problem of how to receive a call from a public statue does not seem to have struck him as worth solving.

The Elvira (Madame Rolla), whose B flat at the end of her aria was perhaps the most excusable of all the inexcusable interpolations, was as good as gold, not indulging once in a scream, and relying altogether on pure vocal tone of remarkable softness. In *Mi tradi* she succeeded in being more pleasing than any Elvira I can remember except Di Murska, who understood the full value of the part and played it incomparably, like the great artist she was. Madame Rolla does not act with the force of Nilsson; and in the quartet she failed to bring off the effect at the end, where Elvira gets louder and angrier whilst the wretched Don gets more and more agitated by the dread of her making a scene; but I think Maurel was a little unequal to the occasion here too. On the whole, Madame Rolla, whose voice reminds one somewhat of Marimon's, is a useful addition to the company. Mr Harris had better now turn his attention to achieving a really serious performance of *Le Nozze di Figaro*.

13 May 1891

The Mozart Centenary, 1891

The Mozart Centenary has made a good deal of literary and musical business this week. Part of this is easy enough, especially for the illustrated papers. Likenesses of Mozart at all ages; view of Salzburg; portrait of Marie Antoinette (described in the text as "the ill-fated"), to whom he proposed marriage at an early age; picture of the young composer, two and a half feet high, crushing the Pompadour with his "Who is this woman that refuses to kiss me? The Queen kissed me! (Sensation)"; facsimile of the original MS. of the first four bars of *Là ci darem*, and the like. These, with copious paraphrases of the English translation of Otto Jahn's great biography, will pull the journalists proper through the Centenary with credit. The critic's task is not quite so easy.

The word is, of course, Admire, admire, admire; but unless you frankly trade on the ignorance of the public, and cite as illustrations of his unique genius feats that come easily to dozens of organists and choir-boys who never wrote, and never will write, a bar of original music in their lives; or pay his symphonies and operas empty compliments that might be transferred word for word, without the least incongruity, to the symphonies of Spohr and the operas of Offenbach; or represent him as composing as spontaneously as a bird sings, on the strength of his habit of perfecting his greater compositions in his mind before he wrote them down—unless you try these well-worn dodges, you will find nothing to admire that is peculiar to Mozart: the fact being that he, like Praxiteles, Raphael, Molière, or Shakespear, was no leader of a new departure or founder of a school. He came at the end of a development, not at the beginning of one; and although there are operas and symphonies, and even pianoforte sonatas and pages of instrumental scoring of his, on which you can put your finger and say, "Here is final perfection in this manner; and nobody, whatever his genius may be, will ever get a step further on these lines," you cannot say, "Here is an entirely new vein of musical art, of which nobody ever dreamt before Mozart." Haydn, who made the mould for Mozart's symphonies, was proud of Mozart's genius because he felt his own part in it: he would have written the E flat symphony if he could, and, though he could not, was at least able to feel that the man who had reached that pre-eminence was standing on his old shoulders. Now, Haydn would have recoiled from the idea of composing—or perpetrating, as he would have put it—the first movement of Beethoven's Eroica, and would have repudiated all part in leading music to such a pass.

The more far-sighted Gluck not only carried Mozart in his arms to within sight of the goal of his career as an opera composer, but even cleared a little of the new path into which Mozart's finality drove all those successors of his who were too gifted to waste their lives in making weak dilutions of Mozart's scores, and serving them up as "classics." Many Mozart worshippers cannot bear to be told that their hero was not the founder of a dynasty. But in art the highest success is ⁺o be the last of your race, not the first. Anybody, almost, can make a beginning: the difficulty is to make an end—to do what cannot be bettered.

For instance, if the beginner were to be ranked above the consummator, we should, in literary fiction, have to place Captain Mayne Reid, who certainly struck a new vein, above Dickens, who simply took the novel as he found it, and achieved the feat of compelling his successor (whoever he may be), either to create quite another sort of novel, or else to fall behind his predecessor as at best a superfluous imitator. Surely, if so great a composer as Haydn could say, out of his greatness as a man, "I am not the best of my school, though I was the first," Mozart's worshippers can afford to acknowledge, with equal gladness of spirit, that their hero was not the first, though he was the best. It is always like that. Praxiteles, Raphael and Co., have great men for their pioneers, and only fools for their followers.

So far everybody will agree with me. This proves either that I am hopelessly wrong or that the world has had at least half a century to think the matter over in. And, sure enough, a hundred years ago Mozart was considered a desperate innovator: it was his reputation in this respect that set so many composers—Meyerbeer, for example—cultivating innovation for its own sake. Let us, therefore, jump a hundred years forward, right up to date, and see whether there is any phenomenon of the same nature in view today. We have not to look far. Here, under our very noses, is Wagner held up on all hands as the founder of a school and the arch-musical innovator of our age. He himself knew better; but since his death I appear to be the only person who shares his view of the matter. I assert with the utmost confidence that in 1991 it will be seen quite clearly that Wagner was the end of the nineteenth century, or Beethoven school, instead of the beginning of the twentieth-century school; just as Mozart's most perfect music is the last word of the eighteenth century, and not the first of the nineteenth. It is none the less plain because everyone knows that Il Seraglio was the beginning of the school of nineteenth-century German operas of Mozart, Beethoven, Weber, and Wagner; that

Das Veilchen is the beginning of the nineteenth-century German song of Schubert, Mendelssohn, and Schumann; and that Die Zauberflöte is the ancestor, not only of the Ninth Symphony, but of the Wagnerian allegorical music-drama, with personified abstractions instead of individualized characters as *dramatis personæ*. But Il Seraglio and Die Zauberflöte do not belong to the group of works which constitute Mozart's consummate achievement—Don Juan, Le Nozze di Figaro, and his three or four perfect symphonies. They are nineteenth-century music heard advancing in the distance, as his Masses are seventeenth-century music retreating in the distance. And, similarly, though the future fossiliferous critics of 1991, after having done their utmost, without success, to crush twentieth-century music, will be able to shew that Wagner (their chief classic) made one or two experiments in that direction, yet the world will rightly persist in thinking of him as a characteristically nineteenth-century composer of the school of Beethoven, greater than Beethoven by as much as Mozart was greater than Haydn. And now I hope I have saved my reputation by saying something at which everybody will exclaim, "Bless me! what nonsense!" Nevertheless, it is true; and our would-be Wagners had better look to it; for all their efforts to exploit the apparently inexhaustible wealth of musical material opened up at Bayreuth only prove that Wagner used it up to the last ounce, and that secondhand Wagner is more insufferable, because usually more pretentious, than even secondhand Mozart used to be.

For my own part, if I do not care to rhapsodize much about Mozart, it is because I am so violently prepossessed in his favor that I am capable of supplying any possible deficiency in his work by my imagination. Gounod has devoutly declared that Don Giovanni has been to him all his life a revelation of perfection, a miracle, a work without fault. I smile indulgently at

Gounod, since I cannot afford to give myself away so generously (there being, no doubt, less of me); but I am afraid my fundamental attitude towards Mozart is the same as his. In my small-boyhood I by good luck had an opportunity of learning the Don thoroughly, and if it were only for the sense of the value of fine workmanship which I gained from it, I should still esteem that lesson the most important part of my education. Indeed, it educated me artistically in all sorts of ways, and disqualified me only in one—that of criticizing Mozart fairly. Everyone appears a sentimental, hysterical bungler in comparison when anything brings his finest work vividly back to me. Let me take warning by the follies of Oublicheff, and hold my tongue.

The people most to be pitied at this moment are the unfortunate singers, players, and conductors who are suddenly called upon to make the public *hear* the wonders which the newspapers are describing so lavishly. At ordinary times they simply refuse to do this. It is quite a mistake to suppose that Mozart's music is not in demand. I know of more than one concert-giver who asks every singer he engages for some song by Mozart, and is invariably met with the plea of excessive difficulty. You cannot "make an effect" with Mozart, or work your audience up by playing on their hysterical susceptibilities.

Nothing but the finest execution—beautiful, expressive, and intelligent—will serve; and the worst of it is, that the phrases are so perfectly clear and straightforward, that you are found out the moment you swerve by a hair's breadth from perfection, whilst, at the same time, your work is so obvious, that everyone thinks it must be easy, and puts you down remorselessly as a duffer for botching it. Naturally, then, we do not hear much of Mozart; and what we do hear goes far to destroy his reputation. But there was no getting out of the Centenary: something had to be done. Accordingly, the Crystal Palace committed itself to the Jupiter Symphony and the Requiem; and the Albert Hall, by way of varying the entertainment, announced the Requiem and the Jupiter Symphony.

The Requiem satisfied that spirit of pious melancholy in which we celebrate great occasions; but I think the public ought to be made rather more sharply aware of the fact that Mozart died before the Requiem was half finished, and that his widow, in order to secure the stipulated price, got one of her husband's pupils, whose handwriting resembled his, to forge enough music to complete it. Undoubtedly Mozart gave a good start to most of the movements; but, suggestive as these are, very few of them are artistically so satisfactory as the pretty *Benedictus*, in which the forger escaped from the taskwork of cobbling up his master's hints to the free work of original composition. There are only about four numbers in the score which have any right to be included in a centenary program. As to the two performances, I cannot compare them, as I was late for the one at the Albert Hall.

The Jupiter Symphony was conducted by Mr Manns in the true heroic spirit; and he was well seconded by the wind band; but the strings disgraced themselves. In the first movement even what I may call the common decencies of execution were lacking: Mr Manns should have sent every fiddler of them straight back to school to learn how to play scales cleanly, steadily, and finely. At the Albert Hall, there was no lack of precision and neatness; but Mr Henschel's reading was, on the whole, the old dapper, empty, *petit-maître* one of which I, at least, have had quite enough. Happily, Mr Henschel immediately redeemed this failure—for such it was— by a really fine interpretation of the chorus of priests from the Zauberflöte. This, with Mr Lloyd's delivery of one of the finest of Mozart's concert arias, Mr Norman Salmond's singing of a capital English version of

Non più andrai, and the Crystal Palace Band's performance of the Masonic Dirge, were the successes of the celebration. I should add that Mr Joseph Bennett, fresh from throwing his last stone at Wagner, modestly wrote a poem for recitation between the Requiem and the Symphony. He appeals to Mozart, with evidently sincere emotion, to accept his lines, in spite of any little shortcomings,

Since tis from the heart they flow,
Bright with pure affection's glow.

Perhaps Dr Mackenzie or Dr Parry, in view of a well-known observation of Beaumarchais, may set Mr Bennett's ode to music some of these days, Mr Herkomer, too, has helped by drawing a fancy portrait of Mozart. I have compared it carefully with all the accredited portraits, and can confidently pronounce it to be almost supernaturally unlike the original.

9 December 1891

Tuneful Little Trifles?

The Philharmonic, I am glad to say, rose to the occasion on Thursday last, when it devoted its first concert of the season to the works of Mozart, whose bust, wreathed with laurel, had the same dissipated air which I remember seeing a lady instantaneously produce in the living Wagner by crowning him, too, with a wreath which had not been made for him. The concert was a great success. The music had been thoroughly rehearsed; the band was on its mettle, the strings going with extraordinary brilliancy and precision; and Mr Cowen did his very best. The result was one of those performances during which, if you happen to turn to the program of the next concert, as I did, and find that the symphony there announced is Beethoven's Seventh, you feel that you really cannot listen to such clumsy and obvious sensationalism after Mozart.

For my part, I heartily wish that the Philharmonic Society would devote not merely one concert but a whole season to the commemoration, with a view to educating our London amateurs. These ladies and gentlemen, having for years known Mozart only by vapid and superficial performances which were worse than complete neglect, or by the wretched attempts made to exploit Don Giovanni from time to time at our opera-houses, have hardly yet got out of the habit of regarding Mozart's compositions as tuneful little trifles fit only for persons of the simplest tastes. I have known people to talk in this fashion whilst they were running after every available repetition of the *Walkürenritt,* the Lohengrin bridal prelude, or the finale to Beethoven's Seventh Symphony—all of them glorified bursts of rum-tum, which any donkey could take in at the first hearing—firmly believing them to be profound compositions, caviare to the general. Much as if a picture-fancier should consider Gustave Doré's and Leon Gallait's work finer and deeper than Carpaccio's, or a literary critic declare Victor Hugo the great master of masters, and Molière an obsolete compiler of trivial farces.

I do not deny that there has been an improvement in popular taste in the last few years, and that mere musical stimulants, from the comparatively innocent whisky-and-water of the Beethoven coda and the Rossini crescendo to the fiery intoxicants of Liszt and Berlioz, are beginning to be recognized for what they really are—that is, excitements which have their use on the stage, in the dance, and in flashes of fun and festivity, but which are as much out of place in the highest class of music as a war-dance would be at a meeting of the Royal Society. The notion that the absence of such stimulants from the symphonies and the chamber-music of Mozart is to be counted against him as a deficiency, is precisely analogous to the disappointment which a sporting collier might experience at going to the Lyceum Theatre and finding that the incidents in Henry VIII did not include a little ratting. And if no such notion has prevailed among our Wagnerians, how is it that when you turn over the programs of the Richter Concerts you find such an inordinate proportion of *Walkürenritt* and Seventh Symphony to such a paltry scrap of Mozart? in spite of the fact that Richter's conducting of the E flat symphony was one of his highest achievements—if not his very highest—here as a conductor.

When no demand arose for a repetition of it, I could not help suspecting that if Richter had tried his followers with the chorus of Janissaries from Il Seraglio, or with a vigorous arrangement of *Viva la libertà*, he might have hit off their Mozartian capacity more happily. On the whole, I have no hesitation in saying that as soon as our Wagnerians (and do not forget that there is no more enthusiastic Wagnerian than I have shewn myself) have had their eyes opened to the fact that Wagnerism may cover a plentiful lack of culture and love of stimulants in music, we shall hear more of Mozart's symphonies and concertos, scandalously neglected now for a whole generation, and yet far more beautiful and interesting than any of their kind produced since, by Beethoven or anyone else.

16 March 1892

His Gentleness

In the ardent regions where all the rest are excited and vehement, Mozart alone is completely self-possessed: where they are clutching their bars with a grip of iron and forging them with Cyclopean blows, his gentleness of touch never deserts him: he is considerate, economical, practical under the same pressure of inspiration that throws your Titan into convulsions. This is the secret of his unpopularity with Titan fanciers. We all in our native barbarism have a relish for the strenuous: your tenor whose B flat is like the bursting of a boiler always brings down the house, even when the note brutally effaces the song; and the composer who can artistically express in music a transport of vigor and passion of the more muscular kind, such as the finale to the Seventh Symphony, the *Walkürenritt*, or the Hailstone chorus, not to mention the orgies of Raff, Liszt, and Berlioz, is always a hero with the intemperate in music, who are so numerous nowadays that we may confidently expect to see some day a British Minister of the Fine Arts introducing a local Option Bill applied to concert rooms.

With Mozart you are safe from inebriety. Hurry, excitement, eagerness, loss of consideration, are to him purely comic or vicious states of mind: he gives us Monostatos and the Queen of Night on the stage, but not in his chamber music. Now it happens that I have, deep in my nature, which is quite as deep as the average rainfall in England, a frightful contempt for your Queens of Night and Titans and their like. The true Parnassian air acts on these people like oxygen on a mouse: it first excites them, and then kills them. Give me the artist who breathes it like a native, and goes about his work in it as quietly as a common man goes about his ordinary business. Mozart did so; and that is why I like him. Even if I did not, I should pretend to; for a taste for his music is a mark of caste among musicians, and should be worn, like a tall hat, by the amateur who wishes to pass for a true Brahmin.

19 April 1893

Mozart and Beethoven

Do you know that noble fantasia in C minor, in which Mozart shewed what Beethoven was to do with the pianoforte sonata, just as in Das Veilchen he showed what Schubert was to do with the song? Imagine my feelings when Madame Backer Gröndahl, instead of playing this fantasia (which she would have done beautifully), set Madame Haas to play it, and then sat down beside her and struck up "an original part for a second piano," in which every interpolation was an impertinence and every addition a blemish. Shocked and pained as every one who knew and loved the fantasia must have been, there was a certain grim ironic interest in the fact that the man who has had the unspeakable presumption to offer us his improvements on Mozart is the infinitesimal Grieg. The world reproaches Mozart for his inspired variation on Handel's "The people that walked in darkness." I do not know what the world will now say to Grieg; but if ever he plays that "original second part" himself to an audience equipped with adequate musical culture, I sincerely advise him to ascertain beforehand that no brickbats or other loose and suitably heavy articles have been left carelessly about the room.

7 March 1890

BEETHOVEN'S CENTENARY

A hundred years ago a crusty old bachelor of fifty-seven, so deaf that he could not hear his own music played by a full orchestra, yet still able to hear thunder, shook his fist at the roaring heavens for the last time, and died as he had lived, challenging God and defying the universe. He was Defiance Incarnate: he could not even meet a Grand Duke and his court in the street without jamming his hat tight down on his head and striding through the very middle of them. He had the manners of a disobliging steamroller (most steamrollers are abjectly obliging and conciliatory); and he was rather less particular about his dress than a scarecrow: in fact he was once arrested as a tramp because the police refused to believe that such a tatterdemalion could be a famous composer, much less a temple of the most turbulent spirit that ever found expression in pure sound. It was indeed a mighty spirit; but if I had written the mightiest, which would mean mightier than the spirit of Handel, Beethoven himself would have rebuked me; and what mortal man could pretend to a spirit mightier than Bach's? But that Beethoven's spirit was the most turbulent is beyond all question. The impetuous fury of his strength, which he could quite easily contain and control, but often would not, and the uproariousness of his fun, go beyond anything of the kind to be found in the works of other composers. Greenhorns write of syncopation now as if it were a new way of giving the utmost impetus to a musical measure; but the rowdiest jazz sounds like The Maiden's Prayer after Beethoven's third Leonora overture; and certainly no negro corobbery that I ever heard could inspire the blackest dancer with such *diable au corps* as the last movement of the Seventh Symphony. And no other composer has ever melted his hearers into complete sentimentality by the tender beauty of his music, and then suddenly turned on them and mocked them with derisive trumpet blasts for being such fools. Nobody but Beethoven could govern Beethoven; and when, as happened when the fit was on him, he deliberately refused to govern himself, he was ungovernable.

It was this turbulence, this deliberate disorder, this mockery, this reckless and triumphant disregard of conventional manners, that set Beethoven apart from the musical geniuses of the ceremonious seventeenth and eighteenth centuries. He was a giant wave in that storm of the human spirit which produced the French Revolution. He called no man master. Mozart, his greatest predecessor in his own department, had from his childhood been washed, combed, splendidly dressed, and beautifully behaved in the presence of royal personages and peers. His childish outburst at the Pompadour, "Who is this woman who does not kiss me? The Queen kisses me," would be incredible of Beethoven, who was still an unlicked cub even when he had grown into a very grizzly bear. Mozart had the refinement of convention and society as well as the refinement of nature and of the solitudes of the soul. Mozart and Gluck are refined as the court of Louis XIV was refined: Haydn is refined as the most cultivated country gentlemen of his day were refined: compared to them socially Beethoven was an obstreperous Bohemian: a man of the people. Haydn, so superior to envy that he declared his junior, Mozart, to be the greatest composer that ever lived, could not stand Beethoven: Mozart, more farseeing, listened to his playing, and said "You will hear of him some day"; but the two would never have hit it off together had Mozart lived long enough to try. Beethoven had a moral horror of Mozart, who in Don Giovanni had thrown a halo of enchantment round an aristocratic blackguard, and then, with the unscrupulous moral versatility of a born dramatist, turned round to cast a halo of divinity round Sarastro, setting his words to the only music yet written that would not sound out of place in the mouth of God.

Beethoven was no dramatist: moral versatility was to him revolting cynicism. Mozart was still to him the master of masters (this is not an empty eulogistic superlative: it means literally that Mozart is a composer's composer much more than he has ever been a really popular composer); but he was a court flunkey in breeches whilst Beethoven was a Sansculotte; and Haydn also was a flunkey in the old livery: the Revolution stood between them as it stood between the eighteenth and nineteenth centuries. But to Beethoven Mozart was worse than Haydn because he trifled with morality by setting vice to music as magically as virtue. The Puritan who is in every true Sansculotte rose up against him in Beethoven, though Mozart had shewn him all the possibilities of nineteenth-century music. So Beethoven cast back for a hero to Handel, another crusty old bachelor of his own kidney, who despised Mozart's hero Gluck, though the pastoral symphony in The Messiah is the nearest thing in music to the scenes in which Gluck, in his Orfeo, opened to us the plains of Heaven.

Thanks to broadcasting, millions of musical novices will hear the music of Beethoven this anniversary year for the first time with their expectations raised to an extraordinary pitch by hundreds of newspaper articles piling up all the conventional eulogies that are applied indiscriminately to all the great composers. And like his contemporaries they will be puzzled by getting from him not merely a music that they did not expect, but often an orchestral hurlyburly that they may not recognize as what they call music at all, though they can appreciate Gluck and Haydn and Mozart quite well. The explanation is simple enough. The music of the eighteenth century is all dance music. A dance is a symmetrical pattern of steps that are pleasant to move to; and its music is a symmetrical pattern of sound that is pleasant to listen to even when you are not dancing to it. Consequently the sound patterns, though they begin by being as simple as chessboards, get lengthened and elaborated and enriched with harmonies until they are more like Persian carpets; and the composers who design these patterns no longer expect people to dance to them. Only a whirling Dervish could dance a Mozart symphony: indeed, I have reduced two young and practised dancers to exhaustion by making them dance a Mozart overture. The very names of the dances are dropped: instead of suites consisting of sarabands, pavanes, gavottes, and jigs, the designs are presented as sonatas and symphonies consisting of sections called simply movements, and labelled according to their speed (in Italian) as allegros, adagios, scherzos, and prestos. But all the time, from Bach's preludes to Mozart's Jupiter Symphony, the music makes a symmetrical sound pattern, and gives us the dancer's pleasure always as the form and foundation of the piece.

Music, however, can do more than make beautiful sound patterns. It can express emotion. You can look at a Persian carpet and listen to a Bach prelude with a delicious admiration that goes no further than itself; but you cannot listen to the overture to Don Giovanni without being thrown into a complicated mood which prepares you for a tragedy of some terrible doom overshadowing an exquisite but Satanic gaiety. If you listen to the last movement of Mozart's Jupiter Symphony, you hear that it is as much a riotous corobbery as the last movement of Beethoven's Seventh Symphony: it is an orgy of ranting drumming tow-row-row, made poignant by an opening strain of strange and painful beauty which is woven through the pattern all through. And yet the movement is a masterpiece of pattern designing all the time.

Now what Beethoven did, and what made some of his greatest contemporaries give him up as a madman with lucid intervals of clowning and bad taste, was that he used music altogether as a means of expressing moods, and completely threw over pattern designing as an end in itself. It is true that he used the old pat-

terns all his life with dogged conservatism (another
Sansculotte characteristic, by the way); but he imposed on them such an overwhelming charge of human energy and passion, including that highest
passion which accompanies thought, and reduces the
passion of the physical appetites to mere animalism,
that he not only played Old Harry with their symmetry but often made it impossible to notice that there
was any pattern at all beneath the storm of emotion.
The Eroica Symphony begins by a pattern (borrowed
from an overture which Mozart wrote when he was a
boy), followed by a couple more very pretty patterns;
but they are tremendously energized, and in the middle of the movement the patterns are torn up savagely;
and Beethoven, from the point of view of the mere
pattern musician, goes raving mad, hurling out terrible chords in which all the notes of the scale are
sounded simultaneously, just because he feels like that,
and wants you to feel like it.

And there you have the whole secret of Beethoven.
He could design patterns with the best of them; he
could write music whose beauty will last you all your
life; he could take the driest sticks of themes and work
them up so interestingly that you find something new
in them at the hundredth hearing: in short, you can
say of him all that you can say of the greatest pattern
composers; but his diagnostic, the thing that marks
him out from all the others, is his disturbing quality,
his power of unsettling us and imposing his giant
moods on us. Berlioz was very angry with an old
French composer who expressed the discomfort Beethoven gave him by saying *"J'aime la musique qui me
berce,"* "I like music that lulls me." Beethoven's is
music that wakes you up; and the one mood in which
you shrink from it is the mood in which you want to
be let alone.

When you understand this you will advance beyond

the eighteenth century and the old-fashioned dance
band (jazz, by the way, is the old dance band Bee-
thovenized), and understand not only Beethoven's
music, but what is deepest in post-Beethoven music as
well.

From *the* RADIO TIMES
18 March 1927

ROSSINI CENTENARY, 1892

The Rossini Centenary passed without any celebration
in London (as far as I know) except an afternoon concert at the Crystal Palace, whither I went, partly for
the sake of old times, and partly because the concert
afforded me an opportunity, now very rare, of hearing
Rossini's overtures, not from a military band, or from a
careless promenade-concert orchestra with an enormous preponderance of string quartet, but from a first-
rate wind-band, balanced by about as many strings
as the composer reckoned upon. The program was
made up of no fewer than four overtures—Siege of
Corinth, La Gazza Ladra, Semiramide, and William
Tell—with an admirable arrangement of the prayer
from Moses for orchestra and organ by Mr Manns, and
two vocal pieces, *Di piacer* and *Una voce*, curiously
chosen, since one is almost an inversion of the intervals
of the other. There was, besides, a selection from William Tell, arranged for the band alone.

This was rather too much for the endurance of the
orchestra, which became a little demoralized towards
the end. Rossini's band parts consist mostly of uninteresting stretches of rum-tum, relieved here and there by
some abominably inconvenient melodic trait; for he
was the most "absolute" of musicians: his tunes came
into his head unconnected with any particular quality

of tone, and were handed over to the instrument they would sound prettiest on, without the least regard to the technical convenience of the player—further, of course, than to recognize the physical limits of possibility, and not write piccolo parts down to sixteen-foot C, or tombone parts up to C in altissimo. Consequently, though the scores of Berlioz and Wagner are in a sense far more difficult than those of Rossini, you do not hear during performances of their works any of those little hitches or hair-breadth escapes which are apt to occur when a player has to achieve a feat, however trifling, which is foreign to the genius of his instrument.

It is true that what I call the genius of the instrument varies with the nationality of the player; so that a French horn, though most refractory to a compatriot of its own, or to an Englishman, will be quite docile in the hands of a German; or twelve violins played by Italians will have less weight in an orchestra than five played by Englishmen, not to mention other and subtler differences. Yet the fact remains that we have at present a sort of international school of orchestration, through which an English player, whatever his instrument may be, finds much the same class of work set for him, whether the composer be the Italian Verdi, the French Gounod or Massenet, the Jew Max Bruch, the Bohemian Dvořák, the Norwegian Grieg, the Dutchman Benoit, and so on to the Irish Villiers Stanford, the Scotch Hamish MacCunn, and the English— well, perhaps I had better not mention names in the case of England. Rossini's scores, especially those which he wrote for Venice and Naples, run off these lines; and the result is, that at a Rossini concert there is more likelihood of actual slips in execution than at a Wagner or Beethoven concert; whilst the eventual worrying, fatiguing, and boring of the executants is a certainty when the program is a long one.

The Crystal Palace band held out brilliantly until the final number, which was the overture and selection from William Tell, in the course of which it occurred to most of them that they had had about enough of the Swan of Pesaro. Yet the Swan came off more triumphantly than one could have imagined possible at this time of day. *Dal tuo stellato soglio* was as sublime as ever. Mr. Manns conducted it as he had arranged it, with perfect judgment and sympathy with its inspiration; and in spite of myself I so wanted to hear it again that after a careful look round to see that none of my brother-critics were watching me I wore away about an eighth of an inch from the ferrule of my umbrella in abetting an encore. Another encore, of which I am guiltless, was elicited by the cabaletta of *Una voce,* which, however, Miss Thudichum did not sing so well as *Di piacer.* The repeats in the overtures were, strange to say, not in the least tedious: we were perfectly well content to hear the whole bag of tricks turned out a second time. Nobody was disgusted, *à la* Berlioz, by "the brutal crescendo and big drum." On the contrary, we were exhilarated and amused; and I, for one, was astonished to find it all still so fresh, so imposing, so clever, and even, in the few serious passages, so really fine.

I felt, not without dread, that the nails were coming out of Rossini's coffin as the performance proceeded; and if I had been seated a little nearer the platform, there is no saying that I might not have seized Mr Manns's arm and exclaimed, "You know not what you do. Ten minutes more and you will have this evil genius of music alive again, and undoing the last thirty years of your work." But after the third overture and the second aria, when we had had six doses of crescendo, and three, including one encore, of cabaletta, I breathed again. We have not heard the last of the overture to Semiramide; but we shall not in future hear grave critics speaking of it as if it were first-cousin to Beethoven's No. 3 Leonora. The general opinion, especially among literary men who affected music, used to be that there was an Egyptian grandeur about Semiramide, a massiveness as of the Great Pyramid, a Ninevesque power and terror far beyond anything that Beethoven had ever achieved. And when Madame Trebelli, as a handsome chieftain in a panther-skin, used to come down to the footlights, exclaiming, "Here I am at last in Babylon," and give us *Ah quel giorno,* with a cabaletta not to be distinguished without close scrutiny from that to Rosina's aria in Il Barbiere, we took it as part of the course of Nature on the operatic stage. We are apt to wonder nowadays why the public should have been so impressed at first by the apparent originality, dramatic genius, depth and daring of Meyerbeer as to be mystified and scandalized when Mendelssohn, Schumann, and Wagner treated him with no more respect than if he had been an old clo' man from Houndsditch.

But the explanation is very simple. We compare Meyerbeer with Wagner: amateurs of 1840 compared him with Rossini; and that made all the difference. If we are to have any Rossini celebrations during the opera season, the best opera for the purpose will be Otello, partly because the comparison between it and Verdi's latest work would be interesting, and partly because it is one of the least obsolete of his operas. When it was last played here at Her Majesty's, with Nilsson, Faure, and Tamberlik, it proved highly bearable, although Faure was then almost at the end even of his capacity for singing on his reputation, and Tamberlik was a mere creaking wreck, whose boasted *ut de poitrine* was an eldritch screech which might just as well have been aimed an octave higher, for all the claim it had to be received as a vocal note in the artistic sense. The only difficulty at present would be to replace Nilsson, who sang Desdemona's music beautifully. William Tell, of course, we may have: Sir Augustus Harris's attempts with it have always ranked among his triumphs from the artistic point of view, probably because (like Rienzi) it is an opera not of heroes and heroines, but of crowds and armies. He is therefore able to deal with it as he deals with his pantomimes and melodramas, which he takes so much more seriously and artistically than he is able to take those unfortunate operas in which his spoiled children of the Paris Opera, lazier than Rossini himself, have to be petted at every turn. However, enough of Rossini for the present. I cannot say "Rest his soul," for he had none; but I may at least be allowed the fervent aspiration that we may never look upon his like again.

9 *March 1892*

WEBER'S DER FREISCHÜTZ

The production of Der Freischütz and Fidelio at the German Opera momentarily transferred the centre of operatic interest, for me at least, from Covent Garden to Drury Lane. It was amusing to find these two masterpieces arousing quite a patronizing interest as old-fashioned curiosities, somewhat dowdy perhaps, but still deserving of indulgence for the sake of tradition. As to the Freischütz, hardly anyone could remember its last performance in London; and I was astonished when the questions addressed to me on this point made me conscious that although the work is as familiar to me as the most familiar of Shakespear's plays, and counts, indeed, as a permanent factor in my consciousness, I could only clearly recollect two actual representations of it, one in Munich, and the other in my

native town, which is not in England. I will not swear
that I have not seen it oftener; for I have long since
given free play to my inestimable gift of forgetting,
and have lost count of the performances I have witnessed almost as completely as I have lost count of my
headaches; but still, even in my case, it is somewhat
significant that I should be unable to recall a representation of Der Freischütz in London. Such a doubt as
to the abysmally inferior Carmen would be a ridiculous
affectation.

Perhaps, therefore, the first question to answer is,
"How has Der Freischütz worn?" To which I am happy
to be able to reply that its freshness and charm delighted everyone as much as its unaffected sincerity
of sentiment impressed them. I will not, of course, pretend that the hermit strikes the popular imagination as
he did in the days when hermits habitually trod the
stage, and were deferred to, at sight of their brown
gowns, rope girdles, and white beards, by all the civil
and military authorities, exactly as if they were modern
French deputies exhibiting their scarves to the police
in *émeutes.*

And it would be vain to conceal the fact that the
terrors of the Wolf's Gulch and the casting of the magic
bullets were received with audible chuckling, although
Sir Augustus Harris had made a supreme effort to en-
sure the unearthliness of the incantation by making the
stage a sort of museum of all the effects of magic and
devilry known in the modern theatre. He had illumi-
nated steam clouds from Bayreuth, and fiery rain from
the Lyceum Faust; he had red fire, glowing hell-mouth
caverns, apparitions, skeletons, vampire bats, explosions, conflagrations, besides the traditional wheels, the
skulls, the owl, and the charmed circle.

And yet nobody could help laughing, least of all, I
should imagine, Sir Augustus himself. The owl alone
would have sufficed to set me off, because, though its

eyes were not red like those of previous stage owls, and it was therefore not so irresistibly suggestive of a railway signal as I had expected, one of its eyes was much larger than the other, so that it seemed to contemplate the house derisively through a single eyeglass. This quaint monocle notwithstanding, the scene produced some effect until the other phenomena supervened. If they had been omitted—if the apparitions had been left to our imaginations and to Weber's music, the effect would have been enormously heightened. Owls, bats, ravens, and skeletons have no supernatural associations for our rising generations: the only function an owl or a bat can now fulfil in such a scene is to heighten that sense of night in a forest which is one of Nature's most wonderful effects.

But this change in public susceptibility makes it necessary to take much greater pains with stage illusions than formerly. When the bat was a mere bogy to terrify an audience of grown-up children, it was, no doubt, sufficient to dangle something like a stuffed bustard with huge moth's wings at the end of a string from the flies to make the pit's flesh creep. Nowadays, unless a manager can devise some sort of aerial top that will imitate the peculiar flitting of the real flittermouse he must forgo bats altogether.

To appeal to our extinct sense of the supernatural by means that outrage our heightened sense of the natural is to court ridicule. Pasteboard pies and paper flowers are being banished from the stage by the growth of that power of accurate observation which is commonly called cynicism by those who have not got it; and impossible bats and owls must be banished with them. Der Freischütz may be depended on to suggest plenty of phantasmagoria without help from out-of-date stage-machinists and property-masters.

Except during the absurdities of the Wolf's Gulch, the performance appeared to me to be an exceptionally successful one. The orchestra has improved greatly since the first week; and though Lohse has one trick which I greatly dislike—that of hurrying at every crescendo—he is equal to his weighty duties as Wagner and Beethoven conductor. His handling of Fidelio was at many points admirable. Beethoven had not any bats or skeletons to contend with; but he had what was quite as bad in its way: to wit, an execrable chorus of prisoners who, on catching sight of the sentinels, would break in on the German text with mistuned howls of "*Silenzio, silenzio.*" In both operas there were moments when the singing was beyond all apology.

Alvary's Florestan, vocally considered, was an atrocious performance; and Klafsky did not finish the aria in the first act without perceptible effort. Weber's music was, of course, far more singable; and even Alvary, saving a few intervals the corruption of which must, I suppose, be put up with from him as part of his mannerism, sang fairly in tune according to his German scale, which, let me point out, not for the first time, is not precisely the southern scale dear to our ears.

But Wiegand, as Caspar, dropped all pretence of singing before he came to the coda of the Revenge song. He simply shouted the words hoarsely through the orchestration, and left the audience to infer that Weber meant it to be done that way—a notion of which I beg somewhat indignantly to disabuse them. Yet in spite of all this and more, these three artists, Klafsky, Alvary, and Wiegand, with Mr Bispham and Rodemund to help them, made Fidelio and Der Freischütz live again. Their sincerity, their affectionate intimacy with the works, their complete absorption in their parts, enable them to achieve most interesting and satisfactory performances, and to elicit demonstrations of respect and enthusiasm from the audience, which, nevertheless, if it has any ears, must know perfectly well that the singing has been at best second-rate, and at worst quite outside the category of music.

18 July 1894

BERLIOZ

The Damnation of Faust

Call no conductor sensitive in the highest degree to musical impressions until you have heard him in Berlioz and Mozart. I never unreservedly took off my hat to Richter until I saw him conduct Mozart's great symphony in E flat. Now, having heard him conduct Berlioz' Faust, I repeat the salutation. I never go to hear that work without fearing that, instead of exquisite threads of melody, wonderful in their tenuity and delicacy, and the surpassingly strange and curious sounds and measures, ghostly in touch and quaint in tread, unearthly, unexpected, unaccountable, and full of pictures and stories, I shall hear a medley of thumps and bumps and whistles and commonplaces: one, two, three, four: one, two, three, four; and for Heaven's sake dont stop to think about what you are doing, gentlemen, or we shall never keep the thing together. Last night there was no such disappointment. The Hungarian March I pass over, though I felt towards the end that if it were to last another minute I must charge out and capture Trafalgar Square single-handed. But when the scene on the banks of the Elbe began—more slowly than any but a great conductor would have dared to take it—then I knew that I might dream the scene without fear of awakening a disenchanted man.

9 July 1889

When the fierce strain put by my critical work on my

powers of attention makes it necessary for me to allow my mind to ramble a little by way of relief, I like to go to the Albert Hall to hear one of the performances of the Royal Choral Society. I know nothing more interesting in its way than to wake up occasionally from a nap in the amphitheatre stalls, or to come out of a train of political or philosophic speculation, to listen for a few moments to an adaptation of some masterpiece of music to the tastes of what is called "the oratorio public." Berlioz' Faust is a particularly stiff subject for Albert Hall treatment. To comb that wild composer's hair, stuff him into a frock-coat and tall hat, stick a hymn-book in his hand, and obtain reverent applause for his ribald burlesque of an Amen chorus as if it were a genuine Handelian solemnity, is really a remarkable feat, and one which few conductors except Sir Joseph Barnby could achieve. Instead of the brimstonish orgy in Auerbach's cellar we have a *soirée* of the Young Men's Christian Association; the drunken blackguardism of Brander is replaced by the decorous conviviality of a respectable young bank clerk obliging with a display of his baritone voice (pronounced by the local pianoforte tuner equal to Hayden Coffin's); Faust reminds one of the gentleman in Sullivan's Sweethearts; the whiskered pandoors and the fierce hussars on the banks of the Danube become a Volunteer corps on the banks of the Serpentine; and all Brixton votes Berlioz a great composer, and finds a sulphurous sublimity in the whistles on the piccolo and clashes of the cymbals which bring Mr Henschel, as Mephistopheles, out of his chair. This does not mean that Berlioz has converted Brixton: it means that Brixton has converted Berlioz. Such conversions are always going on. The African heathen "embrace" the Christian religion by singing a Te Deum instead of dancing a war-dance after "wetting their spears" in the blood of the tribe next door; the English heathen (a much more numerous body) take to reading the Bible when it is edited for them by Miss Marie Corelli; the masses, sceptical as to Scott and Dumas, are converted to an appreciation of romantic literature by Mr Rider Haggard; Shakespear and Goethe become world-famous on the strength of "acting versions" that must have set them fairly spinning in their graves; and there is a general appearance of tempering the wind to the shorn lamb, which turns out, on closer examination, to be really effected by building a badly ventilated suburban villa round the silly animal, and telling him that the frowsy warmth he begins to feel is that of the sunbeam playing on Parnassus, or the peace of mind that passeth all understanding, according to circumstances. When I was young, I was like all immature critics: I used to throw stones at the windows of the villa, and thrust in my head and bawl at the lamb that he was a fool, and that the villa builders—honest people enough, according to their lights—were swindlers and hypocrites, and nincompoops and sixth-raters. But the lamb got on better with them than with me; and at last it struck me that he was happier and more civilized in his villa than shivering in the keen Parnassian winds that delighted my hardier bones; so that now I have become quite fond of him, and love to lead him out when the weather is exceptionally mild (the wind being in the Festival cantata quarter perhaps), and talk to him a bit without letting him see too plainly what a deplorable mutton-head he is. Dropping the metaphor, which is becoming unmanageable, let me point out that the title of Berlioz' work is The Damnation of Faust, and that the most natural abbreviation would be, not Berlioz' Faust, but Berlioz' Damnation. Now the Albert Hall audience would certainly not feel easy with such a phrase in their mouths. I have even noticed a certain reluctance on the part of mixed assemblies of ladies and gentlemen unfamiliar with the German language to tolerate discussions of Wagner's Götterdämmerung, unless it were mentioned only as The Dusk of the Gods. Well, the sole criticism I have to make of the Albert Hall performance is that the damnation has been lifted from the work. It has been "saved," so to speak, and jogs along in a most respectable manner. The march, which suggests household troops cheered by enthusiastic nursemaids, is encored; and so is the dance of sylphs, which squeaks like a tune on the hurdy-gurdy. The students' *Jam nox stellata* sounds as though middle-aged commercial travellers were having a turn at it. On the whole the performance, though all the materials and forces for a good one are at the conductor's disposal, is dull and suburban. The fact is, Berlioz is not Sir Joseph Barnby's affair. On Thursday last (note that the concert night is changed back again from Wednesday to Thursday) Gounod's Religious March was played, as at the Crystal Palace. A printed slip was circulated asking the audience to stand up. What value a demonstration manufactured in this way can have I do not see, especially when the performance of the march at the Crystal Palace had proved that it would not have occurred spontaneously. It jarred on me as a forced and flunkeyish manoeuvre; and I took no part in it. I have sufficient feeling about Gounod not to permit myself to be instructed in the matter by impertinent persons communicating with me by anonymous slips of paper. Besides, I object to confer on a trumpery *pièce d'occasion* the distinction which is the traditional English appanage of Handel's Hallelujah Chorus.

8 November 1893

Mention of Mottl reminds me that my feeling that he should break ground as a Beethoven conductor here by the C minor symphony is evidently shared by Mr

Schulz-Curtius and himself; for the program for the 22nd now includes that work, along with six pieces by Wagner and two by Berlioz. As we never hear Berlioz handled successfully in London, except on one of the scarce visits of the Manchester band, it will be interesting to hear what Mottl, whose appreciation of Berlioz carried him to the length of producing Les Troyens at Carlsruhe, will be able to do with him.

9 May 1894

I must return to the subject of the Hallé orchestra to chronicle a magnificent performance of Berlioz' Fantastic Symphony. At present no London band can touch this work at all, because no London band has learnt it thoroughly. We can get the notes played, and we sometimes do; but, as in the case of the first movement of the Ninth Symphony, only confusion and disappointment come of the attempt. Now the Manchester band, knowing the work through and through, handles it with a freedom, intelligence, and spirit which bring out all its life and purpose, and that, too, without giving the conductor any trouble. It is especially to be hoped that the orchestral students of the Royal College of Music who had a turn at the Harold Symphony in St James's Hall two days before were at this concert. If so, it must have helped them to realize how completely they were beaten, in spite of the highly praiseworthy degree of skill they have attained in using their instruments, and the excellent drill they are getting in *ensemble* playing.

17 December 1890

Meanwhile, we have, outside London, just one first-class orchestra, the result of Hallé's life work at Manchester. And all the music in London last week was its two performances of Berlioz' Faust. One of the advantages of being a critic in London is that at all seasons of rejoicing and holiday making, Music vanishes from the critical sphere and takes to the streets, where she is very vociferous between eleven and two at night. The drunken bachelor sings, four or five strong, beneath my window; and the drunken husband passes doggedly on his way home, with his hardly sober wife one pace behind, nag, nag, nagging, except at such crises of screaming as are produced by the exasperated husband proving himself unworthy the name of a British sailor. This is a leading feature of our English Christmas, with its round of slaughtering, gorging, and drinking, into the midst of which this time comes Hallé with his orchestra, and finds his stalls anything but well filled, though the gallery is faithful even to "standing room only," and not too much of that.

When he first introduced The Damnation of Faust here, there were no rival performances to compare with that of the Manchester band. Now the work is a stock piece at the Albert Hall and the Richter concerts; and it has been heard at the Crystal Palace. The result is that London is utterly eclipsed and brought to naught. In vain does Mr Barnby guarantee metronomic regularity of tempo and accurate execution of every note in the score: the work is usually received at the Albert Hall as an unaffectedly pious composition in the oratorio style. Richter, by dint of incessant vigilance and urgency, only gets here and there a stroke of fancy, power, or delicacy out of his orchestra in its own despite. Mr Manns conducts Faust conscientiously, but without opposing any really sympathetic knowledge to the blank ignorance of the orchestra. Hallé simply indicates the quietest, amblingest tempos at his ease; and the score comes to life in the hands of players who understand every bar of it, and individualize every phrase.

The Hungarian March, taken at about half the speed at which Lamoureux vainly tries to make it "go," is encored with yells—literally with yells—in St James's Hall. Nobody mistakes the Amen parody for a highly becoming interlude of sacred music, nor misses the diabolic *élan* of the serenade, the subtler imaginative qualities of the supernatural choruses and dances, or the originality and pathos of the music of Faust and Margaret. Here is the experimental verification of my contention that no precision in execution or ability in conducting can, in performing Berlioz' music, supply the want of knowledge on the part of the band of the intention of every orchestral touch. Victories over Berlioz are soldiers' victories, not generals'. The long and short of the matter is that our London men do not know the works of Berlioz and the Manchester men do; hence the enormous superiority of the latter on such occasions as the one in question.

13 January 1892

The Trombone

The Valkyrie Ride, which came next, excited the audience furiously; but it also made a lady on the orchestra put her fingers into her ears. The lady was quite right. The Valkyrie Ride requires above all things fine trombone-playing—such playing, for instance, as Mr Manns seldom fails to get at the Crystal Palace from Messrs Hadfield, Geard, and Phasey, who generally contrive to stop short of that brain-splitting bark which detaches itself from the rest of the orchestra, asserting itself rowdily and intrusively in your ear, preventing you from hearing the music, and making you wonder, if you accept the hideous din as inevitable, how Berlioz could ever call such an ignobly noisy instrument "Olympian." No matter how many fortissimo marks the composer writes, there is no use in forcing the tone of the trombone, unless, indeed, you are to be intentionally hellish, as in Liszt's Inferno. But if you want to be majestic, as in the Valkyrie Ride and the Francs Juges overture, then it is not to be done by bawling like a mob orator who does not know his business. Why Richter permits forcing, and even encourages it, not only in the Valkyrie Ride but in the first movement of the Tannhäuser overture, can only be explained as the result of his share of original sin. It is not that his players cannot do better: they are always dignified in the Valhalla motif in the Nibelungen music.

18 June 1890

The Art of Composition

The overture of The Barber of Bagdad, with which the concert opened, made another step forward in popularity. I should like to hear the whole opera again; and, *a fortiori*, the general body of our amateurs, less jaded than I, must be of the same mind. Why does not Mr Carte turn his attention to Cornelius's most popular work, and to the Beatrice and Benedict of Berlioz, the nocturne from which, by the bye, was sung by Mrs Henschel and Madame Hope Temple at the London Symphony concert? The comparative roughness of Mr Henschel's band on that occasion heightened the effect of the finished execution of Mendelssohn's Italian symphony by the Crystal Palace orchestra, which was in its best form on Saturday. I am far from having grown out of enjoying the Italian symphony; but I confess to becoming more and more disagreeably affected by the conventional features of the instrumentation, especially the trumpet parts in the first movement.

I think it must be admitted that even in Beethoven's symphonies the trumpet parts are already in many places mere anachronisms. Perhaps the dots and dashes of trumpet which we learn from "the study of the best masters" between the Bach period of brilliant florid counterpoints for three trumpets, and the modern Berlioz-Wagner style based technically on the essentially melodic character of our cornets and tubas, were always ridiculous to ears unperverted by custom and the pedantry which springs from the fatal academic habit of studying music otherwise than through one's ears. People would compose music skilfully enough if only there were no professors in the world. Literature is six times as difficult an art technically as composition: yet who ever dreams of going to a professor to learn how to write? Anyhow, when Mr Manns next performs the Italian symphony, I hope he will either omit the dots and dashes, or else have them played on those slide trumpets which are always produced with such solemnity when that august classic, the pianoforte concerto in G minor, is in the bill.

2 March 1892

WAGNER

Das Rheingold

After the performance of Das Rheingold last Wednesday at the Opera, I do not think we shall hear much more about the impropriety of beginning the season with Siegfried, which should have come third instead of first. If it be true that it was Alvary who insisted on the transposition, let us admit now that Alvary knew what he was about. Siegfried was a success because there was hardly a moment in the three acts during which Lieban or Alvary, or both, or Sucher and Alvary, were not on the stage to keep things going. Besides, the defects of the orchestra did not matter so much in a score which admits of a certain degree of roughness of treatment. The dullest moment in Siegfried was the dialogue at the beginning of the second act between Wotan and Alberich.

Now imagine our German visitors setting to at a music drama which contains an enormous percentage of Wotan-cum-Alberich, with a score requiring the most delicate handling, and you will be able to understand that the performance of Das Rheingold was none of the liveliest. The band, no longer braced up by the excitement of the first night, did what I hope was its worst. Its playing of the wonderful water music prelude suggested that the Rhine must be a river of treacle —and rather lumpy treacle at that; the gold music was arrant pinchbeck; Freia's return to heaven brought no magical waftings of joy to the audience; and the rainbow music, with its hosts of harps (I distinctly heard one, and was not well placed for seeing whether there were any others), might have been pleasant deck music during a steamboat excursion to Hampton Court, for all the success it attained in providing a splendid climax to the prologue of a mighty drama.

Then the stage arrangements were rather hard to bear. There was nothing to complain of in the first scene, since no better way of doing it has yet been invented. The Rhine daughters waved their arms, and floated up and down and round and round in their aquarium; and if I could only have forgotten the scene as it appeared to those behind the curtain—the three fire-escapes being elongated and shortened and raced round the floor, each with a lady fastened to the top and draped with a modest green skirt of prodigious length—I should have been satisfied. But the orchestra did not make me forget it, nor did Alberich, nor anyone except Flosshilde (Fräulein Heink), who quite fulfilled the promise of her Erda in Siegfried. The really difficult part of the stage management in Das Rheingold is the change from the home of the gods to that of the dwarfs, and the business of Alberich's metamorphoses and final capture.

The way in which these were either bungled or frankly given up in despair shewed with brutal directness what I have so often tried to hint delicately: namely, that if Sir Augustus Harris would dismiss a round dozen of his superfluous singers, and give a fifth of what they cost him to an artistic and ingenious stage-manager, he would double the value of the performances at Covent Garden. The attempts of Herr Lissman, who is, to say the least, no harlequin, to disappear suddenly through a trick shutter, the obviousness of which would have disgraced a cheesemonger's shop in a Christmas pantomime, were not made any the more plausible by the piffling little jet of steam which followed. As to the changes into the dragon and the toad, they were simply taken for granted, although Sir Augustus might easily have taken advice on the subject, not from Bayreuth, but from any provincial manager who has ever put the story of Puss in Boots on the stage. The descent from god-home to dwarf-home was avoided by dropping the curtain and making an interval at the end of the second scene; and the change back again, which should be an ascent into the clouds, was a badly managed attempt at the descent which had been omitted. Evidently the scene-plot had got mixed on its way from Hamburg.

The shortcomings in the staging of the work were all the more depressing because, with two conspicuous exceptions, the principal performers were so averagely German that it is only by repeatedly telling myself not to be rude that I can restrain myself from saying flatly that they might as well have been English, so powerfully mediocre were they. Grengg sang his way loudly and heavily through the part of Wotan with both his eyes wide open (one of them should have been removed). Every line he uttered was exactly like every other line. Alberich did not even sing: he shouted, and seemed content if he came within a half-quarter tone of the highest notes he aimed at. His acting, though conscientious, was that of a pirate in a Surrey melodrama: neither in his ghastly declaration to Loge of his ambition to become master of the world, nor in his frantic despair when Wotan wrests the ring from him, did he make the smallest sensation.

Frau Andriessen failed to make Fricka interesting—small blame to her, perhaps, considering the impossibility of getting any variety of play out of Wotan. Fräulein Bettaque, as Freia, was pretty and pleasing enough to disarm criticism; and the giants, having little to do except to appear clumsy and intellectually and artistically dense, took to their parts with considerable aptitude. But they certainly would not have made the performance endurable but for the two exceptions I have alluded to: namely, Lieban (Mime), whose ten minutes on the stage, including his capital singing of Sorglose Schmiede, sent up the artistic level of the performance with a bound during that too brief period; and Alvary, who, as Loge, the northern Mephistopheles, succeeded by his alertness in making the rest of the gods look anything but quick-witted.

On the whole, it was fortunate for the success of the work that most of us are at present so helplessly under the spell of the Ring's greatness that we can do nothing but go raving about the theatre between the acts in ecstasies of deluded admiration. Even the critics lose their heads: you find the same men who are quite alive to the disparities between Jean de Reszke and Montariol, Maurel or Edouard de Reszke and Miranda or De Vaschetti, Calvé or Giulia Ravogli and Melba or Miss de Lussan, losing all discrimination when the German artists come up for judgment; admiring a third-rate Alberich as devoutly as a first-rate Mime; and meekly accepting the German tendency to coarse singing and wooden declamation as the right thing for Wagner, whose music really demands as much refinement, expression, and vivacity as Mozart's.

As to the band, one hardly knows what to say of the revelation it has made of the fewness of the people who know *by ear* the difference between a second-rate German orchestra reinforced by a number of students from the Guildhall College and first-rate ones like those of London and Manchester.

When the public wakes up from its happy hypnotic trance and resumes its normal freedom of judgment, it will inevitably be bored by Das Rheingold, unless it is smartly and attractively stage-managed and well acted in English. And even then it will remain, like Die Zauberflöte, a mere extravaganza, except to those who see in all that curious harlequinade of gods, dwarfs, and giants, a real drama of which their own lives form part. Herren Wiegand and Litter, raised to gigantic stature on thick-soled boots, and poking at one another with huge cudgels whilst the drum is pounded unmercifully down in the orchestra, may look ridiculous; but the spectacle of good-natured ignorance and serviceable brute force, suddenly roused to lust and greed, and falling to fratricidal murder, is another matter—one that makes the slaying of Fasolt by Fafnir the most horrifying of stage duels.

Wotan is a delicate subject, especially in England, where you do not know whose toes you may tread on if you suggest that the Wagnerian stage is not the only place in which Religion, corrupted by ambition, has bartered away its life-principle for a lordly pleasure-house, and then called in the heartless intellect to rescue it from the consequences of its bargain by hypocrisy, fraud, and force. As to Alberich, renouncing love for gold, and losing all fellow-feeling in his haste to accumulate it, I question whether it is good taste to exhibit him at Covent Garden on "diamond nights."

But I am sure that Das Rheingold must either be read between the lines and through the lines, or else yawned at. Siegfried, Die Walküre, and Götterdämmerung may pass as ordinary dramas, barring a little interruption from time to time by the prolixities of Wotan; but Das Rheingold is either a profound allegory or a puerile fairy tale. Consequently it is hardly worth doing at all unless it is done very well, which is precisely why it was so much less successful at Covent Garden than Siegfried.

29 June 1892

The Tone Poet

It is not often that one comes across a reasonable book about music, much less an entertaining one. Still, I confess to having held out with satisfaction to the end of M. Georges Noufflard's *Richard Wagner d'après lui-même* (Paris, Fischbacher, 2 vols., at 3.50 fr. apiece). Noufflard is so exceedingly French a Frenchman that he writes a preface to explain that though he admires Wagner, still Alsace and Lorraine must be given back; and when he records an experiment of his hero's in teetotalism, he naïvely adds, "What is still more surprising is that this unnatural régime, instead of making Wagner ill, operated exactly as he had expected." More Parisian than this an author can hardly be; and yet Noufflard always understands the Prussian composer's position, and generally agrees with him, though, being racially out of sympathy with him, he never entirely comprehends him. He is remarkably free from the stock vulgarities of French operatic culture: for instance, he washes his hands of Meyerbeer most fastidiously; and he puts Gluck, the hero of French musical classicism, most accurately in his true place.

And here let me give a piece of advice to readers of

books about Wagner. Whenever you come to a statement that Wagner was an operatic reformer, and that
in this capacity he was merely following in the footsteps of Gluck, who had anticipated some of his most
important proposals, you may put your book in the
waste-paper basket, as far as Wagner is concerned,
with absolute confidence. Gluck was an opera composer
who said to his contemporaries: "Gentlemen, let us
compose our operas more rationally. An opera is not
a stage concert, as most of you seem to think. Let us
give up our habit of sacrificing our common sense to
the vanity of our singers, and let us compose and
orchestrate our airs, our duets, our recitatives, and our
sinfonias in such a way that they shall always be appropriate to the dramatic situation given to us by the
librettist." And having given this excellent advice, he
proceeded to shew how it could be followed. How
well he did this we can judge, in spite of our scandalous ignorance of Gluck, from Orfeo, with which Giulia
Ravogli has made us familiar lately.

When Wagner came on the scene, exactly a hundred years later, he found that the reform movement
begun by Gluck had been carried to the utmost limits
of possibility by Spontini, who told him flatly that
after La Vestale, etc., there was nothing operatic left
to be done. Wagner quite agreed with him, and never
had the smallest intention of beginning the reform of
opera over again at the very moment when it had just
been finished. On the contrary, he took the fully reformed opera, with all its improvements, and asked
the nineteenth century to look calmly at it and say
whether all this patchwork of stage effects on a purely
musical form had really done anything for it but expose the absurd unreality of its pretence to be a form
of drama, and whether, in fact, Rossini had not
shewn sound common sense in virtually throwing
over that pretence and, like Gluck's Italian contempo-

raries, treating an opera as a stage concert. The nineteenth century took a long time to make up its mind on the question, which it was at first perfectly incapable of understanding. Verdi and Gounod kept on trying to get beyond Spontini on operatic lines, without the least success, except on the purely musical side; and Gounod never gave up the attempt, though Verdi did.

Meanwhile, however, Wagner, to shew what he meant, abandoned operatic composition altogether, and took to writing dramatic poems, and using all the resources of orchestral harmony and vocal tone to give them the utmost reality and intensity of expression, thereby producing the new art form which he called "music drama," which is no more "reformed opera" than a cathedral is a reformed stone quarry. The whole secret of the amazing futility of the first attempts at Wagner criticism is the mistaking of this new form for an improved pattern of the old one. Once you conceive Wagner as the patentee of certain novel features in operas and librettos, you can demolish him point by point with impeccable logic, and without the least misgiving that you are publicly making a ludicrous exhibition of yourself.

The process is fatally easy, and consists mainly in shewing that the pretended novelties of reformed opera are no novelties at all. The "leading motives," regarded as operatic melodies recurring in connection with the entry of a certain character, are as old as opera itself; the instrumentation, regarded merely as instrumentation, is no better than Mozart's and much more expensive; whereas of those features that really tax the invention of the operatic composer, the airs, the duos, the quartets, the cabalettas to display the virtuosity of the trained Italian singer, the dances, the marches, the choruses, and so on, there is a deadly learth, their place being taken by—of all things—an interminable dull recitative.

The plain conclusion follows that Wagner was a barren rascal whose whole reputation rested on a shopballad, O star of eve, and a march which he accidentally squeezed out when composing his interminable Tannhäuser. And so you go on, wading with fatuous self-satisfaction deeper and deeper into a morass of elaborately reasoned and highly conscientious error. You need fear nothing of this sort from Noufflard. He knows perfectly well the difference between musicdrama and opera; and the result is that he not only does not tumble into blind hero-worship of Wagner, but is able to criticize him—a thing the blunderers never could do. Some of his criticisms: for example, his observation that in Wagner's earlier work the melody is by no means so original as Weber's, are indisputable—indeed he might have said Meyerbeer or anybody else; for Wagner's melody was never original at all in that sense, any more than Giotto's figures are picturesque or Shakespear's lines elegant.

But I entirely—though quite respectfully—dissent from Noufflard's suggestion that in composing Tristan Wagner turned his back on the theoretic basis of Siegfried, and returned to "absolute music." It is true, as Noufflard points out, that in Tristan, and even in Der Ring itself, Wagner sometimes got so rapt from the objective drama that he got away from the words too, and in Tristan came to writing music without coherent words at all. But wordless music is not absolute music. Absolute music is the purely decorative sound pattern: tone poetry is the musical expression of poetic feeling. When Tristan gives musical expression to an excess of feeling for which he can find no coherent words, he is no more uttering absolute music than the shepherd who carries on the drama at one of its most deeply felt passages by playing on his pipe.

Wagner regarded all Beethoven's important instrumental works as tone poems; and he himself, though he wrote so much for the orchestra alone in the course of his music dramas, never wrote, or could write, a note of absolute music. The fact is, there is a great deal of feeling, highly poetic and highly dramatic, which cannot be expressed by mere words—because words are the counters of thinking, not of feeling—but which can be supremely expressed by music. The poet tries to make words serve his purpose by arranging them musically, but is hampered by the certainty of becoming absurd if he does not make his musically arranged words mean something to the intellect as well as to the feeling.

For example, the unfortunate Shakespear could not make Juliet say:

O Romeo, Romeo, Romeo, Romeo, Romeo;

and so on for twenty lines. He had to make her, in an extremity of unnaturalness, begin to argue the case in a sort of amatory legal fashion, thus:

O Romeo, Romeo, wherefore art thou Romeo?
Deny thy father and refuse thy name,
Or, if thou wilt not, etc., etc., etc.

It is verbally decorative; but it is not love. And again:

Parting is such sweet sorrow
That I shall say goodnight till it be morrow;

which is a most ingenious conceit, but one which a woman would no more utter at such a moment than she would prove the rope ladder to be the shortest way out because any two sides of a triangle are together greater than the third.

Now these difficulties do not exist for the tone poet. He can make Isolde say nothing but "Tristan, Tristan, Tristan, Tristan, Tristan," and Tristan nothing but "Isolde, Isolde, Isolde, Isolde, Isolde," to their hearts' content without creating the smallest demand for more definite explanations; and as for the number of times a tenor and soprano can repeat "Addio, addio, addio," there is no limit to it. There is a great deal of this reduction of speech to mere ejaculation in Wagner; and it is a reduction directly pointed to in those very pages of Opera and Drama which seem to make the words all-important by putting the poem in the first place as the seed of the whole music drama, and yet make a clean sweep of nine-tenths of the dictionary by insisting that it is only the language of feeling that craves for musical expression, or even is susceptible of it.

Nay, you may not only reduce the words to pure ejaculation, you may substitute mere roulade vocalization, or even balderdash, for them, provided the music sustains the feeling which is the real subject of the drama, as has been proved by many pages of genuinely dramatic music, both in opera and elsewhere, which either have no words at all, or else belie them. It is only when a thought interpenetrated with intense feeling has to be expressed, as in the Ode to Joy in the Ninth Symphony, that coherent words must come with the music. You have such words in Tristan; you have also ejaculations void of thought, though full of feeling; and you have plenty of instrumental music with no words at all. But you have no "absolute" music, and no "opera."

Nothing in the world convinces you more of the fact that a dramatic poem cannot possibly take the form of an opera libretto than listening to Tristan and comparing it with, say, Gounod's Romeo and Juliet. I submit, then, to Noufflard (whose two volumes I none the less cordially recommend to all amateurs who can appreciate a thinker) that the contradictions into which Wagner has fallen in this matter are merely such verbal ones as are inevitable from the imperfection of language as an instrument for conveying ideas; and that the progress from Der fliegende Holländer to Parsifal takes a perfectly straight line ahead in theory as well as in artistic execution.

17 January 1894

Bayreuth

When I ran across to Bayreuth the other day I was fully aware that the cost of my trip would have been better spent in bringing a German critic to England. And I greatly regret that this article is not written in German, and for a German paper, since it is now evident that, as far as any musical awakening and impulse can come from one country to another, it must come for the present from England to Bayreuth, and not from Bayreuth to England.

First, as to the wonderful Bayreuth orchestra, to the glories of which we have been taught to look with envious despair. I beg to observe here, in the most uncompromising manner, that the Bayreuth orchestra, judged by London standards, is not a first-rate orchestra, but a very carefully worked up second-rate one. The results of the careful working up are admirable: the smoothness, the perfect sostenuto, the unbroken flow of tone testify to an almost perfect orchestral execution in passages which lend themselves to such treatment. But there are two factors in the effect produced by an orchestra: the quality of the execution, and the quality of the instruments on which the execution is done. How much this may vary may be judged by the wide range of prices for musical instruments, even leaving out of account the scarcity values reached by certain exceptionally desirable old fiddles and bassoons.

Take, for example, the cheapest and most popular wind instrument in the orchestra—the cornet. Heaven knows how low the prices of the vilest specimens of cornet may run! but between the cheapest orchestrally presentable cornet and a first-rate one by Courtois or a good English maker the variation in price, without counting anything for electroplating or decoration of any sort, is from about thirty-five shillings to eight or ten pounds. Fiddles range from a few shillings to the largest sums any orchestral player can afford to give for them; and the scale of prices for wood-wind instruments varies from one to three figures.

Now, if there were such a thing as an international musical parliament, I should certainly agitate for a return of the prices of the instruments used in the Bayreuth and Crystal Palace orchestras respectively; and I should be surprised if the German total came to as much as half the English one. In the brass especially, the peculiar dull rattle of inferior thin metal at once strikes an ear accustomed to the smooth, firm tone of the more expensive instruments used in England. There is a difference in brightness too; but that I leave out of the question, as possibly due to the difference between Continental and English pitch, a difference which is all to the bad for us.

In judging the wood-wind I am on less certain ground, since the tone is so greatly affected by the way in which the reed is cut. I have heard in the street what I supposed to be an execrable cracked cornet, and on coming round the corner have found an old man playing a clarinet with an old slack reed as easy for his feeble jaws as the reed one cuts for a child in a cornfield. The tone produced by such ancient men and that produced by Lazarus in his best days (which was, I think, purer, if less rich, than Mühlfeld's) mark the two poles of my experience of clarinet-playing; and I have always found that in German orchestras the standard tone leans more to the man in the street than to Lazarus.

Unfortunately, I am not expert enough to discriminate confidently between the difference due to the cutting of the reed and that due to the quality of the instrument; but except in the case of unusually fine players, who generally take the first chance of coming to England and settling here, the German wood-wind player is content with a cheaper tone than the English one; and Bayreuth is no exception to this rule. The oboe there is as reedy as the *cor anglais* is here. The strings, as compared with ours, are deficient in power and richness; and even in the case of the horns, which we somehow or other cannot play, whilst the Germans can, the tone is much rougher and more nearly allied to that of the Alpine cowhorn than what may be called the standard tone here.

I rather harp on the word standard, because the facts that so many of our best orchestral players are Germans, and that Mr August Manns, the conductor whose band, in the wind section, puts the Germans most completely to shame in point of fineness of tone, is himself not merely a German, but a Prussian, conclusively prove that the inferiority of the German orchestra to the English is not an inferiority in natural capacity, but an inferiority in the current national standard of musical beauty—that is, an inferiority in the higher physical culture, and consequently in the quality of the demand to which the orchestral supply is a response.

That this inferiority is no new thing, and was well weighed by Wagner himself, is clear from the stress which he laid on the superiority of the instruments used by our Philharmonic band, and also by the fact that he always cited the Conservatoire concerts in Paris as the source of what he had learned from actual experience as to fineness of orchestral execution. All the other points he so strenuously urged on conductors have been mastered at Bayreuth; and the superficialities of the Mendelssohnian system have disappeared. But the material of it all—the brute physical sound of the instruments which are so ably handled—still remains comparatively cheap and ugly; and the worst of it is that no German seems to care. As far as I can make out, the payment of an extra five pounds to an instrument-maker for the sake of a finer tone would strike both conductor and player as an unreasonable waste of money.

And yet this German indifference to the final degrees of excellence in instrumental tone is conscientiousness itself compared to their atrocious insensibility to the beauty of the human voice and the graces of a fine vocal touch. The opening performance of Parsifal this season was, from the purely musical point of view, as far as the principal singers were concerned, simply an abomination. The bass howled, the tenor bawled, the baritone sang flat, and the soprano, when she condescended to sing at all, and did not merely shout her words, screamed, except in the one unscreamable song of Herzeleide's death, in which she subsided into commonplaceness.

The bass, who was rather flustered, perhaps from nervousness, was especially brutal in his treatment of the music of Gurnemanz; and it struck me that if he had been a trombone-player in the band, instead of a singer, the conductor, Levi of Munich, would have remonstrated. Indeed, I presently heard a trombone-player, who was helping with the fanfares outside the theatre between the acts, pulled up by the sub-conductor for being "a little too strong." Accordingly, having the opportunity of exchanging a few words with Levi afterwards, I expressed my opinion about the bass in question. Levi appeared surprised, and, declaring that the singer had the best bass voice in Germany, challenged me to find him anyone who would sing the part better, to which I could only respond with sufficient emphasis by offering to sing it better myself, upon which he gave me up as a lunatic.

It had to be explained to him that I was accustomed to the "smooth" singing popular in England. That settled the question for the Bayreuth conductor. Good singing there is merely "glatt," obviously an effeminate, silly, superficial quality, unsuited to the utterances of primeval heroes. The notion that this particular sort of smoothness is one of the consequences of aiming at beauty of tone and singing in tune is apparently as strange in Germany as the notion that it is more truly virile to sing like a man than like a bullock.

If I had passed the whole season listening to Alvary, Klafsky, and Wiegand at Drury Lane, no doubt I should not have noticed any great deficiency in Grengg or Rosa Sucher. Even as it was, after the first three performances my ear became so corrupted that the second performance of Parsifal did not infuriate me as the first one did. I had become accustomed to second-rate intonation, especially after Tannhäuser, in which from beginning to end there was not a vocal note placed, I will not say as Melba or Miss Eames or the De Reszkes would have placed it, but as any tolerable English concert singer would have placed it.

This inveterate carelessness of intonation is only partly due to bad method. It is true that German singers at Bayreuth do not know how to sing: they shout; and you can see them make a vigorous stoop and lift with their shoulders, like coalheavers, when they have a difficult note to tackle, a pianissimo on any note above the stave being impossible to them.

But this system is nothing like so injurious to them as that of many of the operatic singers to whom we are accustomed. Their voices, it is true, get stale and rough; but they last astonishingly in that condition; the singers themselves are as robust as dray horses;

and sixty appears to be about the prime of their shouting life. The thin, worn, shattered voice, with its goat-bleat or tremolo, and its sound as if it had taken to drink and wrecked its nerves and constitution, all shockingly common here, even among quite young singers, is not to be heard, as a rule, at Bayreuth. Singing there, in fact, is exactly like public speaking in England—not a fine art, but a means of placing certain ideas intelligibly and emphatically before the public without any preoccupation as to beauty of voice or grace of manner.

The music dramas are, so to speak, effectively debated; and the exposition of the poetic theme has all the qualities of a good Budget speech; but there is just about as much charm of voice and style as there is at a conference of the National Liberal Federation. The English political speaker learns his business by practice, and has neither the vices of the artificial elocutionist nor the fascinations of the cultivated artist. Nobody will listen to his voice for its own sake; but he does not break it: it lasts him until he is old enough to retire; and his general health is improved by the vigorous exercise of his lungs.

And that is just exactly the case of the German singer. Unfortunately, this disqualifies him from presenting the works of Wagner as completely as Sir William Harcourt is disqualified from playing Hamlet—a matter which will appear more fully when I come to describe the fate of Parsifal and Tannhäuser in the hands of German singers as compared with that of Lohengrin as performed by Belgian, Roumanian, American, and English singers. For I shall require more than one article to make myself sufficiently unpleasant to help those German lovers of music who are in revolt against the coarseness and laxity of German taste in this matter, and who are struggling to awaken the national conscience to the impossibility of a school of art in which the first lesson is one of callous indifference to beauty.

1 August 1894

Sitting, as I am today, in a Surrey farmhouse with the sky overcast, and a big fire burning to keep me from shivering, it seems to me that it must be at least four or five months since I was breathing balmy airs in the scented pine-woods on the hills round Bayreuth. If I could only see the sun for five minutes I could better recall what I have to write about. As it is, I seem to have left it all far behind with the other vanities of the season. I no longer feel any impulse to describe Lohengrin and Tannhäuser as I promised, or to draw morals for Frau Wagner on the one hand, or Sir Augustus Harris on the other. For months I have held the whole subject of musical art in an intense grip, which never slackened even when I was asleep; but now the natural periodicity of my function asserts itself, and compels me to drop the subject in August and September, just as hens moult in November (so they tell me here in the farmhouse).

What I feel bound to record concerning the Bayreuth Lohengrin—remember that this is the first time the work has been done there, and probably the first time it has ever been thoroughly done at all, if we except the earliest attempt under Liszt at Weimar—is that its stage framework is immensely more entertaining, convincing, and natural than it has ever seemed before. This is mainly because the stage management is so good, especially with regard to the chorus. In Lohengrin there are only two comparatively short scenes in which the chorus is not present and in constant action.

The opera therefore suffers fearfully on ordinary occasions from the surprising power of the average

Italian chorister to destroy all stage illusion the moment he shambles on the scene with his blue jaws, his reach-me-down costume, his foolish single gesture, his embarrassed eye on the prompter, and his general air of being in an opera chorus because he is fit for nothing better. At Covent Garden he is, in addition, generally an old acquaintance: it is not only that he is destroying the illusion of the opera you are looking at, but that he has destroyed the illusion of nearly all the operas you have ever seen; so that the conflict of his claim upon you as one of "the old familiar faces" with the claims of the art which he outrages finally weakens your mind and disturbs your conscience until you lose the power of making any serious effort to get rid of him. As to the ladies of our opera chorus, they have to be led by competent, sensible women; and as women at present can only acquire these qualities by a long experience as mothers of large families, our front row hardly helps the romance of the thing more than the men do.

Now I am not going to pretend that at Bayreuth the choristers produce an overwhelming impression of beauty and chivalry, or even to conceal the fact that the economic, social, and personal conditions which make the Covent Garden chorus what it is in spite of the earnest desire of everybody concerned that it should be something quite different, dominate Frau Wagner just as they dominate Sir Augustus Harris, and compel her to allot to Elsa a bevy of maidens, and to Henry the Fowler a band of warriors, about whose charms and prowess a good deal of make-believe is necessary. The stouter build of the men, the prevalence of a Teutonic cast among them, and their reinforcement by a physically and artistically superior class of singers who regard it as an honor to sing at Bayreuth, even in the chorus, certainly help the illusion as far as the Saxon and Brabantine warriors in

Lohengrin are concerned; but this difference in raw
material is as nothing compared with the difference
made by the intelligent activity of the stage-manager.
One example of this will suffice. Those who know
the score of Lohengrin are aware that in the finale to
the first act there is a section, usually omitted in performance, in which the whole movement is somewhat
unexpectedly repeated in a strongly contrasted key, the
modulation being unaccountable from the point of
view of the absolute musician, as it is not at all needed
as a relief to the principal key. At Bayreuth its purpose
is made clear. After the combat with Telramund and
the solo for Elsa which serves musically as the exposition of the theme of the finale, the men, greatly excited
and enthusiastic over the victory of the strange knight,
range themselves in a sort of wheel formation, of which
Lohengrin is the centre, and march round him as they
take up the finale from Elsa in the principal key. When
the modulation comes, the women, in their white robes,
break into this triumphal circle, displace the men, and
march round Elsa in the same way, the striking change
of key being thus accompanied by a correspondingly
striking change on the stage, one of the incidents of
which is a particularly remarkable kaleidoscoping of
the scheme of color produced by the dresses.

Here you have a piece of stage management of the
true Wagnerian kind, combining into one stroke a dramatic effect, a scenic effect, and a musical effect, the
total result being a popular effect the value of which
was proved by the roar of excitement which burst forth
as the curtains closed in. A more complex example of
the same combination was afforded by the last act of
Tannhäuser, which produced the same outburst from
the audience, and which was all the more conclusive
because none of the enthusiasm could be credited to
the principal artists, who had, in the first two acts,
effectually cleared themselves of all suspicion of being

able to produce any effect except one of portentous
boredom.

Here, then, we have the point at which Bayreuth
beats Drury Lane and Covent Garden in staging Wagner and every other composer whose works have been
for some years in our repertory. I have over and over
again pointed out the way in which the heroic expenditure of Sir Augustus Harris gets wasted for want of a
stage-manager who not only studies the stage picture
as it is studied, for instance, at the Savoy Theatre, or
at any of our music-halls where ballets form part of the
entertainment, but who studies the score as well, and
orders the stage so that the spectator's eye, ear, and
dramatic sense shall be appealed to simultaneously.

I have sometimes had to point out, in the case of old
stock operas, that there is often reason to suspect that
the stage-manager either does not even know the story
of the opera he has in hand, or has become cynically
convinced that an opera is in itself such a piece of nonsense that an extra absurdity or two cannot matter
much. This is of course quite a tenable view argumen-
tatively; but it is not the understanding upon which
the public pays for its seats. The moment you take a
guinea, or half-a-crown, or whatever it may be, from
an individual for a performance of an opera, you are
bound to treat the performance as a serious matter,
whatever your private philosophic convictions may be.

At Bayreuth they do take the performance seriously
in all its details: the heroine does not die in the middle
of the street on a lodging-house sofa, nor does the tenor
step out of a window with a rope ladder attached to it,
and openly walk off at the level of the chamber floor.
The rank and file are carefully instructed as to what
they are supposed to be doing; and nobody dreams of
taking any liberties with the work or with the public.
It is quite a mistake to suppose that the makeshifts
which circumstances force upon Covent Garden are

unknown at Bayreuth, or that the stock works are as well rehearsed and prepared as the new works; but there is, at any rate, always the habit of discipline; and though things may be left undone for want of time or ill done for want of rehearsal, nothing is let slide on the assumption that it is not worth doing. I have been tortured there by bad singing, and bored by solemnly prosaic acting; but I have never been offended by wanton trifling.

I have sufficiently explained in my last article how Bayreuth's scrupulous artistic morality is heavily counterbalanced by the callousness of its musical sensibility. The cure for this, however, is not the writing of homilies about it, but the cultivation of the German ear by actual experience of something better than the singing they are accustomed to tolerate. Already the popularity of Van Dyck, a Belgian singer with none of the German bluntness about him, whose charm of voice and style was sufficient, when he appeared as Des Grieux at Covent Garden, to produce on Jean de Reszke, who was at that time taking his supremacy for granted somewhat too lazily, the effect popularly known as "making him sit up," is rendering the Bayreuth stage more accessible to foreigners, who will finally, if the Germans do not realize their own deficiencies, make it difficult for a German singer to get an engagement there. This year we have Nordica and Miss Brema as well as Van Dyck; and it is probable that Frau Wagner will look for more help in the same direction—across the frontier, that is—on future occasions.

I am not quite done with the subject even yet; but as this farmhouse is beyond the sphere of the Post Office, I must conclude, in order to allow three or four days for the journey of thirty miles or so which my communication must make before it reaches London.

8 August 1894

POSTSCRIPT 1931. As it happened I *was* done with the subject. I had already resigned my post as musical critic to The World on the death of its editor Edmund Yates on the 19th May 1894. But his successor pleaded that it would seem a personal slight to himself if I did not go on under his editorship until the end of the season; and this, to save appearances, I consented to do. After the autumn recess my vacant place was filled by Mr Robert Smythe Hichens, who had trained himself as a musician, not knowing that he was destined to be a famous novelist.

I never again undertook regular duties as a critic of music.

VERDI

Falstaff

Easter has afforded me an opportunity for a look through the vocal score of Verdi's Falstaff, now to be had at Ricordi's for sixteen shillings, a price which must obviously be reduced before the opera can get into the hands of the amateur at large. I did not go to Milan to hear the first performance for several reasons, the chief being that I am not enough of a first-nighter to face the huge tedium and probable sickness of the journey from Holborn to Basle (the rest I do not mind) in order merely to knock at the tradesman's door of Italy, so to speak, and turn back after hearing an opera half murdered by La Scala prima donnas with shattering tremolos, and witnessing a Grand Old Man demonstration conducted for the most part by people who know about as much of music as the average worshipper of Mr Gladstone does of statesmanship. In short, being lazy and heavily preoccupied, I cried sour grapes and stayed at home, knowing that the mountain would come to Mahomet soon enough.

Let it be understood, then, that since I have not been present at a complete performance of Falstaff I do not know the work: I only know some things about it. And of these I need not repeat what has already been sufficiently told: as, for instance, that Falstaff is a music drama, not an opera, and that consequently it is by Shakespear, Boito, and Verdi, and not by Verdi alone. The fact that it is a music drama explains the whole mystery of its composition by a man eighty years old. If there were another *Il balen* or *La donna è mobile* in it, I should have been greatly astonished; but there is nothing of the sort: the fire and heroism of his earlier works blazes up now only on strong provocation.

Falstaff is lighted and warmed only by the afterglow of the fierce noonday sun of Ernani; but the gain in beauty conceals the loss in heat—if, indeed, it be a loss to replace intensity of passion and spontaneity of song by fullness of insight and perfect mastery of workmanship. Verdi has exchanged the excess of his qualities for the wisdom to supply his deficiencies; his weaknesses have disappeared with his superfluous force; and he is now, in his dignified competence, the greatest of living dramatic composers. It is not often that a man's strength is so immense that he can remain an athlete after bartering half of it to old age for experience; but the thing happens occasionally, and need not so greatly surprise us in Verdi's case, especially those of us who, long ago, when Von Bülow and others were contemptuously repudiating him, were able to discern in him a man possessing more power than he knew how to use, or indeed was permitted to use by the old operatic forms imposed on him by circumstances.

I have noticed one or two exclamations of surprise at the supposed revelation in Falstaff of a "hitherto unsuspected" humorous force in the veteran tragic composer. This must be the result of the enormous popularity which Il Trovatore first and Aïda afterwards attained in this country. I grant that these operas are quite guiltless of comic relief; but what about Un Ballo, with its exquisitely light-hearted *E scherz' od è follia,* and the finale to the third act, where Renato is sarcastically complimented on his domestic virtue by the conspirators who have just shewn him that the Duke's veiled mistress, whom he is defending from them after devotedly saving the Duke's life, is his own wife. Stupidly as that tragi-comic quartet and chorus has always been mishandled on our wretched operatic stage, I cannot understand anyone who knows it denying Verdi's gift of dramatic humor.

In the first act of Otello, the stretto made in the drinking song by Cassio when he gets drunk is very funny without being in the least unmusical. The grim humor of Sparafucile, the terrible ironic humor of Iago, the agonized humor of Rigoletto: these surely settled the question as to Verdi's capacity for Falstaff none the less because the works in which they occur are tragedies and not comedies. All that could be said on the other side was that Verdi was no Mozart, which was as idle as saying that Victor Hugo was no Molière. Verdi's vein of humor is all the more Shakespearean on that account.

Verdi's worst sins as a composer have been sins against the human voice. His habit of taking the upper fifth of the compass of an exceptionally high voice, and treating that fifth as the normal range, has a great deal to do with the fact that the Italian singer is now the worst singer in the world, just as Wagner's return to Handel's way of using the voice all over its compass and obtaining physical relief for the singer and artistic relief for the audience by the contrast of the upper and lower registers has made the Wagnerian singer now the best singer in the world. Verdi applied his system with special severity to baritones.

If you look at the score of Don Giovanni, you will find three different male voices written for on the bass clef, and so treated as to leave no doubt that Mozart, as he wrote the music, had a particular sort of voice for each part constantly in his head, and that one (Masetto's) was a rough peasant's bass, another (Leporello's) a ready, fluent, copious *basso cantante;* and the third a light fine baritone, the voice of a gentleman. I have heard public meetings addressed successively by an agricultural laborer's delegate, a representative of the skilled artisans, and a university man; and they have taught me what all the treatises on singing in the world could not about the Mozartian differentiation between Masetto, Leporello, and Don Giovanni.

But now please remark that there is no difference of range between the three parts. Any man who can sing the notes of one of them can sing the notes of the others. Let Masetto and the Don exchange characters, and though the Don will be utterly ineffective in the concerted music on Masetto's lower G's and B flats, whilst Masetto will rob the serenade of all its delicacy, yet neither singer will encounter any more impossibility, or even inconvenience, in singing the notes than Mr Toole would have in reading the part of Hamlet. The same thing is true of the parts of Bartolo, Figaro, and Almaviva in Le Nozze; of San Bris and Nevers in Les Huguenots; of Wotan and Alberich in The Niblung's Ring; and of Amfortas and Klingsor in Parsifal. The dramatic distinction between these parts is so strong that only an artist of remarkable versatility could play one as well as the other; but there is practically no distinction of vocal range any more than there is a distinction of physical stature or strength.

But if we turn to Il Trovatore, we find two vocal

parts written in the bass clef, of which the lower,
Ferrando, is not a *basso profondo* like Osmin or Marcel,
but a *basso cantante* like San Bris or Leporello; yet the
baritone part (Di Luna) is beyond the reach of any
normal *basso cantante,* and treats a baritone voice as
consisting of about one effective octave, from G on the
fourth space of the bass stave to the G above. In *Il
balen* there are from two hundred and ten to two hundred and twenty notes, including the cadenza, etc.
Barring five notes in the cadenza, which is never sung
as written, only three are below F on the fourth line,
whilst nearly one hundred and forty lie above the stave
between B flat and the high G. The singing is practically continuous from end to end; and the strain on a
normal baritone voice is frightful, even when the song
is transposed half a tone as it usually is to bring it
within the bare limits of possibility. Di Luna is in this
respect a typical Verdi baritone; and the result has
been that only singers with abnormally high voices
have been able to sing it without effort.

As to the normal baritones who have made a spe-
cialty of bawling fiercely up to G sharp, they have so
lost the power of producing an endurable tone in their
lower octave, or of pitching its notes with even approx-
imate accuracy, that they have all but destroyed the
popularity of Mozart's operas by their occasional appearances as Don Giovanni, Figaro, etc. I have often
wished that the law would permit me to destroy these
unhappy wretches, whose lives must be a burden to
them. It is easy to go into raptures over the superiority
of the Italian master in vocal writing because his
phrases are melodious, easily learned, symmetrical, and
often grandiose; but when you have to sing the melodious well-turned phrases, and find that they lie a tone
higher than you can comfortably manage them, and a
third higher than you can keep on managing them for
five minutes at a stretch (for music that *lies* rather high

is much more trying than music that *ventures* very high occasionally), you begin to appreciate the sort of knowledge of and consideration for the voice shewn by Purcell, Handel, and Wagner, and to very decidedly resent Verdi's mere partiality for the top end of it.

Now comes the question, what sort of voice is needed for the part of Falstaff? Well, Ferrando and the Count di Luna rolled into one—Amonasro, in short. A rich *basso cantante,* who can knock out a vigorous high G and play with F sharp as Melba plays with B flat. Polyphemus in Handel's Acis and Valentine in Gounod's Faust might do it justice between them. Barely reasonable this, even at French pitch, and monstrous at Philharmonic pitch. And yet it is the fashion to say that Verdi is a master of the art of writing singable music.

The score is necessarily occupied to a great extent by the discourses of Falstaff, which are set with the most expert ingenuity and subtlety, the advance in this respect from the declamation of Charles V in Ernani to that of Falstaff being as great as from Tannhäuser's to Parsifal's, or from Vanderdecken's to Hans Sachs's. One capital effect—the negative answers in the manner of Mr Chadband to the repeated questions as to what honor is—is, musically, a happy adaptation from Boito's Mefistofele, and is, as far as I have discovered, the only direct Boitoism in the work, though I imagine that Verdi has profited generally by having so fine an artist and critic as Boito at his elbow when composing Otello and Falstaff. There are some amusing passages of instrumental music: for instance, a highly expressive accompaniment to a colossal drink taken by Falstaff.

During the abundant action and stage bustle of the piece we get a symphonic treatment, which belongs exclusively to Verdi's latest manner. Some tripping figuration, which creates perpetual motion by its ceaseless repetition in all sorts of ingenious sequences, as in

Mendelssohn's scherzos or the finales to his concertos, is taken as the musical groundwork upon which the vocal parts are put in, the whole fabric being wrought with the most skilful elegance. This is a matter for some of our musical pundits to consider rather anxiously. For, if I had said ten years ago that Ernani was a much greater musical composition than Mendelssohn's Scotch symphony or any of his concertos, words could not have conveyed the scorn with which so gross an opinion would have been received. But here, today, is the scorned one, whom even Browning thought it safe to represent as an empty blusterer shrinking amid a torrent of vulgar applause from the grave eye of—of—of—well, of ROSSINI! (poor Browning!) falling back in his old age on the Mendelssohnian method, and employing it with ease and brilliancy.

Perhaps, when Verdi turns a hundred and feels too old for opera composition, he will take to concerto writing, and cut out Mendelssohn and Schumann in the pretty pattern work which the pundits love them for. Which will shew how very easy it is for a good musician, when he happens to be a bad critic, to admire a great composer for the wrong thing.

12 April 1893

A Word More about Verdi

I have read most of the articles on Verdi elicited by his death, and I have blushed for my species. By this I mean the music-critic species; for though I have of late years disused this learned branch I am still entitled to say to my former colleagues "*Anch' io son critico.*" And when I find men whom I know otherwise honorable glibly pretending to an intimate acquaintance with Oberto, Conte di San Bonifacio, with Un Giorno di Regno, with La Battaglia di Legnano; actually comparing them with Falstaff and Aïda, and weighing,

with a nicely judicial air, the differences made by the
influence of Wagner, well knowing all the time that
they know no more of Oberto than they do of the tunes
Miriam timbrelled on the shores of the divided Red
Sea, I say again that I blush for our profession, and ask
them, as an old friend who wishes them well, where
they expect to go to after such shamelessly mendacious
implications when they die.

For myself, I value a virtuous appearance above vain
erudition; and I confess that the only operas of Verdi's
I know honestly right through, as I know Dickens's
novels, are Ernani, Rigoletto, Il Trovatore, Un Ballo,
La Traviata, Aïda, Otello, and Falstaff. And quite
enough too, provided one also knows enough of the
works of Verdi's forerunners and contemporaries to see
exactly when he came in and where he stood. It is inevitable that as younger and younger critics come into
the field, more and more mistakes should be made
about men who lived as long as Verdi and Wagner,
not because the critics do not know their music, but
because they do not know the operas that Wagner and
Verdi heard when they were boys, and are consequently apt to credit them with the invention of many
things which were familiar to their grandfathers.

For example, in all the articles I have read it is assumed that the difference between Ernani and Aïda is
due to the influence of Wagner. Now I declare without
reserve that there is no evidence in any bar of Aïda or
the two later operas that Verdi ever heard a note of
Wagner's music. There is evidence that he had heard
Boito's music, Mendelssohn's music, and Beethoven's
music; but the utmost that can be said to connect him
with Wagner is that if Wagner had not got all Europe
into the habit of using the whole series of dominant
and tonic discords as freely as Rossini used the dominant seventh, it is possible that Falstaff might have
been differently harmonized. But as much might be

said of any modern pantomime score. Verdi uses the
harmonic freedom of his time so thoroughly in his own
way, and so consistently in terms of his old style, that
if he had been as ignorant of Wagner as Berlioz was
of Brahms there is no reason to suppose that the score
of Falstaff would have been an unprepared thirteenth
the worse.

I am, of course, aware that when Aïda first reached
us, it produced a strong impression of Wagnerism. But
at that time nothing of Wagner's later than Lohengrin
was known to us. We thought the Evening Star song
in Tannhäuser a precious Wagnerian gem. In short, we
knew nothing of Wagner's own exclusive style, only his
operatic style, which was much more mixed than we
imagined. Everybody then thought that a recurring
theme in an opera was a Wagnerian Leitmotif, especially if it stole in to a tremolando of the strings and
was harmonized with major ninths instead of sub-dom-
inants; so when this occurred in Aïda's scena, *Ritorna
vincitor*, we all said "Aha! Wagner!" And, as very often
happens, when we came to know better, we quite forgot to revise our premature conclusion. Accordingly,
we find critics taking it for granted to-day that Aïda
is Wagnerized Verdi, although, if they had not heard
Aïda until after Siegfried and Die Meistersinger, they
would never dream of connecting the two composers
or their styles.

The real secret of the change from the roughness of
Il Trovatore to the elaboration of the three last operas,
is the inevitable natural drying up of Verdi's spontaneity and fertility. So long as an opera composer can
pour forth melodies like *La donna è mobile* and *Il
balen,* he does not stop to excogitate harmonic elegan-
cies and orchestral sonorities which are neither helpful
to him dramatically nor demanded by the taste of his
audience. But when in process of time the well begins
to dry up; when instead of getting splashed with the

bubbling over of *Ah si, ben mio,* he has to let down a
bucket to drag up *Celeste Aïda,* then it is time to be
clever, to be nice, to be distinguished, to be impressive, to study instrumental confectionery, to bring
thought and knowledge and seriousness to the rescue
of failing vitality. In Aïda this is not very happily
done: it is not until Otello that we get dignified ac-
complishment and fine critical taste; but here, too, we
have unmistakably a new hand in the business, the
hand of Boito. It is quite certain that Boito could not
have written Otello; but certain touches in Iago's
Credo were perhaps either suggested by Boito, or composed in his manner in fatherly compliment to him;
and the whole work, even in its most authentic passages, shews that Verdi was responding to the claims
of a more fastidious artistic conscience and even a
finer sensitiveness to musical sound than his own was
when he tried to turn Macbeth into another Trovatore,
and made Lady Macbeth enliven the banquet scene
with a florid drinking song. The advance from romantic intensity to dramatic seriousness is revolutionary.
Nothing is more genial in Verdi's character than this
docility, this respect for the demands of a younger
man, this recognition that the implied rebuke to his
taste and his coarseness showed a greater tenderness
for his own genius than he had shown to it himself.

But there is something else than Boito in Otello. In
the third act there is a movement in six-eight time,
Essa t'avvince, which is utterly unlike anything in the
Trovatore period, and surprisingly like a rondo in the
style of Beethoven. That is to say, it is pre-Wagnerian;
which at such a date is almost equivalent to anti-
Wagnerian. In Falstaff, again, in the buck-basket scene
there is a light-fingered and humorous *moto perpetuo*
which might have come straight out of a Mendelssohn
concerto. Unfortunately it is ineffectively scored; for
Verdi, brought up in the Italian practice of using the

orchestra as pure accompaniment, was an unskilled
beginner in German symphonic orchestration. These
are the only passages in the later works which are not
obviously the old Verdi developed into a careful and
thoughtful composer under the influence of Boito and
the effect of advancing age on his artistic resources. I
think they would both be impossible to a composer
who had not formed an affectionate acquaintance with
German music. But the music of Beethoven and Mendelssohn is the music of a Germany still under that
Franco-Italian influence which made the music of
Mozart so amazingly unlike the music of Bach. Of the
later music that was consciously and resolutely German and German only; that would not even write allegro at the head of its quick, or adagio at the head
of its slow movements, because these words are not
German; of the music of Schumann, Brahms, and
Wagner, there is not anywhere in Verdi the faintest
trace. In German music the Italian loved what Italy
gave. What Germany offered of her own music he entirely ignored.

Having now, I hope, purged myself of the heresy
that Verdi was Wagnerized, a heresy which would
never have arisen if our foolish London Opera had
been as punctual with Lohengrin as with Aïda, instead of being nearly a quarter of a century late with
it, I may take Verdi on his own ground. Verdi's genius,
like Victor Hugo's, was hyperbolical and grandiose: he
expressed all the common passions with an impetuosity and intensity which produced an effect of sublimity. If you ask What is it all about? the answer must
be that it is mostly about the police intelligence melo-
dramatized. In the same way, if you check your excitement at the conclusion of the wedding scene in Il
Trovatore to ask what, after all, *Di quella pira* is, the
answer must be that it is only a common bolero tune,
just as *Stride la vampa* is only a common waltz tune.

Indeed, if you know these tunes only through the barrel organs, you will need no telling. But in the theatre, if the singers have the requisite power and spirit, one does not ask these questions: the bolero form passes as unnoticed as the saraband form in Handel's *Lascia ch'io pianga,* whereas in the more academic form of the aria with cabaletta, which Rossini, Bellini, and Donizetti accepted, the form reduces the matter to absurdity. Verdi, stronger and more singly dramatic, broke away from the Rossinian convention; developed the simpler cavatina form with an integral codetta instead of a separated cabaletta; combined it fearlessly with popular dance and ballad forms; and finally produced the once enormously popular, because concise, powerful, and comparatively natural and dramatic type of operatic solo which prevails in Il Trovatore and Un Ballo. A comparison of this Italian emancipation of dramatic music from decorative form with the Wagnerian emancipation shews in a moment the utter unthinkableness of any sort of connection between the two composers. No doubt the stimulus given to Verdi's self-respect and courage by his share in the political activity of his time, is to some extent paralleled by the effect of the 1848 revolution on Wagner; but this only accentuates the difference between the successful composer of a period of triumphant nationalism and the exiled communist-artist-philosopher of The Niblung's Ring. As Wagner contracted his views to a practicable nationalism at moments later on, I can conceive a critic epigrammatically dismissing the Kaiser March as a bit of Verdified Wagner. But the critic who can find Wagner in Otello must surely be related to the gentleman who accused Bach of putting forth the accompaniment to Gounod's *Ave Maria* as a prelude of his own composition.

By this Mascagni-facilitating emancipation of Italian opera, Verdi concentrated its qualities and got rid

of its alloys. Il Trovatore is Italian opera in earnest
and nothing else: Rossini's operas are musical enter-
tainments which are only occasionally and secondarily
dramatic. Moses in Egypt and Semiramis, for example,
are ridiculous as dramas, though both of them contain
one impressively splendid number to shew how nobly
Rossini could have done if the silly conditions of the
Italian opera houses had given their composers any
chance of being sensible. "I could have achieved something had I been a German" said Rossini humbly to
Wagner; *"car j'avais du talent."* Bellini, Donizetti, and
the Italianized Jew Meyerbeer pushed the dramatic
element in opera still further, making it possible for
Verdi to end by being almost wholly dramatic. But
until Verdi was induced by Boito to take Shakespear
seriously they all exploited the same romantic stock-in-
trade. They composed with perfect romantic sincerity,
undesirous and intolerant of reality, untroubled by the
philosophic faculty which, in the mind of Wagner, re-
volted against the demoralizing falseness of their dramatic material. They revelled in the luxury of stage
woe, with its rhetorical loves and deaths and poisons
and jealousies and murders, all of the most luscious,
the most enjoyable, the most unreal kind. They did
not, like Rossini, break suddenly off in the midst of
their grandiosities to write *excusez du peu* at the top
of the score, and finish with a galop. On the contrary,
it was just where the stage business demanded something elegantly trivial that they became embarrassed
and vulgar. This was especially the case with Verdi,
who was nothing if not strenuous, whereas Bellini
could be trivially simple and Donizetti thoughtlessly
gay on occasion. Verdi, when he is simple or gay, is
powerfully so. It has been said, on the strength of the
alleged failure of a forgotten comic opera called Un
Giorno di Regno, that Verdi was incapable of humor;
and I can understand that an acquaintance limited to

Ernani, Il Trovatore, La Traviata, and Aïda (and acquaintances of just this extent are very common) might support that opinion. But the parts of the Duke and Sparafucile in Rigoletto could not have been composed by a humorless man. In Un Ballo again we have in Riccardo the Duke's gaiety and gallantry without his callousness; and at the great moment of the melodrama Verdi achieves a master-stroke by his dramatic humor. The hero has made an assignation with the heroine in one of those romantically lonely spots which are always to be found in operas. A band of conspirators resolves to seize the opportunity to murder him. His friend Renato, getting wind of their design, arrives before them, and persuades him to fly, taking upon himself the charge of the lady, who is veiled, and whose identity and place of residence he swears as a good knight to refrain from discovering. When the conspirators capture him and find that they have the wrong man they propose to amuse themselves by taking a look at the lady. Renato defends her; but she, to save him from being killed, unveils herself and turns out to be Renato's own wife. This is no doubt a very thrilling stage climax: it is easy for a dramatist to work up to it. But it is not quite so easy to get away from it; for when the veil is off the bolt is shot; and the difficulty is what is to be said next. The librettist solves the problem by falling back on the chaffing of Renato by the conspirators. Verdi seizes on this with genuine humorous power in his most boldly popular style, giving just the right vein of blackguardly irony and mischievous mirth to the passage, and getting the necessary respite before the final storm, in which the woman's shame, the man's agony of jealousy and wounded friendship, and the malicious chuckling of the conspirators provide material for one of those concerted pieces in which Italian opera is at its best.

And here may I mildly protest that the quartet in

Rigoletto, with its four people expressing different emotions simultaneously, was not, as the obituary notices almost all imply, an innovation of Verdi's. Such concerted pieces were *de rigueur* in Italian opera before he was born. The earliest example that holds the stage is the quartet in Don Giovanni, *Non ti fidar*; and between Don Giovanni and Rigoletto it would be difficult to find an Italian opera without a specimen. Several of them were quite as famous as the Rigoletto quartet became. They were burlesqued by Arthur Sullivan in Trial by Jury; but Verdi never, to the end of his life, saw anything ridiculous in them; nor do I. There are some charming examples in Un Ballo, of which but little seems to be remembered nowadays.

In Otello and Falstaff there is some deliberate and not unsuccessful fun. When Cassio gets too drunk to find his place in Iago's drinking song it is impossible not to burst out laughing, though the mistake is as pretty as it is comic. The fugue at the end of Falstaff so tickled Professor Villiers Stanford that he compromised himself to the extent of implying that it is a good fugue. It is neither a good fugue nor a good joke, except as a family joke among professional musicians; but since Mozart finished Don Giovanni with a whizzing fughetta, and Beethoven expressed his most wayward fits by scraps of fugato, and Berlioz made his solitary joke fugally, the Falstaff fugue may be allowed to pass.

However, to shew that Verdi was occasionally jocular does not prove that he had the gift of dramatic humor. For such a gift the main popular evidence must be taken from the serious part of Falstaff; for there is nothing so serious as great humor. Unfortunately, very few people know The Merry Wives of Windsor as it was when Falstaff was capably played according to the old tradition, and the playgoer went to hear the actor pile up a mighty climax, culminating in "Think of that, Master Brook." In those palmy days it was the vision of the man-mountain baked in the buck-basket and suddenly plunged hissing hot into the cool stream of the Thames at Datchet that focused the excitement of the pit; and if the two conversations between Ford and Falstaff were played for all they were worth, Shakespear was justified of his creation, and the rest was taken cheerfully as mere filling up. Now, it cannot be supposed that either Boito or Verdi had ever seen such a performance; and the criticisms of modern quite futile productions of The Merry Wives have shown that a mere literary acquaintance with the text will not yield up the secret to the ordinary un-Shakespearean man; yet it is just here, on Ford and Falstaff, that Verdi has concentrated his attack and trained his heaviest artillery. His Ford carries Shakespear's a step higher: it exhausts what Shakespear's resources could only suggest. And this seems to me to dispose of the matter in Verdi's favor.

The composition of Otello was a much less Shakespearean feat; for the truth is that instead of Otello being an Italian opera written in the style of Shakespear, Othello is a play written by Shakespear in the style of Italian opera. It is quite peculiar among his works in this aspect. Its characters are monsters: Desdemona is a prima donna, with handkerchief, confidante, and vocal solo all complete; and Iago, though certainly more anthropomorphic than the Count di Luna, is only so when he slips out of his stage villain's part. Othello's transports are conveyed by a magnificent but senseless music which rages from the Propontick to the Hellespont in an orgy of thundering sound and bounding rhythm; and the plot is a pure farce plot: that is to say, it is supported on an artificially manufactured and desperately precarious trick with a handkerchief which a chance word might upset at any moment. With such a libretto, Verdi was quite at home: his

success with it proves, not that he could occupy Shakespear's plane, but that Shakespear could on occasion
occupy his, which is a very different matter. Nevertheless, such as Othello is, Verdi does not belittle it as
Donizetti would have done, nor conventionalize it as
Rossini actually did. He often rises fully to it; he
transcends it in his setting of the very stagey oath of
Othello and Iago; and he enhances it by a charming
return to the simplicity of real popular life in the
episodes of the peasants singing over the fire after the
storm in the first act, and their serenade to Desdemona
in the second. When one compares these choruses with
the choruses of gypsies and soldiers in Il Trovatore one
realizes how much Verdi gained by the loss of his
power to pour forth *Il balens* and *Ah, che la mortes.*

The decay and discredit which the Verdi operas of
the Trovatore type undoubtedly brought on Italian
opera in spite of their prodigious initial popularity was
caused not at all by the advent of Wagner (for the
decay was just as obvious before Lohengrin became
familiar to us as it is now that Tristan has driven
Manrico from the Covent Garden stage), but by
Verdi's recklessness as to the effect of his works on
their performers. Until Boito became his artistic conscience he wrote inhumanly for the voice and fero-
ciously for the orchestra. The art of writing well for the
voice is neither recondite nor difficult. It has nothing
to do with the use or disuse of extreme high notes or
low notes. Handel and Wagner, who are beyond all
comparison the most skilled and considerate writers of
dramatic vocal music, do not hesitate to employ extreme notes when they can get singers who possess
them. But they never smash voices. On the contrary,
the Handelian and Wagnerian singer thrives on his
vocal exercises and lasts so long that one sometimes
wishes that he would sing Il Trovatore once and die.

The whole secret of healthy vocal writing lies in

keeping the normal plane of the music, and therefore the bulk of the singer's work, in the middle of the voice. Unfortunately, the middle of the voice is not the prettiest part of it; and in immature or badly and insufficiently trained voices it is often the weakest part. There is, therefore, a constant temptation to composers to use the upper fifth of the voice almost exclusively; and this is exactly what Verdi did without remorse. He practically treated that upper fifth as the whole voice, and pitched his melodies in the middle of it instead of in the middle of the entire compass, the result being a frightful strain on the singer. And this strain was not relieved, as Handel relieved his singers, by frequent rests of a bar or two and by long ritornellos: the voice has to keep going from one end of the song to the other. The upshot of that, except in the case of abnormally pitched voices, was displacement, fatigue, intolerable strain, shattering tremolo, and finally, not, as could have been wished, total annihilation, but the development of an unnatural trick of making an atrociously disagreeable noise and inflicting it on the public as Italian singing, with the result that the Italian opera singer is now execrated and banished from the boards of which he was once the undisputed master. He still imposes himself in obscure places; for, curiously enough, nothing dumbs him except well-written music. Handel he never attempts; but Wagner utterly destroys him; and this is why he spread the rumour through Europe that Wagner's music ruined voices.

To the unseductive bass voice, Verdi always behaved well; for since he could not make it sensuously attractive, it forced him to make the bass parts dramatically interesting. It is in Ferrando and Sparafucile, not in Charles V and the Count di Luna, that one sees the future composer of Falstaff. As to the orchestra, until Boito came, it was for the most part nothing

but the big guitar, with the whole wind playing the
tune in unison or in thirds and sixths with the singer.*
I am quite sure that as far as the brass was concerned
this was a more sensible system, and less harshly crushing to the singer, than the dot and dash system of using trumpets and drums, to which the German school
and its pupils in England clung pedantically long after
the employment of valves had made it as unnecessary
as it was ugly and absurd. But beyond this, I do not
feel called upon to find excuses for Verdi's pre-
Boitian handling of the orchestra. He used it unscrupulously to emphasize his immoderate demands for
overcharged and superhuman passion, tempting the
executants to unnatural and dangerous assumptions
and exertions. It may have been exciting to see Edmund Kean revealing Shakespear "by flashes of lightning," and Robson rivalling him in burlesque; but
when the flashes turned out to be tumblers of brandy,
and the two thunder-wielders perished miserably of
their excesses, the last excuse for the insufferable follies and vulgarities of the would-be Keans and Rob-
sons vanished. I speak of Kean and Robson so as not
to hurt the survivors of the interregnum between
Mario and De Reszke, when bawling troopers, roaring
Italian porters, and strangulating Italian newspaper
criers made our summer nights horrible with Verdi's
fortissimos. Those who remember them will understand.

But in his defects, as in his efficiencies, his directness, and his practical common sense, Verdi is a thorough unadulterated Italian. Nothing in his work needs
tracing to any German source. His latter-day develop-

* Elgar, the greatest of all orchestral technicians, maintained that the big guitar business has a genuine skilled
technique, and that, for instance, such scores as Rossini's
Stabat Mater, in the apparently crude and crushing accompaniment to *Cujus animam,* in performance sound exactly
right, and help the singer instead of annihilating him.

ment of declamatory recitative can be traced back through the recitatives in Rossini's Moses right back to the beginning of Italian opera. You cannot trace a note of Wotan in Amonasro or Iago, though you can trace something of Moses in the rhythms of Wotan. The anxious northern genius is magnificently assimilative: the self-sufficient Italian genius is magnificently impervious. I doubt whether even Puccini really studies Schumann, in spite of his harmonic Schumannisms. Certainly, where you come to a strong Italian like Verdi you may be quite sure that if you cannot explain him without dragging in the great Germans, you cannot explain him at all.

At all events, Verdi will stand among the greatest of the Italian composers. It may be that, as with Handel, his operas will pass out of fashion and be forgotten whilst the Manzoni Requiem remains his imperishable monument. Even so, that alone, like Messiah, will make his place safe among the immortals.

THE ANGLO-SAXON REVIEW
March 1901

Spoof Opera
by a Ghost from the 'Eighties

The institution called variously a busman's or a stage-doorkeeper's holiday has never been called a musical critic's holiday. The musician who has been a professional critic knows, better even than Wagner, that music is kept alive on the cottage piano of the amateur, and not in the concert rooms and opera houses of the great capitals. He will not go to public performances when he is no longer paid for his soul-destroying sufferings. I wonder how many of our critics at last become quite clearly conscious that what they have to listen to in these places is not music. Sometimes the horrible thought comes that perhaps

some of them have never heard music in their lives,
but only public performances, and therefore honestly
believe that these sounds, produced for so many
guineas a week, and synchronized by an official called
a conductor, really make music, and that there is no
other sort of music. But such a state of damnation is
hardly possible; for it happens from time to time
within the experience of every opera or concert goer
that the pentecostal miracle recurs, and for a few bars,
or a whole number, or even for a whole evening, the
guineas' worth of notes organize themselves into living
music. Such occasions are very rare; but they are
frequent enough to give every critic some moments
of the real thing to compare with the simulacrum. Yet
the critics seldom venture to face the conclusion that
the difference is not between a bad performance and
a good one, but between the waste and heartbreak of
a vain search, and the supreme satisfaction of a glorious discovery.

Still, the miracle being always possible, there is
hope, as long as the performers are really trying.
Sometimes, if only for a moment, there is success. But
they are not always trying. Worst of all, they are sometimes guying. Our orchestras become so stale with
their endless repetitions of work which contains no
durably interesting orchestral detail nor presents any
technical difficulty, that nothing but a high standard
of artistic self-respect and honesty in their public obligations will make them do their work seriously if the
conductor either sympathizes with their attitude or
lacks the authority which is not to be trifled with.
When these saving conditions are lacking, you get
spoof opera. The accompaniments are a derisive rum-
tum. The fortissimo chords are music-hall crashes, pure
charivari, in which the players play any note that
comes uppermost, and then laugh to one another. The
joke is kept from the audience, partly by its own igno-

rance, and partly by the fact that as the *farceurs* are in a minority, most of the players are playing the notes set down in their parts because that is the easiest thing to do, and because they are not all in the humor for horseplay, not to mention that some of them are artists to whose taste and conscience such tomfoolery is detestable.

Verdi was the victim of a riot of this sort which lately came under my ghostly notice. I haunted a famous London theatre one evening in time to hear the last two acts of what was the most popular opera of the nineteenth century until Gounod's Faust supplanted it: an opera so popular that people who never dreamt of going to the opera as a general habit, and never in all their lives went to any other opera, went again and again to hear Il Trovatore whenever they had a chance.

Il Trovatore is, in fact, unique, even among the works of its own composer and its own country. It has tragic power, poignant melancholy, impetuous vigor, and a sweet and intense pathos that never loses its dignity. It is swift in action, and perfectly homogeneous in atmosphere and feeling. It is absolutely void of intellectual interest: the appeal is to the instincts and to the senses all through. If it allowed you to think for a moment it would crumble into absurdity like the garden of Klingsor. The very orchestra is silenced as to every sound that has the irritant quality that awakens thought: for example, you never hear the oboe: all the scoring for the wind that is not mere noise is for the lower registers of the clarinets and flutes, and for the least reedy notes of the bassoon.

Let us admit that no man is bound to take Il Trovatore seriously. We are entirely within our rights in passing it by and turning to Bach and Handel, Mozart and Beethoven, Wagner and Strauss, for our music. But we must take it or leave it: we must not trifle with it. He who thinks that Il Trovatore can be performed without taking it with the most tragic solemnity is, for all the purposes of romantic art, a fool. The production of a revival of Il Trovatore should be supervised by Bergson; for he alone could be trusted to value this perfect work of instinct, and defend its integrity from the restless encroachments of intelligence.

The costumes and scenery need to be studied and guarded with the most discriminating care. For example, there is only one costume possible for the Count di Luna. He must wear a stiff violet velvet tunic, white satin tights, velvet shoes, and a white turban hat, with a white puggaree falling on a white cloak. No other known costume can remove its wearer so completely from common humanity. No man could sit down in such a tunic and such tights; for the vulgar realism of sitting down is ten times more impossible for the Count di Luna than for the Venus of Milo. The gipsy must be decorated with sequins and Zodiacal signs: as well put a caravan on the stage at once as relate her by the smallest realistic detail to any gipsy that ever sold uncouth horses at St Margaret's Fair or kept a shooting-gallery. The harp of Manrico must be, not "the harp that once," but the harp that never. It should be such an instrument as Adams decorated ceilings with, or modern piano-makers use as supports for the pedals of their instruments. Give Manrico an Erard harp—a thing that he could possibly play—and he is no longer Manrico, but simply Man; and the unplumbed depths of the opera dry up into an ascertained and disilluding shallow. And the scenes in which these unbounded and heart-satisfying figures move must be the scenery of Gustave Doré at his most romantic. The mountains must make us homesick, even if we are Cockneys who have never seen a mountain bigger or remoter than Primrose Hill. The garden must be an enchanted garden: the convent must be a sepulchre for the living:

the towers of Castellor must proclaim the dungeons within.

I should say that a production of Il Trovatore is perhaps the most severe test a modern impresario has to face; and I suggest that if he cannot face it he had better run away from it; for if he pretends to make light of it no one will laugh with him.

Well knowing all this, I haunted, as aforesaid, half a performance of this wonderful opera a few nights ago. It cost me six-and-sixpence.

Let the six-and-sixpence go: I do not ask for my money back, except, perhaps the sixpence that went as tax to the Government, which might have stopped the performance by virtue of Dora, and didnt. But except for the unorganized individual feats of the singers, it was not worth the money. The Count of Luna not only wore an ugly historical costume (German, I think), in which he could have sat down, but actually did sit down, and thereby killed the illusion without which he was nothing. The scenery was the half playful scenery of the Russian opera and ballet. The soldiers, instead of being more fiercely soldierly than any real soldiers ever were on sea or land, were wholly occupied in demonstrating their unfitness to be combed out; and though, unlike the old Italian choristers, they had voices, they seemed to have picked up their music by ear in the course of a demoralizing existence as tramps. Worst of all, the humorists of the orchestra were guying what they regarded as the poor old opera quite shamelessly. There was some honorable and fine playing in the wood wind: Leonora could not have desired a more dignified and sympathetic second than the flute in her opening of the last act; but there were others, of whom I cannot say that they treated Verdi, or the audience, or their own professional honor, handsomely.

In their defence, I will say just this: that the cue was

given to them by mutilations of the score for which the management must be held responsible. In the wedding scene, Verdi demands that Leonora shall wear a bridal veil and make it clear that her intentions are honorable. But here Leonora scandalously wore her walking dress. Manrico shamelessly sang his love song; and then, instead of giving Leonora a chance in the touching little antiphony which introduces the organ and gives the needed ritual character to the scene, besides saving the lady's character, he went straight on to the final war song with the bolero accompaniment, and thus made the whole scene a licentious concert. The end of it was quite senselessly botched in a way that must have given somebody a good deal of unnecessary trouble. The first interlude between the bolero blood-and-thunder song and its repetition was cut out, and replaced by the second; yet the song was repeated, so that when it ended there was nothing to be done but set the chorus and band to demonstrate at random, in the key of C or thereabouts, whilst the tenor brought down the curtain and the house by delivering that note "all out," as motorists say, above the din. If there was any more design in the business than this, all I can say is that it was not discernible: the finish seemed to me to be pure spoof. In any case, I see no reason why any gentleman employed about the theatre should have been called on to improve Verdi, who knew how to arrange that sort of climax very well. As the thrown-open window, and the blaze of red fire which tells the audience that Manrico's high C is extracted from him by the spectacle of his mother at the stake, were omitted (too much trouble in the hot weather, doubtless), nobody had the least notion of what he was shouting about.

Again, in the prison scene, when one was expecting the little stretto for the three singers which leads to Leonora's death, and which is happily not a stunt for any of them, but a very moving dramatic passage

which completes the musical form of the scene, the
lady suddenly flopped down dead; the tenor was be-
headed; and the curtain rushed down: this barbarous
cut announcing plainly that the object was to get the
silly business over as soon as possible when there were
no more solos for the principals.

Yet that is not the worst thing of the kind I have
heard lately. I went to hear Figaro's Wedding, by
Mozart, at another theatre a few weeks ago; and they
not only made a cut of several pages in the finale of
the last act, including one of the most beautiful passages in the whole work, but positively stopped the
music to speak the words set to the omitted music, and
then calmly resumed the finale, leaving me gasping.
They had much better have taken a collection. There
would have been some sense in that. And they began
the proceedings with the National Anthem, which almost makes the matter one of high treason.

And now may I ask the critics why they, the watch-
dogs of music, suffer these misdemeanors to pass un-
mentioned and unreproved? They may know so little
of Italian opera, and have so low an opinion of it, that
the cuts in Il Trovatore may escape them; and they
may really believe that all that spoof and charivari is
genuine Verdi. But if they know anything about the
forms of music at all, they must know that the interruption of a Mozart finale for a spell of dialogue is as
impossible as a step-dance by a dean in the middle of
an anthem. Several numbers of the opera were also
omitted; but the omission of complete separate numbers is not mutilation: circumstances may make it reasonable; for instance, the artists may not be able to sing
them, or it may be desirable to shorten the performance. But if such cuts as I have just described are allowed to pass without remonstrance, we shall soon
have all the connective tissue of opera either left out
or supplied by spoof, the residue consisting of star

turns. Needs there a ghost from the criticism of the eighteen-eighties to tell the public that they are not getting full measure? Why, even the dramatic critics only the other day missed Polonius's blessing from Hamlet when Mr Harry Irving cut it. When his father omitted about a third of King Lear, the critics of that day did not miss a line of it, and only wondered mildly what on earth the play was about. If dramatic criticism can progress, why should musical criticism, which used to be the senior branch, be left behind?

What makes me touchy about Il Trovatore is that the materials for a better performance than I have ever heard were present. In the nineteenth century, Verdi, Gounod, Arthur Sullivan, and the rest wrote so abominably for the human voice that the tenors all had goat-bleat (and were proud of it); the baritones had a shattering vibrato, and could not, to save their lives, produce a note of any definite pitch; and the sopranos had the tone of a locomotive whistle without its steadiness: all this being the result of singing parts written for the extreme upper fifth of voices of exceptional range, because high notes are pretty. But to-day our singers, trained on Wagner, who shares with Handel the glory of being great among the greatest writers for the voice, can play with Verdi, provided they do not have to do it too often. There was no spoof about the singing of Leonora and Manrico: they threw about high Cs like confetti, and really sang their music. I have never heard the music of the prison scene sung as it was by the tenor. He was, by the way, remarkably like Mr Gilbert Chesterton, who would certainly have a very pleasant voice if he took to opera (I hope he will); and the illusion was strongly reinforced by the spectacle of Mr Belloc seated in a box in evening dress, looking like a cardinal in mufti. A better Leonora was impossible: there is nothing more in the part than she got out of it. Though the opera was supposed to be in

English, they all exhorted her to lay a Nora whenever they addressed her; and I am afraid they thought they were pronouncing her name in the Italian manner. I implore them to call her Leeonora, like Sir James Barrie's heroine, in future; for that is at least English. Layanora is nothing but simple mispronunciation. I do not think either the conductor or the chorus knew much about the opera except the tunes they had picked up from the ghosts of the old barrel-organs (where they heard them, goodness only knows); but the Count knew his part; and the result in the trio at the end of the third act, where there is a very jolly counterpoint to be pieced out in mosaic by the Count, Ferrando, and the chorus, was amusing, as the Count got in his bits of the mosaic, whilst the bewildered chorus merely muttered distractedly, and the conductor raced madly to the end to get it all over and enable the gipsy to cover his disgrace by answering repeated curtain calls, which she deserved, not only for her courageous singing against a very unsympathetic accompaniment, but for the self-restraint with which she refrained from committing murder.

England's musical obligations to the artistic director of this enterprise are so enormous that it seems ungrateful to ask him to add to them by taking Il Trovatore in hand himself next time I drop in. But I really can say no less than I have said above. Even at that, I am surprised at my own moderation.

By the way, incredible as it may seem, there really was a Manrico in the fifteenth century who fought a Di Luna, who was not a Count, but a Constable (not a police-constable). Di Luna was not his brother, and did not cut his head off; but as Manrico was the founder of Spanish drama, perhaps it would have been better if he had.

SCHÖNBERG AND ATONALITY

Dear Sir,

Within my lifetime there has been a complete liberation of modulation from its own rules. All the composers, great and small, have now availed themselves fully of this. New modes have been tried, like the whole tone (or organ tuner's) scale of Debussy; and the obsolete modes have been played with a little. But all this music was in terms of some tonality or other, however sudden and frequent its modulations and transitions might be. And the harmonic practice was so free that the scale became a 12 note scale with nothing of the old tonality left but a keynote. Still, as long as there was a keynote there was no fundamental difference between Bach and Richard Strauss.

Schönberg tried to get loose from the keynote by writing pieces in listening to which you could not guess which was to be the final chord, because there was no tonal cadence. The revolutionary young composers rushed in at this new game and dropped key signatures; so that their scores were a mass of accidentals; but Schönberg exhausted the fun of this and relapsed more and more into tonality. This drift is apparent in all the big composers now. It is hard to say that the symphonies of Sibelius are in this key or that; but when we come to know his symphonies by heart as we know those of Mozart and Beethoven they will appear as tonal to us as Elgar's.

In short the post-Wagnerian anarchy is falling into order as all anarchies do pretty soon; and I expect soon to hear the Wagnerian flood of endless melody getting embanked in the melodic *design* of Bach and Handel.

Faithfully

G. Bernard Shaw

To Nicolas Slominsky Esq.

2 August 1936

Musical

Questions

MORE ABOUT OPERA

Acting in Opera

The operatic stage is improving, like other things. But it is still possible for a prima donna to bounce on the stage and throw her voice at the heads of the audience with an insolent insistence on her position as a public favorite, and hardly the ghost of a reference to the character she is supposed to impersonate. An ambitious young artist may easily be misled by illustrious examples of stage misconduct. To tell an average young opera singer that she is a Patti or a Nilsson is to pay her the highest compliment she desires. Yet Madame Patti's offences against artistic propriety are mighty ones and millions. She seldom even pretends to play any other part than that of Adelina, the spoiled child with the adorable voice; and I believe she would be rather hurt than otherwise if you for a moment lost sight of Patti in your preoccupation with Zerlina, or Aïda, or Caterina. Nilsson, a far greater dramatic artist, so far stood on her dignity that she never came before the curtain to bow until there had been applause enough to bring out her rival at least six times (Patti will get up and bow to you in the very agony of stage death if you only drop your stick accidentally); and yet it is not sixteen years since I saw Madame Nilsson, in the wedding scene in Il Trovatore, turn to the tenor at the

end of *Ah, si ben mio,* and slap him on the back with
a loud "Bravo" that was audible—and meant to be audible—all over the house. Try to imagine Miss Ellen
Terry doing that to Mr Irving after the "palace lifting
to eternal summer" speech in The Lady of Lyons; and
you will begin to realize how far the opera house is
behind the theatre in England, and how any young
lady, by the exercise of the simplest good sense and
taste, may attain a higher normal level of dramatic sincerity than the two most famous of her predecessors.

18 April 1890

Rigoletto

I cannot congratulate Lassalle on his Rigoletto last
Thursday at Covent Garden. A massive gentleman
with all the empty pomposity of the Paris Opéra ham-
pering him like an invisible chain and bullet tied to his
ankle, and whose stock-in-trade as an actor consists of
one mock-heroic attitude, cannot throw himself into a
part which requires the activity of a leopard; nor, by
merely screwing up his eyes in an ecstasy of self-ap-
probation, convey the raging self-contempt, the superstitious terror, the impotent fury, the savage vindictive-
ness, the heartbroken grovelling of the crippled jester
wounded in his one vulnerable point—his fierce love of
his child, the only creature who does not either hate or
despise him. In such a character, burnt into music as it
has been by Verdi, Lassalle's bag of hackneyed Parisian tricks makes him egotistical and ridiculous.

Further, he spoils the effect of the great scene with
the courtiers, and makes a most unreasonable demand
on the orchestra, by transposing his music a whole tone
down, a monstrous liberty to take. No one can blame
a singer for requiring a transposition of half-a-tone
from our Philharmonic pitch; but where, as at Covent
Garden, the French pitch is adopted, a demand for "a

tone down" could only be justified in the case of a
singer of very limited range, but with sufficiently remarkable acting power to compensate for the injury
to the musical effect. As Lassalle has neither excuse, it
seems to me that we are entitled to expect that he shall
in future either sing the part as Verdi wrote it, or else
let it alone. At the same time, it is but fair to add that
when an unfortunate baritone has to sing fifty bars in
what is practically twelve-eight time, andante, on the
four or five highest notes in his compass, without a rest
except for two bars, during which he is getting out of
breath in a violent stage struggle, the composer has
only himself to thank when the same artist, who sings
the much longer part of Wagner's Hans Sachs without
turning a hair, flatly declines to submit to the strain of
Rigoletto.

As it was, the honors of the occasion were carried
off by Madame Melba, who ended the famous quartet
on a high D flat of the most beautiful quality, the licence in this instance justifying itself by its effect.
Valero, if he did not realize the masterful egotist, full
of *la joie de vivre*, as conceived by Victor Hugo and
Verdi, yet played with such spirit and humor that he
may put down the Duke as one of his London successes. His singing, to be sure, was only a tasty sort of
yelling, without spontaneity or purity of tone; but it
was pretty enough to bring down the house in *La
donna è mobile*.

2 July 1890

Directing Opera

He [Sir Augustus Harris of Covent Garden] made an initial mistake in engaging five leading tenors and no
stage manager. For want of a stage manager, Orfeo
was murdered. For want of a stage manager, the first
act of Otello was laid waste. For want of a stage man-

ager, Tannhäuser was made a laughing-stock to every German who went to see it, except in the one or two passages which Albani stage-managed. For want of a stage manager, the first scene in Boito's Mefistofele remains so absurd that it is to be hoped that when Edouard de Reszke appears at one of the holes in a ragged cloth, and sends a hearty "Ave, Signor," in the direction of another hole, the audience do not know whom he is supposed to be addressing. For want of a stage manager, no man in Les Huguenots knows whether he is a Catholic or a Protestant; and conversations which are pure nonsense except on the supposition that the parties cannot distinguish one another's features in the gloom are conducted in broad moonlight and gaslight. I have been told that the moon in Die Meistersinger has to be superintended by Jean de Reszke in person; but for the truth of this I cannot vouch. As for the prison doors that will not shut, and the ordinary door that will not open, I do not complain of that: it is the stage way of such apertures. One gets at last to quite look forward to Valentine attempting a dashing exit through an impracticable door into his house opposite the cathedral, and recoiling, flattened and taken aback, to disappear ignominiously through the solid wall at the next entrance. I would not now accept any house as being that in which Rigoletto so jealously immured his daughter, unless the garden door were swinging invitingly open before every onset of the draughts, more numerous than the currents of the ocean, which ventilate the Covent Garden stage, and the courses of which have so often been pointed out to me by the horizontal flames of the guttering candles in the first act of La Traviata.

It must be understood that by a stage manager I do not mean merely a person who arranged the few matters which cannot either be neglected or left to arrange themselves as best they may. I mean rather the man who arranges the stage so as to produce the illusion aimed at by the dramatic poet and musician. Such a one, for instance, would begin his preparation for Mefistofele by reminding the scene-painter of Mesdag's Sunrise in the Museum in Amsterdam, and coaxing him to substitute some great cloud region like that for the dingy cloth with the two holes in it which lames the imagination in spite of Boito's music. He would give some touch of nature to that garden of Margaret's, where, beneath the shade of tall trees, a discordantly gaudy flower-bed blazes in an outrageous glare that never was on sea or land; for, if he could not adapt the light to the scenery, he could at least try to adapt the scenery to the light. He would bring his common sense to bear on La Traviata, his intelligence on Les Huguenots, his reading on Tannhäuser, and his imagination on all the operas. And withal, instead of putting Sir Augustus Harris to any additional expense, he would make fifteen shillings go further than a pound goes now. That is what really offends my economic instincts in the business—that so much money should be wasted. I was able to forgive the shabbiness of Signor Lago's Orfeo, because money was scarce there; but the splendors of the Harrisian Orfeo were infuriating, because the effect was reduced more than the cost was increased.

5 August 1891

Cavalleria Rusticana

Of the music of Cavalleria (with the stress on the penultimate vowel, if you please: it is a mistake to suppose that the Italians call it Cavvlearea) I have already intimated that it is only what might reasonably be expected from a clever and spirited member of a generation which has Wagner, Gounod, and Verdi at its fingers' ends, and which can demand, and obtain, larger

instrumental resources for a ballet than Mozart had at
his disposal for his greatest operas and symphonies. Far
more important than that, it has a public trained to endure, and even expect, continuous and passionate melody, instead of the lively little allegros of the old
school, which were no more than classically titivated
jigs and hornpipes; and to relish the most poignant discords—tonic ninths, elevenths, and thirteenths, taken
unprepared in all sorts of inversions (you see, I can be
as erudite as anybody else when I choose)—without
making a wry face, as their fathers, coddled on the
chromatic confectionery of Spohr and his contemporaries, used to do when even a dominant seventh
visited their ears too harshly.

Even today you may still see here and there a big,
strong, elderly man whimpering when they play the
Tannhäuser overture at him, and declaring that there
is no "tune" in it, and that the harmony is all discord,
and the instrumentation all noise. Our young lions no
longer have this infantile squeamishness and petulance
to contend with, even in Italy. They may lay about
them, harmonically and instrumentally, as hard as they
please without rebuke: even the pedants have given
up calling on them to observe "those laws of form to
which the greatest masters have not disdained to submit"—which means, in effect, to keep Pop Goes the
Weasel continually before them as a model of structure
and modulation. Consequently, opera now offers to
clever men with a turn for music and the drama an
unprecedented opportunity for picturesque, brilliant,
apt, novel, and yet safely familiar and popular com-
binations and permutations of the immense store of
musical "effects" garnered up in the scores of the
great modern composers, from Mozart to Wagner and
Berlioz. This is the age of second-hand music. There is
even growing up a school of composers who are poets
and thinkers rather than musicians, but who have

selected music as their means of expression out of the love of it inspired in them by the works of really original masters. It is useless to pretend that Schumann was a creative musician as Mendelssohn was one, or Boito as Verdi, or Berlioz as Gounod. Yet Schumann's setting of certain scenes from Goethe's Faust is enormously more valuable than Mendelssohn's St Paul; we could spare La Traviata better than Mefistofele; whilst Berlioz actually towers above Gounod as a French composer.

And this because, on the non-musical side of their complex art, Mendelssohn and Gounod were often trivial, genteel, or sentimental, and Verdi obvious and melodramatic, whilst Schumann was deeply serious, Berlioz extraordinarily acute in his plans and heroic in his aims, and Boito refined, subtle, and imaginative. The great composer is he who, by the rarest of chances, is at once a great musician and a great poet—who has Brahms's wonderful ear without his commonplace mind, and Molière's insight and imagination without his musical sterility. Thus it is that you get your Mozart or your Wagner—only here we must leave Molière out, as Wagner, on the extra-musical side, is comparable to nobody but himself. The honor of the second place in the hierarchy I shall not attempt to settle. Schumann, Berlioz, Boito, and Raff, borrowing music to express their ideas, have, it must be admitted, sometimes touched an even higher level of originality than Schubert, Mendelssohn, and Goetz, who had to borrow ideas for their music to express, and were unquestionably superior only in the domain of absolute music.

28 October 1891

Dramatic Singing

Fortunately for Signor Lago, the second act of The Flying Dutchman requires no staging worth mentioning, and lies almost altogether in the hands of the two principal artists. Blanchard, who played Vanderdecken, has the music at his fingers' ends. He was thoroughly in earnest, and did his best all through. He has a sufficiently powerful voice, remarkably equal from top to bottom (an immense advantage for this particular part); and though its steadiness and purity of tone have been much impaired by his continental training, still, as he did what he could to minimize his defects, it carried him through with a very respectable measure of success. His acting was too sentimental: he was rather the piously afflicted widower than the obstinate and short-tempered skipper who declared, in profane terms, that he would get round the Cape in spite of Providence if he had to keep trying until the Day of Judgment. But this fault, again, was relieved a little by his substantial stage presence and effective make-up.

Artistically, I think he had more to do with such effect as the work was able to make under the circumstances than Miss Macintyre, who was, nevertheless, the favorite of the evening. She is undoubtedly an interesting young lady; and the pit, captivated by her auburn hair and her Scottish beauty, resolved, to a man, to see her triumphantly through. And they did. Whenever she threw herself at the footlights in the heroic elation of youth, and sent a vigorous B natural tearing over them, the applause could hardly be restrained until the fall of the curtain. But whether it is that I have seen so many stage generations of brave and bonnie lassies doing this very thing (and too many of them have since lost the power of doing that without ever having acquired the power of doing anything better), or whether because my own hair is more or less auburn, the waves of enthusiasm broke over me as over a rock, damping me without moving or warming me. I can see that Miss Macintyre is a true Scot in her susceptibility to a good story, especially a legend. Tell her all about Gretchen, Senta, or Rebecca, and you find her intelligence and imagination on the alert at once, whereas many an Italian prima donna, under the same circumstances, would barely tolerate the information as an irksome and not very important guide to her stage business.

So far, so good. But the story-teller's instinct may be keen enough in a young lady to make her vividly imagine incidents and emotions, without raising her an inch above the commonplace in her power of imagining and realizing beauty of musical tone, eloquence and variety of musical diction, or grace and dignity of movement and gesture. And here it is that Miss Macintyre breaks down. Her notion of dramatic singing at present hardly goes beyond intensely imagining herself to be the person in the drama, and then using the music to relieve her pent-up excitement. This is better than no notion at all; but, all the same, it is the notion of a schoolgirl, and not of an experienced artist. In unstrained situations it leaves her without ideas; in strenuous ones it results in her simply singing excitably, or standing with every muscle, from her jaw down to her wrists, in a state of tension as utterly subversive of grace as the attitude of a terrified horse, which is a perfect example of sincerity of conception without artistic grace of expression.

4 November 1891

A Bad Opera

The other day an actor published a book of directions for making a good play. His plan was a simple one. Take all the devices which bring down the house in existing plays; make a new one by stringing them all together; and there you are. If that book succeeds, I am prepared to write a similar treatise on opera composition. I know quite a lot of things that would be of great use to any young composer. For instance, when two lovers are on the stage together, be sure you make them catch sight of the moon or stars and gaze up rapturously whilst the violins discourse ravishing strains with their mutes on. Mutes are also useful for spinning-wheel business and for fires, as in Marta and Die Walküre.

For dreamy effects, tonic pedals as patented by Gounod and Bizet are useful. When large orchestras are available, broad melodies on the fourth string of the violins may be relied on for a strong and popular impression. When the heroine is alone on the stage, a rapid, agitated movement, expressive of her anticipation of the arrival of her lover, and culminating in a vigorous instrumental and vocal outburst as he rushes on the stage and proceeds without an instant's loss of time to embrace her ardently, never fails to leave the public breathless. The harmonic treatment of this situation is so simple that nobody can fail to master it in a few lessons. The lady must first sing the gentleman's name on the notes belonging to the chord of the dominant seventh in some highly unexpected key; the gentleman then vociferates the lady's name a peg higher on the notes of a more extreme discord; and, finally, the twain explode simultaneously upon a brilliant six-four chord, leading, either directly through the dominant chord, or after some pretty interruption of the cadence, to a flowing melody in which the gentleman either protests his passion or repeatedly calls attention to the fact that at last they meet again.

The whole situation should be repeated in the last act, with the difference that this time it is the gentleman who must be alone at the beginning. Furthermore, he must be in a gloomy dungeon, not larger at the outside than the stage of Covent Garden Theatre; and he must be condemned to die next morning. The reason for putting the gentleman, rather than the lady, in this situation is to be found in the exclusion of women from politics, whereby they are deprived of the privilege of being condemned to death, without any reflection on their personal characters, for heading patriotic rebellions. The difficulty has nevertheless been successfully got over by making the lady go mad in the fourth act, and kill somebody, preferably her own child. Under these circumstances she may sing almost anything she pleases of a florid nature in her distraction, and may take the gentleman's place in the prison-cell in the next act without forfeiting the moral approval of the audience. Florid mad scenes, though they are very pretty when the lady's affliction is made to take the playful turn of a trial of skill with the first flute, which should partly imitate the voice and partly accompany it in thirds, is now out of fashion; and it is far better, in dramatic opera, to be entirely modern in style.

Fortunately, the rule for modernity of style is easily remembered and applied. In fact, it is one of the three superlatively easy rules, the other two being the rules for writing Scotch and archaic music. For Scotch music, as everyone knows, you sustain E flat and B flat in the bass for a drone, and play at random in some Scotch measure on the notes which are black on the piano. For archaic music you harmonize in the ordinary way in the key of E major; but in playing you make the four sharps of the key natural, reading the music as if it was written in the key of C, which, of course, simplifies the execution as far as the piano is concerned. The effect will be diabolical; but nobody will object if you explain that your composition is in the Phrygian mode. If a still more poignant effect be desired, write in B natural, leaving out the sharps as before, and calling the mode Hypophrygian. If, as is possible, the Phrygian is more than the public can stand, write in D without sharps, and call the mode Dorian, when the audience will accept you as being comfortably in D minor, except when you feel that it is safe to excruciate them with the C natural. This is easy, but not more so than the rule for making music sound modern.

For compositions in the major, all that is necessary is to write ordinary diatonic harmonies, and then go over them with a pen and cross the t's, as it were, by sharpening all the fifths in the common chords. If the composition is in the minor, the common chord must be left unaltered; but whenever it occurs some instrument must play the *major* sixth of the key, *à propos de bottes,* loud enough to make itself heard rather distinctly. Next morning all the musical critics will gravely declare that you have been deeply influenced by the theories of Wagner; and what more can you desire, if modernity is your foible?

But I am neglecting my week's work. Although I repeat that "How to compose a good opera" might be written as easily as "How to write a good play," I must not set about writing it myself in this column, although the above sample will shew every learned musician how thoroughly I am qualified for the task. The fact is, I had been reading the reviews of Mr Frank Archer's book; and it set me thinking of what are called actors' plays, meaning plays which are not plays at all, but compilations consisting of a series of stage effects devised *ad hoc.* Indeed, stage effects is too wide a term: actors' effects would be more accurate. I thought of how hopelessly bad all such works are, even when, as in the case of Cibber's Richard III and Garrick's Katharine and Petruchio, they are saved from instant perdition by a mutilated mass of poetry and drama stolen from some genuine playwright.

And then I fell to considering which would be the worst thing to have to sit out in a theatre—an actor's play or a singer's opera. Before I could settle the point the clock struck; and I suddenly realized that if I lost

another moment I should miss the one-fifty-five train
to the Crystal Palace, where I was due at two-forty-five
to witness the performance of Mr George Fox's new
opera, Nydia. And when I sat down just now to write
an account of Nydia, it naturally reminded me of Mr
Frank Archer, and led to the above tremendous di-
gression on the subject of operatic composition in general.

Nydia is founded on Bulwer-Lytton's Last Days of
Pompeii, a novel which I read when a boy. I remember
nothing of it except the name Arbaces, and the Roman
sentinel, and Pliny—though, indeed, I am not sure that
I did not get the last two out of Chambers's Miscellany.
At all events, I found the libretto of Nydia as new to
me as it is in the nature of any libretto to be to a musical critic of my age. It began with a bustling crowd,
singing:

Water melons, rich and rare,
None excel them we declare;
Olives, figs, and honey sweet,
You will find them hard to beat;
Here is game, wild mountain boar,
Oysters too from Britain's shore,
        Come and buy, come and buy.

This was out of Carmen, tune and all, except the oysters; and even their freshness must have been severely
tried by hawking them in the full blaze of an Italian
sun.

    Then we had a blind girl with a Leitmotif, also rather
like the jealousy motive in Carmen, with a heroine,
lover, and villain, in due course. The villain, a Pompe-
ian archbishop, held a service in a temple on the lines
of the one in Aïda; and the lover came in and dashed
him down the steps of the altar, for which exploit he
was haled away to prison—very properly, as I thought
—in spite of the entreaties of the heroine. In prison he
shared his cell with a Nazarene, who strove hard, not

without some partial success, to make him see the beauty of being eaten by a lion in the arena. Next came the amphitheatre, with a gladiator fight which only needed a gallery full of shrieking vestals with their thumbs turned down to be perfectly *à la* Gérome. Then the hero, kept up to the mark by the Nazarene, was thrown to the lion, whereupon Vesuvius emitted clouds of spangles and red fire. A scene of terror and confusion in the streets followed, the crowd standing stock-still, with its eyes on the conductor, and the villain falling, slain by lightning, and then creeping off on all-fours behind the calves of the multitude.

Finally the clouds parted; and we had a pretty pictorial composition of the hero and heroine at sea in a galley with the blind girl, who presently took a deliberate header into the waves, to the intense astonishment of everybody except the hero, who, without making the smallest attempt to save her, set up a thundering Salve eternum just as I was expecting him to break into

Rosy lips above the water,
Blowing bubbles soft and fine;
As for me, I was no swimmer,
So I lost my Clementine.

Mr Durward Lely sustained the tenor part with great heroism; and Madame Valda, after innumerable high C's, finished the third act with a big big D which brought down the house.

18 May 1892

Opera Burlesqued

The young English composer is having a good time of it just now, with his overtures and symphonies resounding at the Crystal Palace, and his operas at the Olympic. Mr Granville Bantock's Caedmar is an enthusiastic and ingenious piece of work, being nothing less than an adaptation of all the most fetching passages in Wagner's later tragic music dramas to a little poem in which Tristan, Siegmund, Siegfried, Hunding, Isolde, and Sieglinde are aptly concentrated into three persons. The idea is an excellent one; for in the space of an hour, and within a stone's-throw of the Strand, we get the cream of all Bayreuth without the trouble and expense of journeying thither. There is also, for the relief of anti-Wagnerians, an intermezzo which might have been written by the late Alfred Cellier or any other good Mendelssohnian.

The plot, as I understood it, is very simple. A pious knight-errant wanders one evening into the garden of Eden, and falls asleep there. Eve, having had words with her husband, runs away from him, and finds in the sleeping warrior the one thing lacking to her: to wit, somebody to run away with. She makes love to him; and they retire together. Elves appear on the deserted stage, and dance to the strains of the intermezzo. They are encored, not because the audience is particularly charmed, but because Cavalleria has put it into its head that to recognize and encore an intermezzo shews connoisseurship. Then the pair return, looking highly satisfied; and presently Adam enters and remonstrates. Ten minutes later the knight-errant is the sole survivor of the three, whereupon he prays the curtain down.

The whole affair is absurdly second-hand; but, for all that, it proves remarkable musical ability on the part of Mr Granville Bantock, who shews a thorough knowledge of the mechanism of the Wagnerian orchestra. If Caedmar had been produced as a newly discovered work by Wagner, everyone would have admitted that so adroit a forgery implied a very clever penman. After Caedmar, Signor Lago put up the third act of Ernani. Strange to say, a good many people did not wait for it. Just imagine the situation. Here is a baritone singer,

Signor Mario Ancona, who has attracted general notice by his performance of Telramund in Lohengrin and Alfonso in La Favorita. Signor Lago accordingly mounts a famous scene, the classic opportunity for lyric actors of the Italian school (baritone variety), a scene which is not only highly prized by all students of Italian opera, but which had its dramatic import well taught to Londoners by the Comédie Française when they crowded to see Sarah Bernhardt as Doña Sol, and incidentally saw Worms as Charles V. In the play Charles is sublime in feeling, but somewhat tedious in expression. In the opera he is equally sublime in feeling, but concise, grand, and touching in expression, thereby proving that the chief glory of Victor Hugo as a stage poet was to have provided libretti for Verdi.

Every opera-goer who knows chalk from cheese knows that to hear that scene finely done is worth hearing all the Mephistopheleses and Toreadors that ever grimaced or swaggered, and that when a new artist offers to play it, the occasion is a first-class one. Yet, when Caedmar was over there was a considerable exodus from the stalls, as if nothing remained but a harlequinade for the children and the novices. "Now this," thought I, "is pretty odd. If these people knew their Ernani, surely they would stay." Then I realized that they did not know their Ernani—that years of Faust, and Carmen, and Les Huguenots, and Mefistofele, and soi-disant Lohengrin had left them ignorant of that ultra-classical product of Romanticism, the grandiose Italian opera in which the executive art consists in a splendid display of personal heroics, and the drama arises out of the simplest and most universal stimulants to them.

Il Trovatore, Un Ballo, Ernani, etc., are no longer read at the piano at home as the works of the Carmen *genre* are, and as Wagner's are. The popular notion

172 *Part 3* MUSICAL QUESTIONS

of them is therefore founded on performances in which
the superb distinction and heroic force of the male
characters, and the tragic beauty of the women, have
been burlesqued by performers with every sort of dis-
qualification for such parts, from age and obesity to
the most excruciating phases of physical insignificance
and modern cockney vulgarity. I used often to wonder
why it was that whilst every asphalt contractor could
get a man to tar the streets, and every tourist could
find a gondolier rather above the average of the House
of Lords in point of nobility of aspect, no operatic manager, after Mario vanished, seemed to be able to find a
Manrico with whom any exclusively disposed Thames
mudlark would care to be seen grubbing for pennies.
When I get on this subject I really cannot contain myself. The thought of that dynasty of execrable impostors
in tights and tunics, interpolating their loathsome B
flats into the beautiful melodies they could not sing,
and swelling with conceit when they were able to finish *Di quella pira* with a high C capable of making a
stranded man-of-war recoil off a reef into mid-ocean,
I demand the suspension of all rules as to decorum of
language until I have heaped upon them some little
instalment of the infinite abuse they deserve. Others,
alas! have blamed Verdi, much as if Dickens had
blamed Shakespear for the absurdities of Mr Wopsle.

The general improvement in operatic performances
of late years has taken us still further away from the
heroic school. But in due time its turn will come. Von
Bülow, who once contemptuously refused the name of
music to Verdi's works, has recanted in terms which
would hardly have been out of place if addressed to
Wagner; and many who now talk of the master as of a
tuneful trifler who only half-redeemed a misspent life
by the clever artificialities which are added in Aïda
and Otello to the power and freedom of his earlier

works, will change their tone when his operas are once more seriously studied by great artists.

2 *November 1892*

Opera Impresario

I have received a circular letter, which I give here in full, although some of my readers will have already seen it elsewhere. Its reappearance in this column may be the means of adding a few more donations to the one which it announces.

PROPOSED TESTIMONIAL TO SIR AUGUSTUS HARRIS

To the Editor

SIR,—As a very old musician, and one that admires talent, energy, and perseverance, I have watched with keen interest the extraordinary success which has attended the efforts of Sir Augustus Harris to establish in this country an opera worthy of the name, and in accordance with the best traditions of its history. This, in my own opinion, deserves some sort of public recognition, and I have therefore ventured to suggest that all lovers of high-class music, and all admirers of managerial enterprise, should be invited to subscribe towards an appropriate souvenir which shall serve as a testimonial to the Impresario of our Royal Opera House, who, for the reasons just stated, I cannot but regard as a benefactor to his country.

Except for the unceasing exertions of Sir Augustus Harris, and his persistent determination to revive our Covent Garden Opera at any personal cost or sacrifice, that time-honored institution would have long since died a natural death. Indeed, at one period it gave sufficient promise of becoming for ever extinct, in spite of the repeated attempts of La Porte, Lumley, E. T. Smith, Gye, and Mapleson to save it from this doom. At last people began to believe that the failures were due not so much to want of managerial enterprise as to

want of operatic attractions, and it was said that the
"palmy days" of opera—which I myself so well remember—were completely over, never to be revived again.
This was, however, by no means the view taken by the
present Manager of Covent Garden. In his own esti-
mation, there were as many good fish in the operatic
sea as were ever produced out of it. So Sir Augustus
Harris betook himself to the Continent, and ransacked
every leading opera-house there, with the result that
he returned triumphant with a company which, regarded as a whole, I have no hesitation in pronouncing
the completest and most brilliant that has ever yet appeared upon the boards of Covent Garden during her
Majesty's reign.

It is in view of these circumstances that I have proposed to open the fund for the souvenir already re-
ferred to, under the title of "The Operatic Testimonial
Fund," and I shall be pleased to head the list of sub-
scribers to it by a donation of ten guineas. Should the
readers of this letter be disposed to follow my example
in any way, their contributions, whether in the form of
cheques or otherwise, will be received by the National
Bank, Oxford Street Branch, if sent on behalf of "The
Operatic Testimonial Fund."—I am, Sir, yours, etc.

(Signed) Henry Russell

18 HOWLEY PLACE, MAIDA VALE,
July 26th, 1893.

Now I have no objection on general grounds to a
testimonial to Sir Augustus, though I would not, if I
were Mr Russell, call it an "operatic" testimonial. Let
it by all means be a genuine, enthusiastic, munificently
subscribed and influentially patronized tribute; and
since Sir Augustus knows what is due to himself, let us
not insult him with anything meaner than a life-size
statue of solid gold, with suitable quotations from the
opera criticisms in the Sunday Times on the four sides

of the pedestal. And let Mr Henry Russell, as the leader
of the enterprise, inaugurate the monument by once
more singing I am not mad; by heavens! I am not mad.
But it would be a mistake, as well as a very left-
handed compliment, to attribute to our illustrious impresario any design to revive the palmy days. Mr Russell was born more than forty years before I was, and
so belongs to a younger period of the world's history.
I am therefore to all intents and purposes his senior;
and I can assure him, as one who remembers the end
of the palmy days, and whose youth was blighted by
their accursed traditions, that they deserved their fate,
and are not only dead, but—I use the word in the pro-
foundest serious sense—damned. If you discuss them
with one of their veteran admirers, you will find that
all the triumphs which his memory fondles are not feats
of management, but strokes of genius by individual
artists. Indeed, so far is he from being able to conceive
an operatic performance as an artistic whole, that he
will describe the most absurd *contretemps* and the
most disastrous shortcomings in the stage management,
the band, chorus, dresses and scenery, as excellent
jokes.

My readers will remember the examples of this
which I was able to give from Santley's Student and
Singer, culminating in his playing Don Giovanni for
the first time after one rehearsal, at which the tenor
(Mario) did not turn up until it was half over. As to
the mutilations, the spurious scorings, the "additional
accompaniments," and the dozen other violations of
artistic good faith which were played off on palmy
nights as a matter of course, you will find the average
veteran either unconscious of them or utterly uncon-
cerned about them. He is content to remember Am-
brogetti as "the Don" (an almost centenarian reminiscence), Piccolomini as Zerlina, Taglioni as La Sylphide,
Malibran as Amina, Grisi and Rubini, Tamburini and

Lablache in the Puritani quartet; and so on up to Titiens and Giuglini, and those post-Giuglinian days when "the mantle of Mario" was tried on every trooper, porter, or ice-barrow man who could bawl a high C, until at last the jeremiads of Berlioz and Wagner were fulfilled, and palmy Italian opera, which had been corrupt even in its prime, openly putrified and had to be embalmed, in which condition its mummy still draws audiences in the United States and other back-eddies of civilization.

Mr Russell, under the impression that he is paying Sir Augustus a compliment, accuses him of having tried to play the resurrection-man. I believe this to be unjust. I admit that there are certain scattered materials for Mr Russell's case—tentative Favoritas, Lucias, and Trovatores (palmy style, with Signor Rawner as Manrico), which had a somewhat retrograde air; but they cannot outweigh the broad fact that the Italian operas which were the staple of the old repertory are the mere stopgaps and makeshifts of the new. If the testimonial is to be given for palminess, then let it be transferred to Colonel Mapleson, whose gallant attempt to revive the old repertory in competition with Sir Augustus a few years ago utterly failed. And the failure was so certain from the first, that for the sake of old times, I refrained from attending a single performance, although I have no doubt that I could have had three or four rows of stalls any night for the asking. No, Covent Garden has its defects, as I have had occasionally to remark; but such as it is, it has been created by Sir Augustus, and is no mere revival of the palmy imposture which still takes in Mr Russell.

Is Sir Augustus then, as Mr Russell says, "a benefactor to his country"? The standard definition of a national benefactor is "the man who causes two blades of grass to grow where one grew before." Now Sir Augustus, on the contrary, has caused one opera-house to keep open where two kept open before. But I do not think he ought to be disqualified on so highly technical a point. He established an opera where, for the moment, there was no opera at all; and if this was not a benefaction I do not know what is.

Therefore, instead of churlishly asking why he should have a testimonial, let us rather ask why he should not have one, and why Mr D'Oyly Carte should not have one, and why Signor Lago should not have one, and why, above all, I should not have one? Signor Lago discovered Giulia Ravogli and Ancona, Orfeo and Cavalleria; and although Sir Augustus is no doubt right in preferring to take his own discoveries ready-made, still, the original discoverer is useful in his little way too, and should not be overlooked. Mr D'Oyly Carte founded a new school of English comic opera; raised operatic inscenation to the rank of a fine art; and finally built a new English Opera House, and made a magnificent effort to do for English grand opera what he had done for comic opera, with the result that Sir Augustus is now conducting a music-hall on the ruins of the enterprise.

As to my own claims, modesty forbids me to ask whose pen has done more to revive public interest in dramatic music during the past five or six years than mine. It is true that I have done it because I have been paid to do it; but even Sir Augustus does not play the public benefactor for nothing. A man must live. Take the case of August Manns, whose enormous services to music in England do not need the penetrating eye of an octogenarian to discover them: even he does not scorn to accept his bread-and-butter. If there is any spare cash left in the country when the Harris testimonial is fully subscribed, some little token—say a cheap conducting stick—might be offered to the untitled Augustus of Sydenham.

But now that I think of it, such a proceeding might

be construed as a slight to the conducting staff at Covent Garden. And we must not thoughtlessly appear to undervalue what Sir Augustus has done for us in placing his orchestra in the hands of three such *chefs* as Mancinelli, Bevignani, and Randegger. Although they are so devoted to the traditions of the house that Sir Augustus has to send to Germany for help whenever the Nibelungen dramas are performed, yet Mancinelli can conduct Die Meistersinger and Bevignani Tannhäuser in a way that I am sure I for one can never forget. Why not give them testimonials? The stage manager, too—he who staged Gluck's Orfeo and Das Rheingold—that "damned pantomime," as somebody is said to have called it—why should not something be done for him? But I am opening up too vast a field. There are so many public benefactors about.

I should be less than candid on the subject, however, if I were to take the proposal quite uncritically. I do not see how it is possible for an impresario to maintain Covent Garden in such a fashion as to deserve a testimonial as a public benefactor. As I have often pointed out, fashionable grand opera does not pay its own expenses in London any more than it does in Paris or Berlin. A subvention is necessary; and if the State does not provide it, a body of private guarantors must. In England there are so many irrational people who think the National Gallery and the British Museum virtuous and Opera vicious (because it takes place in a theatre), that the State leaves Covent Garden to a knot of rich people for whom Opera is not a form of art but simply an item of fashion. These people pay the piper; and they naturally expect to call the tune.

Now suppose an artist or a clique of artists get at the guarantors behind the impresario's back, they can make it very difficult for him to do anything that they disapprove of, whether it be in the public interest or not. To such means of resistance to the manager must be added the already enormous powers possessed by leading artists in virtue of their personal monopoly of voice and talent. The impresario's one defence is his own monopoly of the power of making London reputations. To preserve this monopoly, and at the same time to provide for the danger always latent in the fact that London will support one guaranteed Opera handsomely, but not two, must strain all his commercial genius to suppress competition; and this means not only taking every theatre large enough to be used as a rival house, but engaging several superfluous artists for the sole purpose of forestalling their possible engagement by someone else, the result being, of course, to waste their talents most frightfully.

Finally, he must by hook or crook, by conciliation or intimidation, gag independent criticism, because his greatest need is prestige, and this the press can mar if it chooses. His prestige is his life-blood: it convinces meddling guarantors and mutinous artists that he is the only possible man to run the Italian Opera; and it paralyses his competitors, making their attempts to raise a rival guarantee unavailing, and stamping them from the outset as second rate. And this prestige, which is at once his sword and shield, propagates itself by all the operations which he undertakes for its sake. The theatres leased and kept closed, or sublet on conditions which bar opera; the magnificent list of artists engaged apparently out of an insatiable artistic enthusiasm which takes no account of salaries; even the running of two sets of performances to prevent the superfluous artists from eating their heads off: all these master-moves, with the huge turnover of money they involve, heap prestige on prestige, until at last the public gets dazzled, and ancient men call for testimonials to the national benefactor.

Then there is only one enemy left; and that is the

unhypnotizable critic who, having his own prestige to look after, persists in explaining the situation to the public and criticizing the performances for just what they are worth, and no more. And such critics are scarce, not because of their Roman virtue, but because they must have an eye for the economics of the situation; and a musical critic who is a bit of an economist as well is a very rare bird.

Under these circumstances I do not see how the public services of Sir Augustus as impresario can run to a testimonial. However high-mindedly and ably he may have struggled to do his best within the limits of his very narrow freedom of action, or however Napoleonically he may have faced and fought the opposing economic forces, the fact remains that Covent Garden, with all its boasted resources, could not put the four Nibelung dramas on the stage last year except by the pure showman's expedient of sending for a German company, orchestra, conductor and all.

I do not blame Sir Augustus for this: I pointed out again and again (before the event as well as after) that the real difficulty was the incorrigible *fainéantise* of the De Reszkes, with their perpetual schoolboy Faust and Mephistopheles, Roméo and Frère Laurent, and their determination to make Covent Garden a mere special edition of the Paris Grand Opera. Sir Augustus did contrive to get one triumph out of Jean de Reszke and Lassalle—Die Meistersinger. But from the moment when Jean allowed Alvary to take Siegfried from him, and Edouard left Wotan to Grengg (I hope I have the name correctly), there was an end of all possibility of a testimonial for Covent Garden.

Give me one performance of Die Walküre or Siegfried by the De Reszkes, Calvé, and Giulia Ravogli, with the orchestral work done by the regular band of the house, and a competent conductor of the calibre of Richter or Faccio in permanent command, and then

Mr Russell may apply again. At present I am not at home.

Let me point out, however, that there may be an opening on the dramatic side, as to which I, of course, cannot speak. Sir Augustus is famous for his pantomimes and popular dramas, in producing which he is unhampered by guarantors or tenors, and can face competition without misgiving. My duties as musical critic make me a stranger to his work in this department. There, where his qualities have fuller scope, no doubt they take effect in the high artistic temper and wholesome moral atmosphere of his productions. If so, perhaps my friend W. A. will give Mr Russell's project his blessing and his subscription.

2 August 1893

The New Italian School

I have been to the Opera six times; and I still live. What is more, I am positively interested and hopeful. Hitherto I have had only one aim as regards Italian opera: not, as some have supposed, to kill it, for it was dead already, but to lay its ghost. It was a troublesome phantom enough. When one felt sure that it had been effectually squeezed out at last by French opera, or Hebraic opera, or what may be called operatic music drama—Lohengrin, for instance—it would turn up again trying to sing *Spirito gentil* in the manner of Mario, raving through the mad scene in Lucia amid childish orchestral tootlings, devastating Il Trovatore with a totally obsolete style of representation, or in some way gustily rattling its unburied bones and wasting the manager's money and my patience.

The difficulty was to convince those who had been brought up to believe in it (as I was myself) that it was all over with it: they *would* go on believing that it only needed four first-rate Italian singers to bring

the good old times back again and make the rum-tum
rhythms, the big guitar orchestration, the florid cabalettas, the cavatinas in regular four-bar lines, the choruses in thirds and sixths, and all the rest of it swell
out to their former grandeur and sweep Wagner off
the boards. I have no doubt they believe it as devoutly
as ever, and that if Mr Mapleson were to start again
tomorrow, he would announce Lucia and Il Barbiere
and Semiramide with unshaken confidence in their
freshness and adequacy, perhaps adding, as a concession to the public demand for novelty, a promise of
Ponchielli's La Gioconda.

But now an unlooked-for thing has happened. Italian opera has been born again. The extirpation of the
Rossinian dynasty, which neither Mozart nor Wagner
could effect, since what they offered in its place was
too far above the heads of both the public and the
artists, is now being accomplished with ease by Mascagni, Leoncavallo, Puccini, and Verdi. Nobody has
ever greeted a performance of Tristan und Isolde by
such a remark as "We shall never be able to go back to
L'Elisir d'Amore after this," or declare that Lucrezia
was impossible after Brynhild. The things were too far
apart to affect one another: as well might it be supposed that Ibsen's plays could be accepted as a substitute for popular melodrama, or Shakespear wean
people from the circus. It is only by an advance in
melodrama itself or in circuses themselves that the
melodrama or circus of today can become unpresent-
able to the audiences of ten years hence.

The same thing is true of Italian opera. The improvement of higher forms of art, or the introduction
of new forms at a different level, cannot affect it at all;
and that is why Tristan has no more killed L'Elisir
than Brahms' symphonies have killed Jullien's British
Army Quadrilles. But the moment you hear Pagliacci,
you feel that it is all up with L'Elisir. It is true that

Leoncavallo has shewn as yet nothing comparable to the melodic inspiration of Donizetti; but the advance in serious workmanship, in elaboration of detail, in variety of interest, and in capital expenditure on the orchestra and the stage, is enormous. There is more work in the composition of Cavalleria than in La Favorita, Lucrezia, and Lucia put together, though I cannot think—perhaps this is only my own old-fashionedness—that any part of it will live as long or move the world as much as the best half-dozen numbers in those three obsolete masterpieces.

And when you come to Puccini, the composer of the latest Manon Lescaut, then indeed the ground is so transformed that you could almost think yourself in a new country. In Cavalleria and Pagliacci I can find nothing but Donizettian opera rationalized, condensed, filled in, and thoroughly brought up to date; but in Manon Lescaut the domain of Italian opera is enlarged by an annexation of German territory. The first act, which is as gay and effective and romantic as the opening of any version of Manon need be, is also unmistakably symphonic in its treatment. There is genuine symphonic modification, development, and occasionally combination of the thematic material, all in a dramatic way, but also in a musically homogeneous way, so that the act is really a single movement with episodes instead of being a succession of separate numbers, linked together, to conform to the modern fashion, by substituting interrupted cadences for full closes and parading a Leitmotif occasionally.

Further, the experiments in harmony and syncopation, reminding one often of the intellectual curiosities which abound in Schumann's less popular pianoforte works, shew a strong technical interest which is, in Italian music, a most refreshing symptom of mental vigor, even when it is not strictly to the real artistic point. The less studied harmonies are of the most modern and stimulating kind. When one thinks of the old school, in which a dominant seventh, or at most a minor ninth, was the extreme of permissible discord, only to be tolerated in the harsher inversions when there was a murder or a ghost on hand, one gets a rousing sense of getting along from hearing young Italy beginning its most light-hearted melodies to the chord of the thirteenth on the tonic.

Puccini is particularly fond of this chord; and it may be taken as a general technical criticism of the young Italian school that its free use of tonic discords, and its reckless prodigality of orchestral resources, give its music a robustness and variety that reduce the limited tonic and dominant harmonic technique of Donizetti and Bellini, by contrast, to mere Christy minstrelsy. No doubt this very poverty of the older masters made them so utterly dependent on the invention of tunes that they invented them better than the new men, who, with a good drama to work on, can turn out vigorous, imposing, and even enthralling operas without a bar that is their own in the sense in which *Casta diva* is Bellini's own; but Puccini, at least, shews no signs of atrophy of the melodic faculty: he breaks out into catching melodies quite in the vein of Verdi: for example, *Tra voi, belle,* in the first act of Manon, has all the charm of the tunes beloved by the old operatic guard.

On that and other accounts, Puccini looks to me more like the heir of Verdi than any of his rivals. He has arranged his own libretto from Prevost d'Exiles' novel; and though the miserable end of poor Manon has compelled him to fall back on a rather conventional operatic death scene in which the prima donna at Covent Garden failed to make anyone believe, his third act, with the roll-call of the female convicts and the embarkation, is admirably contrived and carried

out: he has served himself in this as well as Scribe
ever served Meyerbeer, or Boito Verdi.

If now it is considered that this opening week at
Covent Garden began with Manon, and ended with
Falstaff; Cavalleria and Pagliacci coming in between,
with nothing older than Faust and Carmen to fill up
except the immortal Orfeo, it will be understood how
I find myself with the startling new idea that Italian
opera has a future as well as a past, and that perhaps
Sir Augustus Harris, in keeping a house open for it,
has not been acting altogether as an enemy of the human race, as I used sometimes to declare in my agony
when, in a moment of relenting towards that dreary
past, he would let loose some stout matron to disport
herself once more as Favorita, or spend untold gold
in indulging Jean de Reszke with a revival of that concentrated bore and outrage, Le Prophète, when I
wanted to see the prince of tenors and procrastinators
as Siegfried or Tristan.

Falstaff drew an enormous house on Saturday, and
was received with an enthusiasm which was quite un-
forced up to the end of the clothes-basket scene. After
that the opera suffered for a while from the play out-
lasting the freshness of the subject, a fate that invariably overtakes The Merry Wives of Windsor, except
when the actor who plays Falstaff has an extraordinary
power of inventing humorous and varied character-
traits.

The first scene of the third act was undeniably a little dull. The merry wives cackled wearisomely; Pessina's comic stock was exhausted, so that he could do
nothing but repeat the business of the earlier scenes;
and Mrs Quickly, who had been charming for the first
ten minutes in the novel character of the youthful and
charming Signorina Ravogli, gave the final blow to the
dramatic interest of the scene by not being her detestable old self.

Fortunately, the excitement revived in the forest scene at the end, which is full of life and charm. It ends with a sort of musical practical joke in the shape of a fugue which is everything that a fugue ought not to be, and which, failing more rehearsal than it is worth, has to be execrably sung in order to get the parts picked up. It was listened to with deep reverence, as if Verdi, in his old age, had clasped hands with Sebastian Bach. Always excepting the first scene of the third act, the opera went like wildfire.

Boito's libretto is excellent as far as it is a condensation of Shakespear, except that he has not appreciated the great stage effectiveness of Falstaff's description to Ford of his misadventure in the basket, with its climaxes, dear to old Shakespearean actors, of "Think of that, Master Brook." His alterations, notably the screen business in the basket scene, make some fun; but they also make the scene in Ford's house quite outrageously impossible. As far as acting is concerned, the weight of the whole opera lies in the scene between Ford and Falstaff at the Garter Inn; and here Pessina played with considerable humor and vigor, though without any particular subtlety.

Pini-Corsi's acting was better than operatic acting generally is; but it hardly satisfied those of us who have seen anything like an adequate impersonation of Ford on the English stage. The women were rather unintelligently and monotonously merry; and on the whole the success was, past all question, a success of the musical setting, which is immensely vivacious and interesting. The medieval scenery is attractive, especially the garden and the room in Ford's house. The interior of the inn is not sunny enough: modern painting, with its repudiation of the studio light, and its insistence on work in the open air, has made the traditional stage interior look old-fashioned in this respect. The company at Covent Garden is a very strong one. The representations of Cavalleria and Pagliacci derive an altogether exceptional dramatic force from the acting of De Lucia and Ancona in parts which are in constant danger of being handed over to a second-rate tenor and baritone. Beduschi, who plays Des Grieux in Manon with success, is another tenor of the Gayarré school, without the goat-bleat and tremolo of its extreme disciples. He is a capable actor, small in figure, with a face which will probably be described as dark and ugly by a good many people, nevertheless by no means an unprepossessing face. Cossira, a tenor of heavier build than Beduschi, made some effect by his passion and sincerity in the love scene in the second act of Carmen. Albers, a baritone, made his first appearances as Valentine in Faust and the Toreador in Carmen. His treatment of Bizet's daintily written scene between José and Escamillo before the fight in the third act gave me an extremely unfavorable impression of the delicacy of his musical sense; but the rougher part of his work was presentably done. Bonnard, a French tenorino, made a satisfactory Philémon in Philémon et Baucis, in which, however, the honors went to Plançon for a splendid appearance as Jupiter.

Philémon brought back Mlle Simonnet, whose voice is somewhat thicker and richer, especially in the middle, than when she charmed us first in Bruneau's Le Rêve. I am not sure that the same remark does not apply, in a slight degree, to Mlle Simonnet's figure, though she was certainly as trim and youthful as could be desired as Micaela in Carmen. She also played Marguerite in Faust, of which I saw only the last act and a half. Her Micaela was not good: she slipped through the music in a pointless way, apparently finding the part trivial and uninteresting, and certainly making it so. Her Marguerite—what I saw of it—was clever and pretty, but prosaic. It was only as Baucis that she fully justified the admiration excited by her

first performances in this country, though none of her
three appearances passed without a burst of applause
for some happily sung passage. The leading parts in
the two new operas were taken by Olga Olghina, a
clever Russian lady with chiselled features and a
somewhat courtly fastidiousness of manner, just a little
too ladylike for Manon and a little too mundane for
Anne Page, but able to make a distinct mark in both
by her acting in the embarkation scene of the one
opera and her singing in the forest scene of the other.
Mlle Pauline Joran played Siebel and Lola in Cavalleria, the latter cleverly. Of Bauermeister the invalu-
able, the inevitable, I need not speak; and of Signorine
Zilli and Kitzu I shall perhaps speak later on, when
my impressions of them are more definite. Of the two
great dramatic artists of the company, Giulia Ravogli
struck me as suffering from underwork; and as to the
incomparable Calvé, at least a week must elapse before I can trust myself to speak of her Carmen and
her Santuzza, or, indeed, of herself, with a decent pretence of critical coolness.

The Amsterdam Choir, after a brief spell at St Martin's Hall, is singing this week at Queen's Hall. The
expectations I expressed last week have been far surpassed. The choir now consists of twenty-two singers,
each of them a singer in a thousand. In England we
should set the whole thousand bawling together, and
then brag all over Europe about our supremacy in
choral music.

Mr Daniel de Lange eliminates the worst nine hundred and ninety-nine from each thousand, and produces with the remainder a choir the fortissimo of
which would drown the biggest of our feebly monstrous choral societies, and the pianissimo of which almost embraces perfect silence. I wish I had space to
do justice to the extraordinary excellence of their execution and the surpassing interest and beauty of

the music, sacred and secular, of Josquin, Orlando, Sweelinck, and the rest of the heroes of the old Netherlandish school.

23 May 1894

We live in an age of progress. Patti has been singing a song by Wagner. Never shall I forget the sensation among the critics at the Albert Hall when, on turning over the pages of their programs, they saw among the names there that of The Master, cropping up like a modest crocus among those of Mozart, Rossini, and other contemporaries of Madame Patti's grandmother. There is now no denying the fact that Madame Patti —Adelina Patti—*the* Patti—the lady who used to appear and reappear as Rosina in Il Barbiere at Covent Garden until the old régime died of it, actually did, on the afternoon of Saturday, May 19, 1894, sing the study on Tristan und Isolde, No. 5 of the Five Poems composed by Richard Wagner, late of Bayreuth, in 1862. What is more, she sang it extremely well, and, when the inevitable encore came, repeated it instead of singing Home, Sweet Home or Within a Mile.

And yet there was something exasperating in the thought that this demonstration by a fine singer that Wagner's music is as singable as Mozart's came just twenty years after it was most needed. Nobody now supposes that in Wagner's works the women must shriek and the men howl, and that no human voice can stand the wear and tear for more than a year or two. But that was once a very common opinion, most devoutly acted on by many operatic artists, with, of course, fully corroborative results as far as the prophesied wear and tear was concerned. What was Madame Patti doing in those dark days, when she might have rescued Tannhäuser from the horrors of its first performance at Covent Garden in the decline and fall

of the seventies? Alas! in those days she sang *Bel raggio* in the key of A, and did not sing Wagner at all.
It was left to Jean de Reszke, by his Walther in Die
Meistersinger, to give the final proof that Wagner requires and repays the most delicate lyrical treatment;
and now Madame Patti, with the ground made safe
for her, comes forward and, having first propitiated
the first quarter of the expiring century by singing *Bel
raggio* in the key of G, at last ventures on this simple
little *Träume*, and is perhaps surprised to find that the
thrill is deeper and the applause more sincere than
that which follows Rossini's shallow bravura. For my
part, I regard Patti's brilliancy as a singer of florid
decorative music as one of her greatest misfortunes. In
the first place, she has never done it superlatively well:
it has always been a little jerky and tricky in comparison with the finest execution of such a perfect singer
of roulade as Marimon, for instance, not to mention
others.

I never fully appreciated Patti until one night at
Covent Garden when I heard her sing, not *Una Voce*
or anything of that sort, but God save the Queen. The
wonderful even soundness of the middle of her voice,
its beauty and delicacy of surface, and her exquisite
touch and diction, all qualify her to be great in expressive melody, and to occupy a position in the re-
public of art high above the pretty flummery of newspaper puffs, flowers, recalls, encores, and so forth
which makes it so difficult for people who take art
seriously to do justice to the talent and the artistic
pains with which she condescends to bid for such
recognition.

I am so far from regretting that Time has stolen some
of the five or six notes above the high B flat which
she once possessed, and has made the rest hardly safe
for everyday use, that I shall heartily congratulate her
when the day comes when *Bel raggio* and *Ah, non*

giunge, in any key whatsoever, must be dropped, and replaced in her repertory by more such songs as *Träume;* for it is my firm belief that Patti is capable of becoming a great singer, though the world has been at such pains and expense to spoil her for the last thirty-five years. At her concert on the 19th, her voice was better than at last year's concerts; and altogether she was brighter, more efficient, more successful—if there can be said to be degrees in Patti's success—than when I last heard her.

The difference between the old order in opera and the new suggests to my imagination such a vast period of time, that it seems odd to me that I should have witnessed Patti's latest triumph on the morrow of Calvé's appearance at Covent Garden as Carmen. It is only fair that I should warn the public against attaching too much importance to anything I may say about Madame Calvé. As I have often explained, it is one of the conditions of that high susceptibility which is my chief qualification as a critic, that good or bad art becomes a personal matter between me and the artist.

I *hate* performers who debase great works of art: I long for their annihilation: if my criticisms were flaming thunderbolts, no prudent Life or Fire Insurance Company would entertain a proposal from any singer within my range, or from the lessee of any opera-house or concert-room within my circuit. But I am necessarily no less extreme in my admiration of artists who realize the full value of great works for me, or who transfigure ordinary ones. Calvé is such an artist; and she is also a woman whose strange personal appearance recalls Titian's wonderful Virgin of the Assumption at Venice, and who has, in addition to that beauty of aspect, a beauty of action—especially of that sort of action which is the thought or conception of the artist made visible —such as one might expect from Titian's Virgin if the picture were made alive. This description will perhaps sufficiently shew the need for a little discount off such eulogies as I may presently be moved to in speaking of her performances in detail.

But I have no eulogies for her Carmen, which shocked me beyond measure. I pointed out on a previous occasion, when dealing with a very remarkable impersonation of that character by Giulia Ravogli, that the success of Bizet's opera is altogether due to the attraction, such as it is, of seeing a pretty and respectable middle-class young lady, expensively dressed, harmlessly pretending to be a wicked person, and that anything like a successful attempt to play the part realistically by a powerful actress must not only at once betray the thinness and unreality of Prosper Merimée's romance, but must leave anything but a pleasant taste on the palate of the audience. This was proved by the fact that Giulia Ravogli's Carmen, the most powerful that had then been seen in England, was received with a good deal of grumbling, and was shelved to make way for that pretty little imposition, the Carmen of Miss de Lussan, who was, as everybody could see, a perfect young lady innocently playing at being naughty.

And yet Giulia Ravogli flattered Carmen by exhibiting her as a woman of courage and strength of character. Calvé makes no such concession. Her Carmen is a superstitious, pleasure-loving good-for-nothing, caught by the outside of anything glittering, with no power but the power of seduction, which she exercises without sense or decency. There is no suggestion of any fine quality about her, not a spark of honesty, courage, or even of the sort of honor supposed to prevail among thieves. All this is conveyed by Calvé with a positively frightful artistic power of divesting her beauty and grace of the nobility—I had almost written the sanctity —which seems inseparable from them in other parts.

Nobody else dare venture on the indescribable allurements which she practises on the officers in the first act, or such touches as the attempt to get a comprehensive view of her figure in Lillas Pastia's rather small lookingglass, or her jealously critical inspection of Micaela from the same point of view in the third act.

Her death-scene, too, is horribly real. The young lady Carmen is never so effectively alive as when she falls, stage dead, beneath José's cruel knife. But to see Calvé's Carmen changing from a live creature, with properly coordinated movements, into a reeling, staggering, flopping, disorganized thing, and finally tumble down a mere heap of carrion, is to get much the same sensation as might be given by the reality of a brutal murder. It is perhaps just as well that a great artist should, once in a way, give our opera goers a glimpse of the truth about the things they play with so lightheartedly. In spite of the applause and the curtain calls, it was quite evident that the audience was by no means as comfortable after the performance as Miss de Lussan would have left them.

But nothing would induce me to go again. To me it was a desecration of a great talent. I felt furious with Calvé, as if I had been shewn some terrible caricature by Hogarth of the Titian. That, however, may have been a personal sentiment. What I am perfectly sure was a legitimate critical sentiment was my objection to Carmen carrying her abandonment to the point of being incapable of paying the smallest attention to the score. I have never seen, at Bayreuth or anywhere else, an operatic actress fit her action more perfectly and punctually to its indication in the orchestra than Giulia Ravogli did as Carmen. And I have never seen, even at Covent Garden, the same artistic duty so completely disregarded as it was by Calvé. She acted out of time the whole evening; and I do not see why artists should act out of time any more than sing out of time.

I go back with relief from Carmen to Cavalleria, in which her Santuzza was irresistibly moving and beautiful, and fully capable of sustaining the inevitable comparison with Duse's impersonation of the same part. But Duse makes the play more credible, not because an opera is less credible than a spoken play—for though that can be proved logically, the facts are just the other way, the superior intensity of musical expression making the opera far more real than the play—but because Duse makes the woman not only intensely pitiable, but hopelessly unattractive, so that Turiddu's perference for Lola seems natural, whereas in the opera his desertion of Calvé is not to be tolerated as the act of a sane man: one cannot take any interest in such an ass.

The desolating Arctic wind which parched the liver of London last week swept blightingly through the ranks of Mottl's band at his second concert, and laid the program waste. Himself in something less than his highest spirits, he nevertheless made a brave effort to rally his prostrated forces. But he got nothing like the response they made to him at the previous concert. The effect of this general indisposition was unfortunately emphasized by the change from Wagner to Berlioz and Beethoven. Beethoven did not know how to get his effects with the orchestra as Wagner did: some of the most powerful traits in his musical designs are disappointing in orchestral execution. Berlioz, of whom this cannot be said, is a Frenchman; and though Mottl's freedom from anything like German heaviness makes him as good a Berlioz conductor as it is in the nature of any German who lives and works in his own country to be, yet he simply sent me asleep with the extracts from Roméo et Juliette; for his fine reflective handling took all the passion and pathos out of Roméo's brainless reveries, and his splendid self-possession equally took all the brimstone out of the dance music, which makes but a poor show in the vein of Die Meistersinger.

With all these deductions, and the slackness of the band, the hateful wind, and the somewhat injudicious order and excessive length of the program into the bargain, Mottl made a strong impression on those who had not been present at his first appearance as a conductor in England; and I have nothing to retract or modify in the opinion I then expressed of his ability.

30 May 1894

LIGHT ENTERTAINMENT

Sturgis and Sullivan

On second thoughts I have resolved to suppress my notice of Ivanhoe. I was upon my high horse last week when I wrote it; and when I went on Saturday, and saw how pleasantly everything went off, and how the place was full of lovely and distinguished persons, and how everybody applauded like mad at the end, and, above all, how here at last was an English opera-house superbly equipped for its purpose, I felt what a brute I had been to grumble—and that, too, after having been indulged with peeps at the proofs of the score, admission to rehearsals, and every courtesy that could pass betwixt myself and the management, without loss of dignity on either side. Just as a sort of penance, and to shew what I am capable of, I give a couple of paragraphs from the discarded notice. Here they are:

"Proceeding then at once to the faults of Ivanhoe, I maintain that it is disqualified as a serious dramatic work by the composer's failure to reproduce in music the vivid characterization of Scott, which alone classes the novel among the masterpieces of fiction. It would hardly be reasonable to demand that Sir Arthur should have intensified the work of Scott as Mozart intensified that of Beaumarchais and even of Molière; but he might at least have done as much for him as he has done for Mr Gilbert in Patience and its forerunners: that is, before the Savoy operas became machine-made like The Gondoliers. Take for example Scott's Bois Guilbert, the fierce Templar, the original 'bold, bad man,' tanned nearly black, disfigured with sword-cuts, strong, ambitious, going on for fifty, a subject for Verdi or Velasquez. Is it possible to sit patiently and hear the music of the drawing room, sensuous and passionate without virility or intelligence, put into the mouth of such a figure? Not with all the brass and drum sauce in the world. Then there is that gallant scamp De Bracy, for whom we all have a sneaking fondness because he broke down ignominiously when Rowena began to cry, and then went out and stood up like a man to King Richard's terrific horseplay. Did he deserve nothing better than to be treated as a mere fop out of Princess Ida? And Richard himself, whose occasional attempts to behave like a king were so like Mr Pickwick's famous attempt to sneer: surely, though it is quite conceivable that he should be singing the same sentimental ballad whenever he is neither drinking nor killing anybody, yet the ballad should not be a mere paraphrase of the Wandering Minstrel song in The Mikado, as if Cœur de Lion had picked up that subtle strain by ear, and not picked it up quite accurately. As to Cedric singing the most arrant modern tum-tum in honor of the Crusaders—no, Sir Arthur: it may be very pretty and very popular; but it is not Ivanhoe."

"I have here condemned the composer, and not the bookmaker, because, with Scott's novel to work upon, it was clearly the composer's business to dramatize it musically himself, resorting to a librettist's aid only for the filling in of the lyrics, and of such speeches as could not be taken verbatim from Scott. The task would not, I grant, have been an easy one; for though the material of the story is dramatic enough, yet, being a story, it is told with a disregard of stage conditions which no play-wright's ingenuity could entirely overcome. It is true that the resources of music drama surpass those of narrative in some respects: the castle of Torquilstone might have been exhibited in three compartments, with the scene between Rowena and De Bracy in one, that between Bois Guilbert and Rebecca in another, and Front de Bœuf and the Jew in the cellar, all three couples proceeding simultaneously to the point at which they are interrupted by the horn of the besiegers. Some polyphonic skill would have been required in the composition of the music; and only a comprehensive *coup d'œil* and *coup d'oreille* could have taken it all in; but then Sir Arthur is an accomplished contrapuntist, and the London public has had some training at Barnum's in the practice of watching several shows at the same time. Yet this disposes of but one difficulty. The tournament—and what would Ivanhoe be lacking the tournament?—is obviously impracticable without adjourning to the Agricultural Hall. Still, though the jousting must perforce be done by description, it is hard to have to exchange the inimitable commentary of Isaac of York—'Father Abraham! how fiercely that Gentile rides!' etc.—for alternate characterless fragments of recitative from Locksley and Friar Tuck, officiating as a pair of bawling showmen. This, however, is but a trivial sample of the way in which the story has been gutted of every poetic and humorous speech it contains. Here is a piece of Scott's dialogue in the scene in the lists in Templestowe, with Mr Sturgis's 'restorations' (in the architectural sense) of the same:

'REBECCA. Say to the Grand Master that I maintain my innocence, and do not yield me as justly condemned, lest I become guilty of mine own blood. Say to him that I challenge such delay as his forms will permit, to see if God, whose opportunity is in man's extremity, will raise

me up a deliverer; and when such uttermost space is
passed, may His holy will be done!

'GRAND MASTER. God forbid that Jew or Pagan should
impeach us of injustice! Until the shadows be cast from
the west to the eastward will we wait to see if a champion
shall appear for this unfortunate woman.

'BOIS GUILBERT. Rebecca, dost thou hear me?

'REBECCA. I have no portion in thee, cruel, hard-hearted
man.

'BOIS GUILBERT. Ay, but dost thou understand my words?
for the sound of my voice is frightful in mine own ears. I
scarce know on what ground we stand, or for what purpose they have brought us hither. . . . But hear me,
Rebecca: a better chance hast thou for life and liberty
than yonder knaves and dotard dream of. Mount thee behind me on my steed—on Zamor, etc., etc.'

"Mr Sturgis 'adapts' the above to the stage as follows:

'REBECCA. I am innocent. Now, if God will, even in this
last dark hour He will appoint a champion. But if no
champion come, I bow before His holy will and am content to die.

'GRAND MASTER. Sound trumpets! . . . Now, since no
champion makes answer here, draw near and bind the
maiden to the stake, for surely she shall die.

. 'BOIS GUILBERT. It shall not be! Fools, dotards, will ye
slay the innocent? Butchers and burners, she is mine, I say!
I say she shall not burn! Back, as you hope to live! . . .
Swear to be mine, and I will save thee now. My horse is
nigh at hand, etc., etc.'

If the noble dialogue of Scott is not more suitable for
English music than the fustian of Mr Sturgis, then so
much the worse for English music. Purcell would have
found it so. I protest, in the name of my own art of letters, against a Royal English Opera which begins by
handing over a literary masterpiece for wanton debase-
ment at the hands of a journeyman hired for the job."

Now all this was evidently mere temper. Poor Mr
Sturgis, I suppose, knew no better: he unquestionably
meant to improve on the book; and if, when he came
forward hand in hand with the composer amid thun-

ders of applause on Saturday night, nobody had a brick-
bat to break on him for love of Scott, why should I
spoil the harmony of the occasion by striving to belittle
him? But the fact is, I must have been possessed by a
demon when I wrote that notice, for I find lower down
in it that even the building did not please me.

"The scene-painters," I wrote, "have alone dreamt of
going to Scott for inspiration; and they stand forth as
gods in consequence; though even to them I will say
that if Mr Ryan will go round to the front, and look at
that pointed doorway under the Norman arch in the
scene where Rebecca describes the siege from the window, he will agree with me that it was not a happy
thought. Otherwise, the Torquilstone architecture con-
trasts most favorably with the curious absence of any
architectural idea in the auditorium. The view of the
stage from all parts of the house, as far as I was able
to test it, is capital; and the acoustical conditions are of
the happiest. Also the upholstery and materials are luxurious and costly to excess; but as to any beauty of
form or individuality of design, I have been in hydraulic lifts of much higher excellence in these respects.
Even the exterior has been disfigured by a glass and
iron rain-shelter, which I can hardly believe to be the
work of human hands, so utterly destitute is it of any
trace of the artist's sense. But people who are not particular about these matters will find every comfort and
convenience that money can buy; and the majority, I
fear, will find that a sufficient recommendation. Indeed, I should not go out of the way to complain myself if it were not for the ostentation of artistic effort
everywhere, challenging me at all points to give my
opinion—as a musical critic—whether the building is not
really handsome."

But enough of this unsociable document. The truth
is that the theatre is very pretty; and so is the opera.
I do not say that the ceiling is equal to that of Henry

VII's chapel in Westminster, or that the score is in any essential point an advance upon that of Macfarren's Robin Hood, which had a long run at Her Majesty's thirty years ago; but who ever said they were? My business is to praise them for what they are, not to disparage them for what they are not. Ivanhoe, then, has plenty of charming songs in it; and the crash-bang and the top notes in the exciting situations are as stirring as heart could wish. The score is as neat as a new pin. The instrumentation, from the big drum upwards, is effective, practised, and stylish, with all the fullness given by the latest improvements; the tone-colors, though rich, are eminently gentlemanly; there is no Bohemian effervescence, no puerile attempts at brilliancy or grandiosity; all is smooth, orderly, and within the bounds of good breeding. There are several interesting examples of that coincidence of inspiration which is so common in music. For instance, the third act of Ivanhoe begins like Berlioz' Faust, with a scene before sunrise for the tenor. And the musical expression found by both composers is practically identical. Again, when Rebecca presently comes in, and sings *Ah! would that thou and I might lead our sheep!* we hear through the music a delightful echo of that other *pastorale* in the first act of Orphée aux Enfers. Then the hag Ulrica no sooner begins her invocation of Zernebock than we recognize her as first cousin to Ulrica in Un Ballo, with her *Re dell' abisso affrettati.* The rousing prelude to the Friar's drinking song might be a variation on *Vivat Bacchus* from Mozart's Seraglio. The chief stroke of humor in the opera is the patriotic chorus in the tournament scene, to which, with a sly reference to Mr Macdermott, Sir Arthur has imparted an unmistakeable music-hall swing, which must have sorely tempted the gallery to join in.

4 February 1891

Gilbert and Offenbach

Since Monday, when I saw Offenbach's Brigands at the Avenue Theatre, I have been trying to make up my mind whether I run any serious risk of being damned for preferring the profligacy of Offenbach, Meilhac, and Halévy to the decorum of Cellier and the dulness of Stephenson. Perhaps an item more or less in the account can make no very great difference to me personally; but I warn others solemnly that Offenbach's music is wicked. It is abandoned stuff: every accent in it is a snap of the fingers in the face of moral responsibility: every ripple and sparkle on its surface twits me for my teetotalism, and mocks at the early rising of which I fully intend to make a habit some day.

In Mr Cellier's scores, music is still the chastest of the Muses. In Offenbach's she is—what shall I say?—I am ashamed of her. I no longer wonder that the Germans came to Paris and suppressed her with fire and thunder. Here in England how respectable she is! Virtuous and rustically innocent her 6-8 measures are, even when Dorothy sings *Come, fill up your glass to the brim!* She learnt her morals from Handel, her lady-like manners from Mendelssohn, her sentiment from the Bailiff's Daughter of Islington. But listen to her in Paris, with Offenbach. Talk of 6-8 time: why, she stumbles at the second quaver, only to race off again in a wild Bacchanalian, Saturnalian, petticoat spurning, irreclaimable, shocking cancan. Nothing but the wit of a Frenchman shining through the chinks in the materialism of English comic opera artists could make such music endurable and presentable at the same time.

When Mr Gilbert translated Les Brigands for Messrs Boosey, years ago, he must have said to himself: "This Meilhac-Halévy stuff is very funny; but I could do it just as well in English; and so I would too, if only I

could find an English Offenbach." In due time he did
find his Offenbach in Sir Arthur Sullivan. Accordingly,
when Falsacappa the brigand chief exclaims: "Marry
my daughter to an honest man! NEVER!" we are, not
surprised to recognize in him a missing link in the an-
cestry of the Pirate King of Penzance. The relationship
of the carbineers to the policemen is too obvious to be
worth dwelling on; but there are other ties between the
two phases of musical farce. The extremely funny song
in the second act, *Nous avons, ce matin, tous deux,* is
closely allied to *When I First Put This Uniform On,* in
Patience; and the opening chorus *Deux par deux ou
bien par trois* is first cousin to *Carefully on Tiptoe
Stealing* in H.M.S. Pinafore.

I cannot, however, suppose that Mr Gilbert's objection to the use of his libretto was founded on an idiotic
desire to appear "original." The people who regard the
function of a writer as "creative" must surely be the
most illiterate of dupes. The province of the fictionist
is a common which no man has a right to enclose. I
cultivate that common myself; and when someone
claims to have grown a new plant there, different from
all the rest, I smile sardonically, knowing that the self-
same plant grows in all our plots, and grew there before he was born. And when he discovers in my plot a
plant which he has raised in his own or seen in his
neighbor's, and thereupon cries out "Stop thief! Stop
plagiarist! Stop picker of other men's brains!" I only
smile the widelier. What are brains for, if not to be
picked by me and the rest of the world? In my business
I know *me* and *te,* but not *meum* and *tuum.*

Mr Gilbert's book as played at the Avenue is much
nearer in spirit to the original than Henry Leigh's.
Leigh's lyrics sometimes flowed more smoothly than
Mr Gilbert's; but his libretti were silly and raffish: the
fun too often degenerated into tedious tomfoolery: his
feeble and fleshy whimsicalities are inferior in grit and

sparkle to even the most perfunctory paradoxes of Mr
Gilbert. His Royal Horse Marines, commanded by
Marshal Murphi, and his brigands Jacksheppardo,
Dickturpino, and Clauduvallo, only shew how French
wit of no very high order can yet be degraded by translation into English fun. The horse-collar bar-loafing
buffoonery is not in the least like the genuine Meilhac
and Halévy *opera bouffe*, in which the characters, primarily persons of engaging culture, reasonableness,
amiability, and address, are made irresistibly ridiculous
by an exquisite folly, an impossible frivolity of motive,
which exhibit them as at once miracles of wit and
sensibility and monsters of moral obtuseness. Mr Gilbert has given us the English equivalent of this in his
own operas; and a curiously brutalized, embittered,
stolidified, middle-classical, mechanical equivalent it
is; but the essential wit and incongruity are preserved.
In translating Les Brigands, he naturally did not wholly
miss these qualities; though, oddly enough, his version
makes hardly anything of a couple of points which
might have been expected to appeal specially to him:
to wit, the family sentiment of Falsacappa, and the
conscientious scruples of Fiorella on the subject of rob-
bing handsome young men (just as the Pirates of
Penzance drew the line at orphans).

20 September 1889

Gilbert and Solomon

On thinking it over I am inclined to conclude that Mr
D'Oyly Carte did not quite accurately measure the
vacancy made at the Savoy by the withdrawal of his
dramatic poet and his tone poet. His wish to continue
on the old lines as closely as possible is obvious; but instead of trying to find another Gilbert and another
Sullivan, he has tried to find another Mikado, which,
I admit, is exactly what nobody wanted, one Mikado

being enough for any reasonable generation. Perhaps Mr Carte may have found that another Gilbert does not exist. That may very well be the case; for Mr Gilbert, at his best, was a much cleverer man than most of the playwrights of his day: he could always see beneath the surface of things; and if he could only have seen through them, he might have made his mark as a serious dramatist instead of having, as a satirist, to depend for the piquancy of his ridicule on the general assumption of the validity of the very things he ridiculed. The theme of The Pirates of Penzance is essentially the same as that of Ibsen's Wild Duck; but we all understood that the joke of the pirate being "the slave of duty" lay in the utter absurdity and topsyturviness of such a proposition, whereas when we read The Wild Duck we see that the exhibition of the same sort of slave there as a mischievous fool is no joke at all, but a grimly serious attack on our notion that we need stick at nothing in the cause of duty.

Nevertheless, there was a substratum of earnest in Mr Gilbert's joking which shewed that he was not exactly the sort of writer whom Mr Carte could have replaced by merely going into the Strand in the usual managerial way and hailing the first librettist he met there. Now, in the case of the musician, matters were on a very different footing. Sir Arthur Sullivan made his reputation as a composer of comic operas by a consummate *savoir-faire* which was partly, no doubt, a personal and social talent, but which had been cultivated musically by a thorough technical training in the elegant and fastidious school of Mendelssohn, and by twenty years' work in composing for the drawing room, the church, the festival, and the concert room. In 1875, when he composed Trial by Jury, no manager would have dreamt of approaching him with a commission for an Offenbachian opera: he was pre-eminently a sentimental and ecclesiastical composer, whose name suggested Guinevere and Thou'rt Passing Hence, Nearer, My God, to Thee, and Onward, Christian Soldiers, In Memoriam and the additional accompaniments to Handel's Jephtha. When he plunged into the banalities and trivialities of Savoy opera he carried his old training with him. He taught the public to understand orchestral fun; but his instrumental jokes, which he never carried too far, were always in good taste; and his workmanship was unfailingly skilful and refined, even when the material was of the cheapest.

Why, under these circumstances, Mr Carte should have looked to Mr Solomon to replace Sir Arthur is a problem which reason cannot solve. The right man, Mr Villiers Stanford, was ready to his hand—for I presume that the composer of the Irish symphony would not disdain to follow in the footsteps of Mozart any more than Sir Arthur did. He has the technical training and the culture which stood Sullivan in such good stead; and there must be still alive in him something of the young Irishman of genius who wrote those spirited Cavalier tunes, not to mention some numbers from The Veiled Prophet, before he was forced back into the dismal routine of manufacturing impossible trash like The Revenge for provincial festival purposes, and into conducting, which is so little his affair that when I lately described his Bach choir work in my unliterary way from the point of view of a person whose business it is to use his ears, the only champion who ventured to say a word in his defence did not dare to sign it. But I do not want to force Mr Stanford on Mr Carte. I might have cited Mr Cowen with equal point. He, also, is no more fitted to be a conductor than the majority of brilliant and popular writers are to be editors. My interest in getting both gentlemen back to their proper work, which I take to be intelligent and vivacious dramatic composition, is that it would then become a pleasure to

criticize them, instead of, as it generally is at present,
a disagreeable duty.

All this may seem rather hard on poor Mr Solomon,
the composer upon whom Mr Carte's choice has actually fallen. But then Mr Solomon has been very hard
on me. He has given me the worst headache I ever had
in a theatre by an instrumental score which is more
wearisome than the conversation of an inveterate pun-
ster, and more noisy than the *melodrame* which accompanies the knockabout business in a music-hall. Mr
Carte had better remove the bassoon, the piccolo, the
cymbals, the triangle, and the drums, both timpani and
tamburo, from the theatre; for Mr Solomon is clearly
not to be trusted with them. If Sir Arthur Sullivan used
these instruments in an artistically comic way once in
a thousand bars or so, is that any reason why Mr Solomon should use them in an inartistically comic way
nine hundred and ninety-nine times in the same period? Besides, Sir Arthur only did it to point an allusion. Mr Solomon does it, allusion or no allusion, out
of a mere schoolboyish itching to lark with the instruments. When he has an allusion to excuse him, he does
not make it with anything like the neatness which he
shewed once or twice in his Penelope. Sometimes he
simply stops the opera whilst the band play a fragment
from some familiar work, and then calmly resumes.
This is how he manages the phrase from the Hallelujah
Chorus which follows the reference to the Salvation
Army, a jape which is open to the double objection
that the warriors of the Salvation Army never sing the
Hallelujah Chorus, and that Mr Solomon ought to have
more regard for his own music than to remind people
of Handel's whilst it is proceeding. In the end this topical sort of orchestration becomes distracting, worrying,
even exasperating. I do not insist on this to disparage
Mr Solomon's incessant inventive activity, or to drive
him back into routine instrumentation. But I certainly

do wish to recall him to the necessity of exercising that
activity under strictly artistic conditions, the first of
these being that the score shall be at least agreeable
to the ear, if it is too much to ask that it shall be beautiful.

Nothing in The Nautch Girl sustains the orchestral
traditions of comic opera—the delicacy and humor of
Auber, the inimitable effervescence of Offenbach, or
the musicianly smoothness and charm of Sullivan and
Cellier, all of whom felt that the function of the orchestra was primarily to make music, and only secondarily
to make fun. If Mr Solomon ever had that feeling, he
has allowed it to become blunted; and for want of its
guidance he has now landed himself in mere horseplay, and brought the artistic standard at our leading
comic opera house down with a run. The remedy for
him is by no means to acquire the polite but unpro-
gressive technique of our Mendelssohn scholars, which,
though it would carry him a safe distance, would then
stop him dead, but simply to cultivate the sense of
beauty in music until it becomes an infallible monitor
as to the point at which those twitches on the piccolo,
and grunts on the bassoon, and slams on the drum
cease to amuse, and become offensive disfigurements of
the tone-fabric instead of eccentric ornaments upon it.

Of the opera as an artistic whole I cannot very well
speak, because it hardly *is* an artistic whole. The book
was evidently selected for the sake of its resemblance
to The Mikado, of which it might almost be called a
paraphrase if it were not that the secession of Mr
Grossmith and his replacement by Mr Wyatt has neces-
sitated the substitution of a second edition of the Duke
of Plaza Toro for the Lord High Executioner. The
managerial argument evidently was that since The
Mikado had been so unlike externally to any previous
Savoy opera, the way to secure a repetition of its success was to produce the most slavish possible imitation

of the best known previous Savoy opera. Managers always reason in this way. The result on the first night was that when the rather characterless equivalents of the Mikado opening chorus, and of *A wandering minstrel I*, and of the three girls' trio had been sung, there were signs of the settling down of an ominous dullness, which was only dispelled by the appearance of Mr Rutland Barrington, who changed the fortunes of the evening, and, in fact, saved the opera. At this point, too, the dialogue brightened a good deal; and thenceforth, though there was a plentiful lack of freshness, there was liveliness enough and to spare. Miss Snyders, the only member of the cast whose accomplishments are not too well known to need description, owed her success chiefly to a truly Circassian beauty; for, though she has sufficient taste and address to do her business very presentably, she is not as yet specially interesting as a singer or actress. As usual at the Savoy, the piece has been well rehearsed; the *mise-en-scène* is of exceptional excellence; and Mr Charles Harris, the stage-manager, was received with a cordiality which, I hope, convinced him that he has lost nothing by getting rid of the ballets of infants and the interminable processions in which he formerly delighted. As to the music, it is, to say the least, not distinguished; but it is obvious, lively, and easily caught up by the amateur strummer. Those who rejoiced in *An everyday young man* will be enchanted with *Vive la liberté;* and if here and there a number is a little too stale and vulgar for even such words as *It was all my eye,* on the other hand the mosquito song, and one or two others in the same vein, are by no means graceless.

It will not escape observation that the utmost that can be said for The Nautch Girl amounts to no more than can be said for any piece at the Lyric or the Prince of Wales's. In other words, the Savoy has lost its speciality. This, I think, is a misfortune; and if Mr

Carte wishes to remedy it, and cannot discover two new geniuses, he had better make up his mind at once to give a commission to Mr Grundy for his next libretto, and to Mr Stanford or Mr Cowen for his next score.

8 July 1891

Gilbert and Cellier

Need I say anything more in justification of The Mountebanks, a Gilbert opera with Cellier as composer *vice* Sullivan, retired, than that it made me laugh heartily several times. The brigands whose motto is "Heroism without Risk"; the alchemist who pays his bills with halfpence, accompanied by a written undertaking to transmute them into gold as soon as he discovers the philosopher's stone; the girl who thinks herself plain and her lover handsome, but has to confess to him that she finds herself in a hopeless minority on both subjects; the unsuccessful Hamlet who so dreads to be ever again laughed at by the public that he has turned clown; the mountebank who, pretending that he has swallowed poison and is in the agonies of stomach-ache, is forced to swallow an elixir which has the magic property of turning all pretences into realities; the transformation by this same elixir of the brigands into monks, the clown and columbine into automatic clockwork figures, the village belle into an old hag, the heroine into a lunatic, and the rustic hero into a duke: —if all these went for no more than one laugh apiece, the opera would come out ahead of many of its rivals in point of fun. With them, however, the merit of the piece stops: every line that goes a step further is a line to the bad.

Mr Gilbert has gone wrong in his old way: he has mixed his *genres*. In this Shakespear-ridden land one cannot be a stickler for the unities of time and place; but I defy any dramatist to set the fantastic and the conventional, the philosophic and the sentimental, jostling one another for stage-room without spoiling his play. Now The Mountebanks begins in an outrageous Sicily, where the stage-struck people want to play Shakespear, and where impossible brigands, prosecuting farcical vendettas, agree to hold a revel for twenty-four days on wine ordered from the chemist's, and not to cheer during all that time above a whisper, because of a bedridden alchemist upstairs, shattered by the repeated explosions which have attended his researches into the transmutation of metals. As aforesaid, brigands, mountebanks, and everyone else become enchanted by drinking a magic potion, and are restored to their natural, or rather normal, condition by the burning of the label of the bottle which contains the philtre.

Clearly there is no room here for the realism of Ibsen or the idealism of Drury Lane. That a man so clever as Mr Gilbert could have supposed that the atmosphere of such a Sicily could be breathed by a figure from the conventional drama is a startling example of the illusions of authorship. He undoubtedly did suppose it, however; for one of the characters, a girl who loves the hero and is cordially detested by him, might have been turned out by Tom Taylor himself. When Alfredo impersonates the duke, and is caught in that assumption by the action of the elixir, she impersonates the duchess and shares his fate, thereby becoming his adored wife. Incidentally she delays the action, bores the audience, and, being quite unfancifully conceived, repeatedly knocks the piece off its proper plane. In the second act, she goes to the incredible length of a sentimental *dénouement*. She "relents" at the entreaty of the heroine, not in the fashion of the Pirates of Penzance on learning that his prisoner is an orphan—the only variety of ruth conceivable in Gilbertland—but actually in the orthodox manner of Hubert in King John.

I am afraid that Miss Lucille Saunders will think me grossly inconsiderate when I say, as I must, that if her part were completely cut out, the opera would be vastly improved; but that is certainly my opinion. Alfredo could quite Gilbertianly be represented as devoted to an absent duchess whom he had never seen; and the incident of Pietro losing the charm might easily be managed otherwise, if not wholly omitted. Under these circumstances, it is little to be thankful for that Ultrice, though she is ugly, is at least not old. The old woman of the play is happily not a new Lady Jane or Katisha, but a young maiden who takes the elixir when simulating octogenarianism, and pays the penalty like the rest.

Another weakness in the scheme is that there is no dramatic action in the second act—nothing but a simple exhibition of the characters in the plight to which the elixir reduced them at the end of the first. They walk on in twos; sing comic duets recounting the anomalies of their condition in Gilbertian verse; and go off again, all except the incorrigibly malapropos Ultrice, who sings a tragic *scena* which nobody wants to hear. And nothing else happens except an incident planned in the first act and deprived of its *raison d'être* by the charm, and the sentimental *dénouement,* which is dragged in by the ears (if I may so mix my metaphors) when the fun begins to wear out. The result is that the opera is virtually over ten minutes before the curtain falls; and this means that the curtain falls rather flatly, especially as the composer signally failed to come to the rescue at this particular point.

Cellier's strength never lay in the working up of finales; but this one flickers and goes out so suddenly that one can almost hear ghostly muffled drums in the orchestra. The rest of the score is what might have been expected from the composer—that is, better than the occasion required it to be; and in this very superfluity

of musical conscience one recognizes his want of the
tact which has saved Sir Arthur Sullivan from ever
wasting musical sentiment on Mr Gilbert. Musicians
will not think the worse of Cellier for this. There are
many points, such as the graceful formalism of the little
overture, with its orthodox "working out," and the
many tender elaborations in the accompaniments, all
done from sheer love of music, which will shield Cellier
more effectually than his new dignity of *de mortuis*
from that reproach of musical unscrupulousness which
qualifies every musician's appreciation of the Sul-
livanesque *savoir-faire*.

But from the more comprehensive standpoint which
is necessary in judging an opera, it must be confessed
that, since Sullivan is spontaneously vivacious where
Cellier was only energetic—and that, too, with an effort
which, though successful, was obvious—and since Sullivan is out of all comparison more various in his moods,
besides being a better song-writer, Mr Gilbert cannot,
on the whole, be said to have changed for the better
when he left the Savoy for the Lyric. Only, Cellier's
master, Sterndale Bennett, would not have thought the
worse of him on that account; nor do I set it down here
as any disparagement to him.

In speaking of Cellier as generally less vivacious than
Sullivan, I do not of course imply that he is behindhand in those musical facetiousnesses which tickled
the public so hugely at the Savoy. The duet for the
automata with the quaint squeaking accompaniment,
the clockwork music, and the showman's song with big
drum obbligato by Mr Monkhouse, are quite up to the
Savoy standard—if, indeed, that does not prove too
modest an appreciation of the popularity of Put a
penny in the slot. The old and easy expedient of making the men sing a solemn chorus and the women a
merry one successively (or vice versa, as in Patience),
and then repeat them simultaneously, is achieved in

the second act to the entire satisfaction of those who regard it as one of the miracles of counterpoint. One of the operatic jokes is the best in the whole Gilbertian series. The monkized brigands receive the Duke with a mock ecclesiastical chorus on the syllable La. He expresses his acknowledgments by an elaborate recitative in the same eloquent terms, and, having to finish on the dominant, and finding himself at a loss to hit that note, explains that he is "in want of a word," whereupon they offer him La on the tonic. He shakes his head, and a monk gives him La on the dominant, which he immediately accepts with an air of relief, and so finishes triumphantly. Not to damp my readers too much, I may add that anybody with an ear can appreciate the joke when they hear it without in the least knowing what "the dominant" means.

6 January 1892

Gilbert, Sullivan & Others

Now that Mr D'Oyly Carte has at last given us the right sort of theatre for musical comedy, it is too late for Auber: we have had enough of the serenade in Fra Diavolo and the Crown Diamonds galop, and can no longer stand the Scribe libretto which sufficed to keep our fathers from grumbling. We want contemporary work of the Auber class. The difficulty, so far, has been to find a contemporary Auber. The Gilbertian opera did not exactly fill the vacancy: it was an altogether peculiar product, extravagant and sometimes vulgar, as in the case of the inevitable old woman brought on to be jeered at simply because she was old, but still with an intellectual foundation—with a certain criticism of life in it. When the Gilbert-Sullivan series came to an end, the attempt to keep up the school at second-hand produced the old vulgarity and extravagance without the higher element; and Savoy opera instantly

slipped down towards the lower level. Sir Arthur Sullivan, meanwhile, made a spring at the higher one by
trying his hand on Ivanhoe, which is a good novel
turned into the very silliest sort of sham "grand opera."
I hardly believed that the cumulative prestige of Sir
Walter Scott, Sir Arthur Sullivan, Mr D'Oyly Carte
with his new English Opera House, and the very strong
company engaged, not to mention log-rolling on an unprecedented scale, could make Ivanhoe pay a reasonable return on the enormous expenditure it cost. Yet it
turns out that I either overrated the public or under-
rated the opera. I fancy I overrated the public.

Now La Basoche [by Messager] is exactly what
Ivanhoe ought to have been. Though it is a comic
opera, it can be relished without several years' previous
initiation as a bar loafer. The usual assumption that the
comic-opera audience is necessarily a parcel of futile
blackguards, destitute not only of art and scholarship,
but of the commonest human interests and sympathies,
is not countenanced for a moment during the performance. The opposite, and if possible more offensive and
ridiculous, assumption that it consists of undesirably
naïve schoolgirls is put equally out of the question: you
can take your daughter to see it without either wishing
that you had left her at home or being bored to death.
You attain, in short, to that happy region which lies between the pity and terror of tragic opera and the licentious stupidity and insincerity of *opera bouffe*.

27 April 1892

Gilbert and Sullivan

Pleasant it is to see Mr Gilbert and Sir Arthur Sullivan
working together again full brotherly. They should be
on the best of terms; for henceforth Sir Arthur can always say, "Any other librettist would do just as well:
look at Haddon Hall"; whilst Mr Gilbert can retort,

"Any other musician would do just as well: look at The Mountebanks." Thus have the years of divorce cemented the happy reunion at which we all assisted last Saturday. The twain still excite the expectations of the public as much as ever. How Trial by Jury and The Sorcerer surprised the public, and how Pinafore, The Pirates, and Patience kept the sensation fresh, can be guessed by the youngest man from the fact that the announcement of a new Savoy opera always throws the middle-aged playgoer into the attitude of expecting a surprise. As for me, I avoid this attitude, if only because it is a middle-aged one. Still, I expect a good deal that I could not have hoped for when I first made the acquaintance of comic opera.

Those who are old enough to compare the Savoy performances with those of the dark ages, taking into account the pictorial treatment of the fabrics and colors on the stage, the cultivation and intelligence of the choristers, the quality of the orchestra, and the degree of aristic good breeding, so to speak, expected from the principals, best know how great an advance has been made by Mr D'Oyly Carte in organizing and harmonizing that complex co-operation of artists of all kinds which goes to make up a satisfactory operatic performance. Long before the run of a successful Savoy opera is over Sir Arthur's melodies are dinned into our ears by every promenade band and street piano, and Mr Gilbert's sallies are quoted threadbare by conversationalists and journalists; but the whole work as presented to eye and ear on the Savoy stage remains unhackneyed.

Further, no theatre in London is more independent of those executants whose personal popularity enables them to demand ruinous salaries; and this is not the least advantageous of the differences between opera as the work of a combination of manager, poet, and musician, all three making the most of one another in their concerted striving for the common object of a completely successful representation, and opera as the result of a speculator picking up a libretto, getting somebody with a name to set it to music, ordering a few tradesmen to "mount" it, and then, with a stage manager hired here, an acting manager hired there, and a popular prima donna, comedian, and serpentine dancer stuck in at reckless salaries like almonds into an underdone dumpling, engaging some empty theatre on the chance of the affair "catching on."

If any capitalist wants to succeed with comic opera, I can assure him that he can do so with tolerable security if he only possesses the requisite managerial ability. There is no lack of artistic material for him to set to work on: London is overstocked with artistic talent ready to the hand of anyone who can recognize it and select from it. The difficulty is to find the man with this power of recognition and selection. The effect of the finer artistic temperaments and talents on the ordinary speculator is not merely nil (for in that case he might give them an engagement by accident), but antipathetic. People sometimes complain of the indifference of the public and the managers to the highest elements in fine art. There never was a greater mistake. The Philistine is not indifferent to fine art: he *hates* it.

The relevance of these observations will be apparent when I say that, though I enjoyed the score of Utopia more than that of any of the previous Savoy operas, I am quite prepared to hear that it is not as palatable to the majority of the human race—otherwise the mob —as it was to me. It is written with an artistic absorption and enjoyment of which Sir Arthur Sullivan always had moments, but which seem to have become constant with him only since he was knighted, though I do not suggest that the two things stand in the relation of cause and effect. The orchestral work is charmingly humorous; and as I happen to mean by this only

what I say, perhaps I had better warn my readers not
to infer that Utopia is full of buffooneries with the bassoon and piccolo, or of patter and tum-tum.

Whoever can listen to such caressing wind parts—
zephyr parts, in fact—as those in the trio for the King
and the two Judges in the first act, without being
coaxed to feel pleased and amused, is not fit even for
treasons, stratagems, and spoils; whilst anyone whose
ears are capable of taking in more than one thing at a
time must be tickled by the sudden busyness of the orchestra as the city man takes up the parable. I also
confidently recommend those who go into solemn academic raptures over themes "in diminution" to go and
hear how prettily the chorus of the Christy Minstrel
song (borrowed from the plantation dance Johnnie,
get a gun) is used, very much in diminution, to make
an exquisite mock-banjo accompaniment. In these examples we are on the plane, not of the bones and tam-
bourine, but of Mozart's accompaniments to *Soave sia
il vento* in Così fan tutte and the entry of the gardener
in Le Nozze di Figaro. Of course these things are as
much thrown away on people who are not musicians
as a copy of Fliegende Blätter on people who do not
read German, whereas anyone can understand mere
horseplay with the instruments.

But people who are not musicians should not intrude
into opera-houses: indeed, it is to me an open question
whether they ought to be allowed to exist at all. As to
the score generally, I have only one fault to find with
Sir Arthur's luxurious ingenuity in finding pretty tim-
bres of all sorts, and that is that it still leads him to
abuse the human voice most unmercifully. I will say
nothing about the part he has written for the unfortunate soprano, who might as well leave her lower
octave at home for all the relief she gets from the use
of her upper one. But take the case of Mr Scott Fishe,
one of Mr Carte's most promising discoveries, who did

so much to make the ill-fated Jane Annie endurable. What made Mr Fishe's voice so welcome was that it was neither the eternal callow baritone nor the growling bass: it rang like a genuine "singing bass"; and one felt that here at last was a chance of an English dramatic *basso cantante,* able to "sing both high and low," and to contrast his high D with an equally fine one an octave below. Unfortunately, the upper fifth of Mr Fishe's voice, being flexible and of excellent quality, gives him easy command (on occasion) of high passages; and Sir Arthur has ruthlessly seized on this to write for him an excessively specialized baritone part, in which we get not one of those deep, ringing tones which relieved the Jane Annie music so attractively. I have in my time heard so many singers reduced by parts of this sort, in the operas of Verdi and Gounod, to a condition in which they could bawl F sharps *ad lib.* at high pressure, but could neither place a note accurately nor produce any tolerable tone from B flat downwards, that I always protest against vocal parts, no matter what voice they are written for, if they do not employ the voice all over its range, though lying mainly where the singer can sing continuously without fatigue.

A composer who uses up young voices by harping on the prettiest notes in them is an ogreish voluptuary; and if Sir Arthur does not wish posterity either to see the stage whitened with the bones of his victims or else to hear his music transposed wholesale, as Lassalle transposes Rigoletto, he should make up his mind whether he means to write for a tenor or a baritone, and place the part accordingly. Considering that since Santley retired from the stage and Jean de Reszke turned tenor all the big reputations have been made by *bassi cantanti* like Edouard de Reszke and Lassalle, and that all the great Wagner parts in which reputations of the same calibre will be made for some time to

come are impossible to completely specialized baritones, I venture, as a critic who greatly enjoys Mr
Fishe's performance, to recommend him to ask the
composer politely not to treat him worse than Mozart
treated Don Giovanni, than Wagner treated Wolfram,
or than Sir Arthur himself would treat a clarinet. Miss
Nancy McIntosh, who was introduced to us, it will be
remembered, by Mr Henschel at the London Symphony Concerts, where she sang in a selection from
Die Meistersinger and in the Choral Symphony, came
through the trials of a most inconsiderate vocal part
very cleverly, evading the worst of the strain by a treatment which, if a little flimsy, was always pretty. She
spoke her part admirably, and, by dint of natural tact,
managed to make a positive advantage of her stage in-
experience, so that she won over the audience in no
time. As to Miss Brandram, Mr Barrington (who by
means of a remarkable pair of eyebrows transformed
himself into a surprising compound of Mr Goschen and
the late Sir William Cusins), Messrs Denny, Kenning-
ham, Le Hay, Gridley, and the rest, everybody knows
what they can do; and I need only particularize as to
Miss Owen and Miss Florence Perry, who gave us some
excellent pantomime in the very amusing lecture scene,
contrived by Mr Gilbert, and set to perfection by Sir
Arthur, in the first act.

The book has Mr Gilbert's lighter qualities without
his faults. Its main idea, the Anglicization of Utopia by
a people boundlessly credulous as to the superiority of
the English race, is as certain of popularity as that
reference to England by the Gravedigger in Hamlet,
which never yet failed to make the house laugh.
There is, happily, no plot; and the stage business
is fresh and well invented—for instance, the lecture already alluded to, the adoration of the troopers by the
female Utopians, the Cabinet Council "as held at the
Court of St James's Hall," and the quadrille, are capital

strokes. As to the "Drawing Room," with *débutantes,* cards, trains, and presentations all complete, and the little innovation of a cup of tea and a plate of cheap biscuits, I cannot vouch for its verisimilitude, as I have never, strange as it may appear, been present at a Drawing Room; but that is exactly why I enjoyed it, and why the majority of the Savoyards will share my appreciation of it.

11 October 1893

Jane Annie

The new Savoy opera would not occupy me very long here if the comic-opera stage were in a reasonably presentable condition. If I ask Messrs Barrie and Conan Doyle whether I am to regard their reputations as founded on Jane Annie, or Jane Annie on their reputations, I have no doubt they will hastily declare for the second alternative. And, indeed, it would ill become me, as a brother of the literary craft, to pretend to congratulate them seriously upon the most unblushing outburst of tomfoolery that two responsible citizens could conceivably indulge in publicly. Still less can I, as a musical critic, encourage them in their want of respect for opera as an artistic entertainment. I do not mean that a comic-opera writer would be tolerable if he bore himself reverently; but there is a conscientious irreverence which aims at comic perfection, and a reckless irreverence which ridicules its own work and throws away the efforts of the composer and the artists; and I must say that there is a good deal of this sort of irreverence in Jane Annie.

After all, nothing requires so much gravity as joking; and when the authors of Jane Annie begin by admitting that they are not in earnest, they literally give the show away. They no doubt secure from the public a certain indulgence by openly confessing that their work will not bear being taken soberly; but this confession is a throwing up of the sponge: after it, it is idle to talk of success. A retreat may be executed with great tact and humor, but cannot thereby be turned into a victory. The question then arises, Is victory possible on purely humorous lines? Well, who is the great fountain-head of the modern humorous school, from Artemus Ward down to Messrs Barrie and Doyle themselves? Clearly Dickens, who has saturated the whole English-speaking world with his humor. We have whole squadrons of humorous writers who, if they had never read him, would have produced nothing but sectarian tracts, or, worse still, magazine articles. His ascendancy is greater now than ever, because, like Beethoven, he had "a third manner," in which he produced works which influenced his contemporaries as little as the Ninth Symphony influenced Spohr or Weber, but which are influencing the present generation of writers as much as the Ninth Symphony influenced Schumann and Wagner. When I first read Great Expectations I was not much older than Pip was when the convict turned him upside down in the churchyard: in fact, I was so young that I was astonished beyond measure when it came out that the convict was the author of Pip's mysterious fortune, although Dickens took care to make that fact obvious all along to every reader of adult capacity. My first acquaintance with the French Revolution was acquired at the same age, from A Tale of Two Cities; and I also struggled with Little Dorrit at this time. I say struggled; for the books oppressed my imagination most fearfully, so real were they to me. It was not until I became a cynical *blasé* person of twelve or thirteen that I read Pickwick, Bleak House, and the intervening works. Now it is pretty clear that Dickens, having caught me young when he was working with his deepest intensity of conviction, must have left his mark on me far more deeply than on his own contemporaries, who read Pickwick when they were twenty, and Our Mutual Friend when they were fifty, if indeed they kept up with him at all. Every successive generation of his readers had a greater advantage. The generation twenty years younger than his was the first that knew his value; and it is probable that the generation which will be born as the copyrights of his latest works expire, and leave the market open to sixpenny editions of them, will be the most extensively Dickensized of any.

Now I do not see why the disciples should not be expected to keep up to the master's standard of hard work, as far as that can be done by elbow grease, which is a more important factor in good art work than lazy artists like to admit. The fun of Dickens without his knowledge and capacity for taking pains can only end in what I have called Jane Annie—mere tomfoolery. The pains without the humor, or, indeed, any other artistic quality, as we get it occasionally from an industrious "naturalist" when he is not also an artist, is far more respectable. There are a fair number of humorists who can throw off conceits as laughable as Mr Silas Wegg's comments on the decline and fall of the Roman Empire, or his version of Oh, weep for the hour! But Wegg himself is not to be had so cheaply: all the "photographic realism" in the world is distanced by the power and labor which gave us this study of a rascal, so complete inside and out, body and soul, that the most fantastic playing with it cannot destroy the illusion it creates.

You have only to compare Dickens's pictures of people as they really are with the best contemporary pictures of people as they imagine each other to be (Trollope's, for instance) to understand how Dickens, taking life with intense interest, and observing, analysing, remembering with amazing scientific power, got more hard work crammed into a thumbnail sketch than ordinary men do into colossal statues. The high privilege of joking in public should never be granted except to people who know thoroughly what they are joking about—that is, to exceptionally serious and laborious people. Now, in Jane Annie the authors do not impress me as having taken their work seriously or labored honestly over it. I make no allowances for their performances in ordinary fiction: anybody can write a novel. A play—especially a music-play—is a different matter—different, too, in the sense of being weightier, not lighter.

Messrs Doyle and Barrie have not thought so: they have, with a Philistinism as to music of which only literary men are capable, regarded their commission as an opportunity for a lark, and nothing more. Fortunately, they have larked better than they knew. Flimsy as their work is compared to the fiction of the founder of their school, they have made something like a revolution in comic opera by bringing that school on to the comic-opera stage. For years past managers have allowed themselves to be persuaded that in comic-opera books they must choose between Mr Gilbert's librettos and a style of writing which would have disgraced the Cities of the Plain.

In all populous places there is a currency of slang phrases, catch words, scraps from comic songs, and petty verbal indecencies which get into circulation among bar loafers, and after being accepted by them as facetious, get a certain vogue in that fringe of the sporting and dramatic worlds which cannot be accurately described without an appearance of Puritanism which I wish to avoid. An operatic style based on this currency, and requiring for its complete enjoyment nothing else except an exhaustive knowledge of the names and prices of drinks of all kinds, and an almost inconceivable callousness to, and impatience of, every other subject on the face of the earth, does not seem

possible; but it certainly exists, and has, in fact, prevailed to the extent of keeping the comic-opera stage
in a distinctly blackguardly condition for some time
past.

Now the fun in Jane Annie, senseless as some of it
is, is not in the least of this order. If anyone had offered
at the end of the performance to introduce me to the
authors, I should not have hastily declined; and this is
saying a good deal. Further, the characters, always excepting the pageboy, whose point lies in his impossibility, and who is a most degenerate descendant of
Bailey junior, are so sketched as to make it not only
possible but necessary for the performers to act,
thereby departing from the tradition of the "good acting play," the goodness of which consists in the skill
with which it is constructed so as to require no acting
for its successful performance.

24 May 1893

Music Hall

As to the general question of the quality of music-hall
entertainment, I have nothing to say about that: I am
not a representative of the true music-hall public,
which consists partly of people whose powers of imaginative apprehension and attention are too limited to
follow even the most incoherent melodrama, and partly
of people who like to sit smoking and soaking in lazy
contemplation of something that does not greatly matter. What astonishes a theatre-goer at a music hall, or
an educated woman when she realises one of her most
cherished dreams by at last persuading either her husband or the man-about-towniest of his friends to take
her to the London Pavilion or the Empire, is the indifference of the audience to the performance. Five out
of six of the "turns" are of the deadliest dulness: ten
minutes of it would seal the fate of any drama; but the

people do not mind: they drink and smoke. Under these circumstances the standard of interest, much less of art, is low, the strain on the management or the artists to keep it up being of the slightest. It is rising slowly, in spite of the influence of that detestable product of civilization, the rich man's son, who now represents a distinct class, technically described as "masher," and growing with the accumulation of riches in idle hands produced by our idiotic industrial system. If left to develop freely, our best music halls would in course of time present a combination of promenade concert, theatre, and circus (minus the horses): that is, you would have a good band, decent concert singers, acrobats, jugglers, ballets, and dramatic sketches, all in the same evening. And the refreshment department will probably develop also, as 'Arry develops into the noble Juggins, and begins to prefer the aerated bread shop to the public-house.

18 October 1889

Christmas Pantomime

The other day, passing Her Majesty's Theatre, I saw by the placards that a Christmas pantomime was going on inside. I had not been to a pantomime for fourteen years at least. So I went in; and now I do not think I shall go to one for fourteen years more. It was terribly stupid. The investment it represented may have been anything between ten and twenty thousand pounds. Every thousand of it produces about a farthingsworth of enjoyment, net. I say net, because a balance has to be struck between positive and negative results. In estimating that the entertainment exceeds the annoyance and tedium by a tenth of a farthing per cent, I am making a generous allowance for the inferior tastes of my fellow creatures. As far as I am personally concerned, the balance is on the other side; for I am sorry I went; and wild horses could not drag me thither again.

What struck me most was the extraordinary profusion of artistic talent wasted through mere poverty of purpose. One fiftieth part of it placed at the disposal of a man with the right sort of head on his shoulders would have sufficed for a quite satisfactory pantomime. The scene painters, costumiers, property makers, armorers, and musicians are for the most part capable artists; a few of the players are actors; and the dancers do not all walk like irresolute ostriches. But they might almost as well have been walking up and down the Strand with their hands in their pockets—or in Mr Leslie's pockets—for all the use that is made of their ability in the Haymarket. In the Strand they would bore nobody but themselves: in the Haymarket they bored Me—Me, that never injured them.

The whole affair had been, according to the playbill, "invented and arranged by Charles Harris." I have no animosity towards that gentleman; but I must say I wish he would invent a little more and arrange a little less. Take the procession of beetles, for instance. When I was a small boy there was in the house a book on entomology, with colored plates. The beetles depicted in them were so gorgeous and fantastic that it was delightful to turn over ten plates or so. After that they palled, rapid and easy as the turning over of a book-leaf is; for the mind thirsted for a new idea. Now it was a capital notion of Mr Harris's, that of having a processional ballet of beetles. But he has worn the notion to death—or, to put it tropically, he turns over too many plates. The first five minutes are interesting, the second tedious, the third wearisome, the fourth exasperating, and the fifth sickening. As of old, I craved for a fresh idea, and was given a stale beetle. The character of the color scheme never varied, the drill never varied, the music never varied; so that at last I felt as if Mr Harris were brushing my hair by machinery for half an hour on the strength of my having enjoyed it for the first half minute. The fairy tale procession and the Shakespearean procession were far more successful; for here was a world of ideas annexed as cheaply as a slice of Africa by the British Empire.

Perhaps I may seem a little rough on the pantomime, in view of all the praise the papers have lavished on it. But you must remember the fourteen years which have elapsed since my last experience in this line. I have not been let down gently from Christmas to Christmas by a ladder of fourteen steps: I have come down the whole distance with a crash. I used to regret that the performers were merely ordinary actors and not pantomimists as well. Imagine my feelings on finding that they are now not ordinary actors, but "variety artists" without any dramatic training whatever. The reduction of the harlequinade to three or four scenes lasting only an hour or so seemed inevitable owing to the curious scarcity of the sort of talent required to make it really funny. I have never seen a good clown (this is without prejudice to Mr Payne, to whose clowning I am a stranger); and I have my doubts as to whether the character was not as purely idiosyncratic with Grimaldi as Dundreary was with Sothern. I remember one brilliant harlequin—Mr Edward Royce— who donned the spangles one evening in an emergency. Also one solitary pantaloon, a member of the Lauri troupe, an imposing old gentleman, punctiliously mannered and beautifully dressed, whose indignant surprise at the reverses which overtook him was irresistibly ludicrous.

But even in its decay, with stupid and vulgar clowning, and harlequins and columbines who had never seen Dresden China or Watteau pictures, the harlequinade still consisted of a string of definite incidents, involving distinct parts for an old woman, a masher (then known as a swell), a policeman, and a nursery-maid. The policeman still plotted, the clown counter-plotted, the pantaloon muddled everything he attempted, and the harlequin at least danced. At Her Majesty's I found to my astonishment that all this has dwindled to a single scene, lasting about twenty minutes, during which two clowns, two pantaloons, two policemen, and a crowd, without distinct functions, improvise random horseplay in the feeblest and most confusing way simultaneously in opposite corners of the stage.

This idea of doubling the clown and pantaloon is about as sensible as if Mr Irving were to invite Edwin Booth to come back to the Lyceum and revive Othello with two Othellos and two Iagos.

The question now is, shall we leave it there, and shall I never see a pantomime again? Such a solution is impossible. When Mr Harris and Mr Leslie have gone on for a few years more egging each other on to greater expenditure behind the curtain for the sake of greater weariness before it; when even the grown-up people who have learnt to be thankful for small mercies begin to echo the sneers of the cynical little children for whose sake the entertainment is professedly got up; when the essential squalor of the whole affair becomes so obvious that even the dramatic critics will grow tired of writing strings of goodnatured lies about it, then some manager will suddenly strike his forehead and say, "Suppose I try a real pantomime! Suppose I get rid of my foulmouthed, illiterate, ignorant stage-manager, who, though he dips thousands deep into my treasury, cannot with all his swearing get two supers to walk across the stage in step, much less tread the boards like self-respecting men! Suppose I take the matter in hand myself as an artist and a man of culture!"

Well, suppose he does, how could he set to work? I

had better give explicit directions, since it appears that nobody else will. First, then, Mr Manager, get rid of your "literary adviser," if you have such a thing. The theatres which harbor such persons at once become conspicuous by their illiteracy. This done, think over the whole profession as far as you know it, with a view to selecting dancers, acrobats, and comedians who are good pantomimists. At Her Majesty's, for instance, there is a ballet of young ladies who are supposed to represent rabbits. You can pick out at a glance the girls who ever saw a rabbit and who have the faculty of suggesting the peculiar movement of the creature's head and paws. These are the girls to select for the new departure in pantomime. Leading artists are to be found everywhere. At a circus in Amsterdam I saw a troupe which made music out of kitchen utensils. Their leader was a capital pantomimist: his imitation of an orchestral conductor was immense; and his posturing as the ringmaster on a sham horse outdid nature itself. In Le Voyage en Suisse there was a Frenchman, Agouste by name if I mistake not, who was a most artistic pantomimist. When Offenbach's Voyage dans la Lune was produced at the old Alhambra, Madame Rose Bell, a lively French lady, distinguished herself therein, not more by the qualities which endeared her to the Alhambra audience than by the vivacity and expressiveness of her pantomime. Such examples show how a company of pantomimists could be selected by a good judge. It must finally contain a pair of young and beautiful dramatic dancers for lover and sweetheart (harlequin and columbine), a good comedian for the intriguing valet (clown), a good old man for the tyrannical father, the rich old suitor (pantaloon), or anything except the detestable Ally Sloper of today. Finally, you must get a dramatic poet who is a born story teller and who knows the Arabian Nights better than Two Lovely Black Eyes. The poet will tell you the rest.

17 January 1890

Bands

The concert last week in aid of the project for establishing a municipal band in London reminded me of the late Edmund Gurney's demand for an orchestra for the East End. If I had my way in the matter the money should not be raised by a concert and a subscription list, as if the London County Council were a distressed widow: a fitter course would be to levy the cost by the strong hand of the tax-collector on the thousands of well-to-do people who never go to a concert because they are "not musical," but who enjoy, all the same, the health-giving atmosphere which music creates. Just as the river is useful to men who do not row, the bridges to West Enders who never cross them, and the railways to the bedridden, so the provision of good music and plenty of it smooths life as much for those who do not know the National Anthem from Rule Britannia, as for those who can whistle all the themes in the Ninth Symphony. Now that we have renounced the hideous absurdity of keeping up Waterloo Bridge out of the halfpence of the people who actually go over it, it is pitiable to have to go back to that ridiculous system for a town band. We certainly want such a band, though not because private enterprise has been behindhand in the matter. On the contrary, it is because private enterprise every Sunday sends a procession, religious or Radical, past my windows every five minutes or so, each headed by a band, that I feel the need for some model of excellence to hold up to these enthusiastic instrumentalists. In Lancashire and Yorkshire there are, it is computed, twenty thousand bandsmen.

When I was in Bristol some time ago, a fifteen minutes' walk through the working-class quarter on Sunday morning brought me across three bands, two of them by no means bad ones. In London you can, on the occasion of a big "demonstration," pass down a procession miles long without ever being out of earshot of at least two bands. The cultured class sometimes, when suffering from an attack of nerves, wants the band-playing class to be dispersed and silenced; but this cannot now be effectively done, for the band-playing outnumber the cultured five to one, and two-thirds of them have votes.

Whether we like the bands or not, we must put up with them: let us therefore, in self-defence, help them to make themselves fairly efficient. It is certain that they are not so good as they might be at present, and that as long as they never hear anything better than their own music they will remain much as they are. Their instruments are not so bad as might be supposed. They may not come from the first-class stocks of Mahillon, Courtois, or Boosey; but the competition between instrument-makers has resulted in the production of fairly good brass instruments of the simpler types (cornets, saxhorns, etc.) at reasonable prices payable by instalments. Hence the fortuitous German bombardon with cylinders, bought at a pawnshop, and pitched nearly half-a-tone lower than its British companions in the band, is now scarcer than it used to be, though unhappily it is not yet extinct.

But even in bands in which the instruments are all manufactured to English military pitch and of endurable quality, with players whose ears are not satisfied until they have adjusted their tuning-slides and their blowing so as to get the notes made with the pistons tolerably in tune, chaos sets in the moment the music goes beyond the simplest diatonic harmonies. At the occurrence of one of the series of tonic discords which are so freely used in modern music, and which make the six old gentlemen who form the anti-Wagner party in Paris put their fingers to their ears, the working-class bandsman not only does not know whether he is in tune or out, but he actually does not know whether he is playing the right note, so strange is the chord to his ear. Consequently he is limited to the banal quicksteps and tiresome Boulanger marches which confirm him in his vulgar and obvious style of execution. Even a Schubert march is beyond him, because the modulations, simple and brilliantly effective as they are, are not solely from tonic to dominant and back again. The only way to rescue him from his groove is to familiarize him with the sound of modern polyphony in all its developments. A gentleman can do this for himself at his pianoforte; but a wage-earner who has to buy a modest two-guinea cornet by laborious instalments is as likely to learn driving on his own four-in-hand as modern music at his own Steinway.

You must send round to Victoria Park, Finsbury Park, Battersea Park, Peckham Rye, Hampstead Heath, and Blackheath a numerous, well paid, honorably esteemed, highly skilled, and splendidly equipped band, with a conductor who puts music before applause, the chance of a knighthood, loyalty, morals, religion, and every other earthly or unearthly consideration—a municipal August Manns, in short. This is the only way to teach the bandsman of the street and his patrons how his quicksteps with their three chords and one modulation have been improved on by Schubert, Offenbach, Auber, and Rossini, by Weber, Mendelssohn, and Goetz, and finally by Beethoven and Wagner. Let him pick all this up through his ears, and he will come out with a much sounder knowledge than that of the literate person who knows that Wagner is "marvellous" by reading statements to that effect in the critical scriptures of the day. In the end he will pay back the outlay; for when he is qualified as a consumer and producer of good music, the resultant cheapness and plenty will bring down the exorbitant cost of even the Opera. Think of that, ye golden ones whose Oriental names I read on the box-doors as I stroll about Mr Harris's corridors of an evening during the *entr'actes;* and do not let the Municipal Band Fund fall through for lack of subscriptions.

2 July 1890

Comic Opera

The musical season took advantage of the nuptial festivities at Court to fall down in a swoon; and it may now, I suppose, be regarded as stone-dead. It ended piously with a cantata at the Crystal Palace, on the Handel Festival scale, at popular prices, relieved by a mild fling at the Criterion in the evening, where Mr Wyndham has revived La Fille de Madame Angot for the benefit of the autumnal visitor. Whether it has been a good season or not I cannot say: the usual number of assurances that it has been "the worst ever known" are to hand; but it has been quite busy enough for me, even though my labors have been lightened by the retirement of some of our *entrepreneurs* from an unequal combat with my criticism. On looking back over it I recall, with a certain hopeful satisfaction, the failure of innumerable comic operas. They were not worse than the comic operas which used to succeed— quite the contrary. On the musical side, both as to composition and execution, there has been a steady improvement. The comic-opera stage now exchanges artists with the grand-opera stage and the oratorio platform; and the orchestras, compared to their predecessors, are exquisite and imperial.

The difficulty lies on the dramatic side. I have often expressed my opinion of the average comic-opera li-

brettist with pointed frankness; and I have not changed
my mind in the least. Mr D'Oyly Carte's attempt to
keep the Savoy stage up to the Gilbertian level by calling in Messrs Grundy, Barrie, and Conan Doyle is part
of a sound policy, however this or that particular application of it may fail. But for the moment the effect
on our younger comic-opera artists of having been
trained so extensively at bad dramatic work is that the
rank and file of them cannot act; and when good work
is put into their hands, they are unable to execute it
effectively. On the ordinary stage the incapacity of the
actors is got over by the ingenuity of the authors, who,
by adroitly contriving a constant supply of effective
lines, situations, and passages of pure stage management, reduce the function of the actor to the display
of fairly good stage manners; but the ordinary opera
librettist has not the skill thus to substitute good parts
for good acting, nor the imagination to write drama of
the order which stimulates actors to genuine feats of
impersonation, and eventually teaches them their business.

And so a comic opera, on its dramatic side, has come
to mean mostly an inane and occasionally indecorous
play, performed by self-satisfied bunglers who have all
the amateur's ineptitude without his disinterestedness,
one or two experienced and popular comedians being
thrown in to help the rest out by such fun as they can
improvise.

The effect on the public of the long degeneration
from La Grande Duchesse, with its witty book and
effervescent score, down to the last dregs of that school
(tainted as it was from its birth, one must admit, with
a certain dissoluteness which we soon turned into
graceless rowdyness) seems now to be nearly complete.
In the days when La Grande Duchesse was shuddered
at as something frightfully wicked, when improper
stories about Schneider formed the staple of polite con-

versation, and young persons were withheld from the interpolated *can-can* in the second act as from a spectacle that must deprave them for ever, the many-headed received a rapturous impression of opera bouffe as a delightful and complete initiation into life—the very next thing, in fact, to a visit to the Paris of Napoleon III, represented in the British imagination chiefly by the Mabille Gardens.

Now the theatre-going public may be divided roughly into three classes. First, a very small class of experts who know the exact value of the entertainment, and who do not give it a second trial if it does not please them. Second, a much larger class, which can be persuaded by puffs or by the general curiosity about a novelty which "catches on," to accept it at twice or thrice its real value. Third, a mob of persons who, when their imaginations are excited, will accept everything at from ten times to a million times its real value, and who will, in this condition, make a hero of everybody who comes within their ken—manager, composer, author, comedian, and even critic. When a form of art, originally good enough to "catch on," begins to go down hill as opera bouffe did, the first class drops off at once; and the second, after some years, begins to follow suit gradually.

But the third class still worships its own illusion, and enjoys itself rather more than less as the stuff becomes more and more familiar, obvious, and vulgar; and in this folly the managers keep speculating until that generation passes away, and its idols are too degraded to attract fresh worshippers. Managers are still trying to pick profits out of the dregs of the Offenbach movement; and the question of the day for Mr D'Oyly Carte is, how to keep the Gilbert-Sullivan movement from following the Offenbach movement into the abyss.

This being the situation, up comes an interesting question. Why not go back and begin over again? Gen-

erations of playgoers are happily shorter than generations of men; for most men only begin to go to the
theatre when they arrive at the stage of having a latch-
key and pocket money, but no family; and they leave
off when they arrive at the stage of a family and (consequently) no pocket money. As for myself, I can be
proved by figures to have completely outgrown that
boyish shyness which still compels me to regard myself
as a young man; but I am not so very old—nothing like
what you would suppose from the wisdom and serenity
of my writing. Yet I have the flight of time brought
home to me at every theatrical "revival" by the number
of men, to all appearance my contemporaries, for
whom the operas and plays and artists which seem to
me those of yesterday are as Edmund Kean's Richard
or Pasta's Medea. I have hardly yet lost the habit of
considering myself a child because I never saw Charles
Kean, Macready, or even Grisi; yet I am confronted
already with a generation which is in the same predicament with regard to Titiens and Costa, Julia Mathews
and Stoyle. Twenty years of playgoing makes you a
veteran, an oldest inhabitant, an authority to your face
and an old fogey behind your back—all before you are
forty—long before you begin to be spoken of outside as
a callow young man. Under these circumstances La
Grande Duchesse and La Fille de Madame Angot may
surely be produced today as absolute novelties. La
Grande Duchesse and La Belle Hélène belong to the
sixties, Madame Angot to the early seventies. Compared to them Madame Favart, Le Voyage dans la
Lune, and La Fille du Tambour Major are quite recent
works, although these last three are also ripe for revival
—that is, if revival proves a practicable expedient.
Somehow the Zeitgeist, as it stalks along, brushes the
sparkling bloom off operas just as it does off pastel
drawings; and even an "opera buffa" like Mozart's Don
Juan, which turns out to be not for an age but for all

time (meaning a few hundred years or so), survives as a repertory opera, to be heard once a year or so, instead of being boomed into a furorious run of five hundred nights.

And Don Juan is a very different affair from Madame Angot. I wish I had some music type at my disposal to shew exactly what Lecocq would have made out of *Là ci darem la mano*. To begin with, he would have simply composed the first line and the fourth, and then repeated them without altering a note. In the sixties and seventies nobody minded this: Offenbach is full of it; and Sir Arthur Sullivan was not ashamed to give us a most flagrant example of it in the sailors' chorus which opens H.M.S. Pinafore. It not only saved the composer the trouble of composing: it was positively popular; for it made the tunes easier to learn. Besides, I need hardly say that there are all sorts of precedents, from The Vicar of Bray to the finale of Beethoven's choral symphony, to countenance it. Still, there is a difference between the repetition of a phrase which is worth repeating and one which is not; and the song in which the market-woman describes the career of Madame Angot in the first act of Lecocq's opera may be taken as a convincing sample of a series of repetitions of phrases which are not worth hearing once, much less twice. They delighted 1873; but I am happy to say that on last Saturday 1893 saw through their flimsiness at once, and would have damned the whole opera as *vieux jeu* if the rest of it had been no better.

Probably Wagner has a good deal to do with this advance; for even our comic-opera composers have become so accustomed by him to associate unprecedented persistence in repetition with apparently inexhaustible variation and development, that they are now too sensible of the absurd woodenness of the repetitions of Offenbach and Lecocq to resort to them so impudently. Anyhow, it was clear on Saturday night that the old quadrille padding, in spite of its mechanical vivacity, will no longer pass muster, even in an opera bouffe, as lyric or dramatic music. As to the conspirators' chorus, its original success seems to have vaccinated the English nation against a recurrence of the epidemic; for it was not even encored.

And we nourish our orchestral accompaniments so much better nowadays that the score sounded a little thin; although that was partly due to the fact that Mr Wyndham, who, as frequenters of his theatre know, is not a judge of a band, has made no such orchestral provision as would be a matter of course at the Lyric or Savoy. Still, the band did well enough to shew that we now expect more substance and color in accompaniments, and will not be put off with mere movement and froth.

In other respects the opera stood the test of revival very well. The mounting was, for a West End theatre, decidedly modest, the whimsicalities of the *incroyable* period being cheaply and uninventively represented. The choristers sang but little: they for the most part bawled, screamed, and shouted in a manner that would have been trying in a large theatre, and was intolerable in the Criterion. The men were especially objectionable; and I implore Mr Wyndham to send them all for a week to a respectable cathedral, to learn how to make some passably civilized sort of noise. The success of the performance was due altogether to the principals. Everything depends in Madame Angot on Clairette and Lange; and Miss Decima Moore took unsparing trouble with Clairette, and brought off the first act triumphantly, though in the third her attempt at the gay vulgarity and braggart combativeness of the daughter of the market was rather forced, and, as far as it was successful, hopelessly British.

26 July 1893

Yvette Guilbert

Another great artist has come. I suppose I ought to have been quite familiar with her performances already when I went to her reception of the English Press (musical critics *not* included) at the Savoy Hotel last week; but as a matter of fact I had never heard her before. The fact is I am a very bad Parisian. I have never been to the Chat Noir: I have looked at its advertisements on the Boulevards time after time without the least conviction that my sense of being in the fastest forefront of the life of my age would culminate there. To me, going to Paris means going back fifty years in civilization, spending an uncomfortable night, and getting away next morning as soon as possible. I know, of course, that there must be places and circles in Paris which are not hopelessly out of date; but I have never found them out; and if I did, what figure could I make in them with my one weapon, language, broken in my hand?

Hence it is that I had never seen Mlle Yvette Guilbert when Monsieur Johnson, of the Figaro, introduced her to a carefully selected audience of the wrong people (mostly) at the Savoy Hotel as aforesaid. Monsieur Johnson, as a veteran, will not feel hurt at any comment which only goes to prove that "the power of beauty he remembers yet"; therefore I need have no delicacy in saying that the remarks which he addressed to the audience by way of introducing Mlle Guilbert were entirely fatuous when his emotion permitted them to be heard. When the young lady appeared, it needed only one glance to see that here was no mere music-hall star, but one of the half-dozen ablest persons in the room. It is worth remarking here, that in any society whatever of men and women there is always a woman among the six cleverest; and this is why I, who have a somewhat extensive experience of work on the committees of mixed societies, have been trained to recognize the fact that the Efficient Person in this world is occasionally female, though she must not on that ac-

count be confounded with the ordinary woman—or the
ordinary man, for that matter—whom one does not
privately regard as a full-grown responsible individual
at all.

You do not waste "homage" on the female Efficient
Person; you regard her, favorably or unfavorably, much
as you regard the male of the Efficient species, except
that you have a certain special fear of her, based on
her freedom from that sickliness of conscience, so
much deprecated by Ibsen, which makes the male the
prey of unreal scruples; and you have at times to defend yourself against her, or, when she is an ally, to
assume her fitness for active service of the roughest
kinds, in a way which horrifies the chivalrous gentlemen of your acquaintance who will not suffer the winds
of heaven to breathe on a woman's face too harshly lest
they should disable her in her mission of sewing on
buttons.

In short, your chivalry and gallantry are left useless
on your hands, unless for small-talk with the feminine
rank and file, who must be answered according to their
folly, just like the male rank and file. But then you get
on much better with the female masterspirits, who will
not stand chivalry, or gallantry, or any other form of
manly patronage. Therefore let others, who have not
been educated as I have been, pay Mlle Guilbert gallant compliments: as for me, no sooner had the lady
mounted the platform with that unmistakable familiarity with the situation and command of it which shews
itself chiefly by the absence of all the petty affectations
of the favorite who has merely caught the fancy of the
public without knowing how or why, than I was on the
alert to see what an evidently very efficient person was
going to do.

And I was not at all deceived in my expectancy. It
amuses her to tell interviewers that she cannot sing,
and has no gestures; but I need not say that there
would be very little fun for her in that if she were not
one of the best singers and pantomimists in Europe.
She divided her program into three parts: Ironic songs,

Dramatic songs, and—but perhaps I had better use the French heading here, and say Chansons Legères. For though Mlle Guilbert sings the hymns of a very ancient faith, profusely endowed and sincerely upheld among us, we deny it a name and an establishment. Its Chansons Ironiques are delivered by her with a fine intensity of mordant expression that would not be possible without profound conviction beneath it; and if there is anything that I am certain of after hearing her sing Les Vierges, it is the perfect integrity of her self-respect in an attitude towards life which is distinctly not that of the British matron.

To kindle art to the whitest heat there must always be some fanaticism behind it; and the songs in which Mlle Guilbert expresses her immense irony are the veil of a propaganda which is not the propaganda of asceticism. It is not my business here to defend that propaganda against the numerous and highly respectable British class which conceives life as presenting no alternative to asceticism but licentiousness: I merely describe the situation to save people of this way of thinking from going to hear Mlle Yvette, and proposing to treat her as their forefathers treated Joan of Arc.

Perhaps, however, they would only laugh the innocent laugh of the British lady who, not understanding French, and unwilling to let that fact appear, laughs with the rest at the points which prevented Mlle Guilbert from inviting the episcopal bench as well as the Press to her reception. In spite of her superb diction, I did not understand half her lines myself. Part of what I did understand would have surprised me exceedingly if it had occurred in a drawing-room ballad by Mr Cowen or Sir Arthur Sullivan; but I am bound to add that I was not in the least shocked or disgusted, though my unlimited recognition of an artist's right to take any side of life whatsoever as subject-matter for artistic treatment makes me most indignantly resentful of any attempt to abuse my tolerance by coarse jesting.

The fact is, Mlle Guilbert's performance was for the most part much more serious at its base than an

average Italian opera scena. I am not now alluding to
the avowedly dramatic songs like Le Conscrit and
Morphinée, which any ordinary actress could deliver
in an equally effective, if somewhat less distinguished,
manner. I am thinking of Les Vierges, Sur la Scène,
and the almost frightful La Pierreuse. A *pierreuse*, it
appears, is a garrotter's decoy. In the song she describes
how she prowls about the fortifications of Paris at night,
and entraps some belated bourgeois into conversation.
Then she summons her principal with a weird street
cry; he pounces on his prey; and the subsequent operations are described in a perfect war dance of a refrain.

Not so very horrible, perhaps; but the last verse
describes not a robbery, but the guillotining of the
robber; and so hideously exquisite is the singing of this
verse that you see the woman in the crowd at La
Roquette; you hear the half-choked repetition of the
familiar signal with which she salutes the wretch as he
is hurried out; you positively see his head flying off;
above all, you feel with a shudder how the creature's
impulses of terror and grief are overcome by the bestial
excitement of seeing the great State show of killing a
man in the most sensational way.

Just as people would not flog children if they could
realize the true effect of the ceremony on the child's
pet playmates, to whom it is supposed to be a wholesome warning, so the French Government would certainly abolish public executions *sans phrase* (and perhaps private ones too) if only they would go and hear
Mlle Guilbert sing La Pierreuse.

Technically, Mlle Guilbert is a highly accomplished
artist. She makes all her effects in the simplest way,
and with perfect judgment. Like the ancient Greeks,
not to mention the modern music-hall artists, she relies
on the middle and low registers of her voice, they being
the best suited for perfectly well-controlled declamation; but her cantabile is charming, thanks to a fine ear
and a delicate rhythmic faculty. Her command of every
form of expression is very remarkable, her tones rang-

ing from the purest and sweetest pathos to the cockniest Parisian cynicism.

There is not a trace of the rowdy restlessness and forced "go" of the English music-hall singer about her; and I suggest to those members of the London County Council who aim at the elevation of the music-hall, that they could not do better than offer Mlle Guilbert handsome terms to follow up her reception of *la Presse anglaise* by a series of receptions of Miss Marie Lloyd, Miss Katie Lawrence, and other eminent English prima donnas, in order that they might be encouraged to believe that there is room in music-hall singing for art of classic self-possession and delicacy without any loss of gaiety, and that the author of a music-hall song may not be the worse for being a wit, or even a poet.

16 May 1894

MUSIC AND RELIGION

What is Religious?

It is one of the inevitable evils of my profession that I am asked to go to all manner of places; but hitherto I have drawn the line at going to church. Among the pious I am a scoffer: among the musical I am religious. What has a man who knows Die Zauberflöte, the Schiller Ode to Joy as set in the Ninth Symphony, and Parsifal to do with your collects and rubrics and Jackson in F and all the rest of it? I do not believe that many of the people who compound for their essential irreligiousness by putting in a couple of penitential hours in church once or twice every Sunday have any better motive than escaping damnation, in which case they are plainly damned up to the neck already, though they do not know it. However, since I know it, I am bound to look on the poor devils in a friendly and forbearing spirit, as becomes a happier and more fortunate soul. Anyhow I went to church on Tuesday last, to St Nicholas Cole Abbey.

I had some difficulty in finding St Nicholas. He has an old Tower in Thames Street, among the warehouses; but a glance at it convinced me that if there was an organ inside, there would be no room for me. Besides, there was no sign of its having been opened since the great fire of London; so I made for a red brick mansion which I took to be the Saint's private house, and was there directed by a young lady to go back to Queen Victoria Street and look about me, which I had no sooner done than I perceived St Nicholas staring me in the face on the other side of that spacious thoroughfare. Inside I found some sixty people listening to Mr John Runciman, who was compelling a loud-mouthed intractable organ to discourse to the following effect: 1. *Andante con moto* from Beethoven's C minor symphony. 2. The Parsifal prelude. 3. Bach's organ fugue in A minor. 4. The Death March from the Götterdämmerung. 5. Mr Marshall-Hall's Witenagemot music. 6. The prelude to the third act of Lohengrin.

This is exactly the right sort of program for an organ recital in a church. An organist who plays Guilmant and Lemmens, finishing up with a transcription of the Hallelujah chorus, and perhaps throwing in the fugue which he wrote for his Doctor's degree, would be much better employed outside with a mechanical piano, to which the girls could at least dance. But he who sticks to Wagner and Bach, and can play them, as Mr Runciman did, in an imaginative way, will eventually get the choicest spirits in the parish into the way of coming to the church and learning something there. In some churches it might even end in the organist educating the parson; though that is not necessary at Cole Abbey, where, I blush to say it, the parson (Canon Shuttleworth, a muscular Christian Socialist) sometimes finds it hard enough to educate the organists.

25 March 1890

Handel's Messiah

Christmas being the season of mirth, music, the great English killjoy, with its intolerable hypocrisies, is gladly put away until it is time to return to work and duty and mental improvement and other unpleasantnesses; consequently my critical machinery has got out of gear somewhat. I might have kept off the rust by attending the regulation Christmas performance of The Messiah; but I have long since recognized the impossibility of obtaining justice for that work in a Christian country. Import a choir of heathens, restrained by no considerations of propriety from attacking the choruses with unembarrassed sincerity of dramatic expression, and I would hasten to the performance if only to witness the delight of the public and the discomfiture of the critics. That is, if anything so indecent would be allowed here. We have all had our Handelian training in church, and the perfect churchgoing mood is one of pure abstract reverence. A mood of active intelligence would be scandalous. Thus we get broken in to the custom of singing Handel as if he meant nothing; and as it happens that he meant a great deal, and was tremendously in earnest about it, we know rather less about him in England than they do in the Andaman Islands, since the Andamans are only unconscious of him, whereas we are misconscious. To hear a thousand respectable young English persons jogging through *For He shall purify the sons of Levi* as if every group of semiquavers were a whole bar of four crotchets a capella, or repeating *Let Him deliver Him if He delight in Him* with exactly the same subdued and un-

covered air as in *For with His stripes we are healed,*
or lumbering along with *Hallelujah* as if it were a
superior sort of family coach: all this is ludicrous
enough; but when the nation proceeds to brag of these
unwieldy choral impostures, these attempts to make
the brute force of a thousand throats do what can only
be done by artistic insight and skill, then I really lose
patience. Why, instead of wasting huge sums on the
multitudinous dullness called a Handel Festival does
not somebody set up a thoroughly rehearsed and exhaustively studied performance of The Messiah in St
James's Hall with a chorus of twenty capable artists?
Most of us would be glad to hear the work seriously
performed once before we die.

However, if I did not go to The Messiah, I ventured
on a pantomime, although in London we are unable to
produce an endurable pantomime for exactly the same
reasons that prevent us from achieving an endurable
performance of The Messiah. Therefore I did not
make the experiment in London. I found myself one
evening in Bristol with nothing better to do than to
see whether pantomime is really moribund. I am
bound to say that it seems to me to be as lively as it
was twenty-five years ago. The fairy queen, singing In
Old Madrid with reckless irrelevance at the entrance
to the cave where Aladdin found the lamp, was listened to with deep respect as an exponent of the
higher singing; and in the cave itself The Bogie Man,
in about fifty verses, took immensely. A street scene
at night, with Chinese lanterns and a willow-pattern
landscape, were stage pictures with just the right
artistic quality for the occasion; and the absurdity of
the whole affair on the dramatic side was amusing
enough from an indulgent holiday point of view.
There were no processions presenting one silly idea
over and over again in different colored tights, until
a thousand pounds had been wasted in boring the

audience to distraction. And—though here I hardly expect to be believed—there was not a single child under ten on the stage. I told Mr Macready Chute, the manager, that he should come to London to learn from our famous stage-managers here how to spend ten times as much money on a pantomime for one-tenth of the artistic return. I bade him, if he thirsted for metropolitan fame, to take for his triple motto, Expenditure, inanity, vulgarity, and that soon no spectacular piece would be deemed complete without him. With these precepts I left him, assuring him that I felt more than ever what a privilege it was to live in a convenient art-centre like London, where the nearest pantomime is at Bristol, and the nearest opera at Bayreuth.

21 January 1891

The Messiah Again

Fundamentally my view of the Handel Festival is that of a convinced and ardent admirer of Handel. My favorite oratorio is The Messiah, with which I have spent many of the hours which others give to Shakespear, or Scott, or Dickens. But for all this primary bias in favor of Handel, my business is still to be that of the critic, who, invited to pronounce an opinion on the merits of a performance by four thousand executants, must judge these abnormal conditions by their effect on the work as open-mindedly as if there were only four hundred, or forty, or four. And I am bound to add that he who, so judging, delivers a single and unqualified verdict on the Festival, stultifies himself. The very same conditions which make one choral number majestic, imposing, even sublime, make another heavy, mechanical, meaningless. For instance, no host could be too mighty for the Hallelujah Chorus, or See the Conquering Hero. In them every individual chorister knows without study or instruction what he has to do and how he has to feel. The impulse to sing spreads even to the audience; and those who are old hands at choral singing do not always restrain it. I saw more than one of my neighbors joining in the Hallelujah on the first day; and if my feelings at that moment had permitted me to make a properly controlled artistic effort, I think I should have been no more able to remain silent than Santley was. Under the circumstances, however, I followed the example of Albani, who, knowing that she had to save her voice for *I know that my Redeemer liveth*, kept a vocal score tightly on her mouth the whole time, and looked over it with the expression of a child confronted with some intolerably tempting sweetmeat which it knows it must not touch.

But The Messiah is not all Hallelujah. Compare such a moment as I have just described with the experience of listening to the fiercely tumultuous *He trusted in God*, with its alternations of sullen mockery with high-pitched derision, and its savage shouts of *Let Him deliver Him if He delight in Him*, jogging along at about half the proper speed, with an expression of the deepest respect and propriety, as if a large body of the leading citizens, headed by the mayor, were presenting a surpassingly dull address to somebody. There may be, in the way of the proper presentation of such a chorus as this, something of the difficulty which confronted Wagner at the rehearsals of Tannhäuser in Paris in 1861, when he asked the ballet master to make his forces attack the Bacchanal in a bacchanalian way. "I understand perfectly what you mean," said the functionary; "but only to a whole ballet of *premiers sujets* dare I breathe such suggestions."

No doubt Mr Manns's three thousand five hundred choristers might better his instructions so heartily as to go considerably beyond the utmost licence of art if he told them that unless they sang that chorus like a howling bloodthirsty mob, the utter loneliness of *Thy rebuke hath broken his heart,* and *Behold and see,* must be lost, and with it the whole force of the tragic climax of the oratorio. Besides which, there is the physical difficulty, which only a skilled and powerful orator could fully surmount, of giving instruction of that kind to such a host. But I see no reason why matters should not be vastly improved if Mr Manns would adopt throughout the bolder policy as to speed which was forced on him after four on Selection day by the silent urgency of the clock, and persisted in to some extent—always with convincing effect—in Israel. Increased speed, however, is not all that is wanted. To get rid completely of the insufferable lumbering which is the curse of English Handelian choral singing, a spirited reform in style is needed.

For instance, Handel, in his vigorous moods, is fond of launching the whole mass of voices into florid passages of great brilliancy and impetuosity. In one of the most splendid choruses in The Messiah, *For He shall purify the sons of Levi,* the syllable "fy" comes out in a single trait consisting of no less than thirty-two semiquavers. That trait should be sung with one impulse from end to end without an instant's hesitation. How is it actually done in England? Just as if the thirty-two semiquavers were eight bars of crotchets taken alla breve in a not very lively tempo. The effect, of course, is to make the chorus so dull that all the reputation of Handel is needed to persuade Englishmen that they ought to enjoy it, whilst Frenchmen go away from our festivals confirmed in their scepticism as to our pet musical classic. When I had been listening for some minutes on Wednesday to the festival choristers trudging with ludicrous gravity through what they called *Tellit Outa Mongthe Hea-ea Then,* I could not help wishing that Santley, who roused them to boundless enthusiasm by his singing of *Why do the nations,* had given them a taste of their own quality by delivering those chains of triplets on the words "rage" and "counsel," as quavers in twelve-eight time in the tempo of the Pastoral Symphony. The celestial *Lift up your heads, O ye gates,* lost half its triumphant exultation from this heaviness of gait.

Again, in the beginning of *For unto us,* the tenors and basses told each other the news in a prosaic, methodical way which made the chorus quite comic until the thundering *Wonderful, Counsellor,* one of Handel's mightiest strokes, was reached; and even here the effect was disappointing, because the chorus, having held nothing in reserve, could make no climax. The orchestra needed at that point about twenty more of the biggest of big drums. Another lost opportunity was the pathetically grand conclusion of *All we like sheep.* Nothing in the whole work needs to be sung with more intense expression than *But the Lord hath laid on Him the iniquity of us all.* Unless it sounds as if the singers were touched to their very hearts, they had better not sing it at all. On that Monday it came as mechanically as if the four entries of the voices had been produced by drawing four stops in an organ. This was the greater pity, because it must be conceded to our young Handel-sceptics that the preceding musical portraiture of the sheep going astray has no great claims on their reverence.

I am aware that many people who feel the shortcomings of our choral style bear with it under the impression, first, that the English people are naturally too slow and shy in their musical ways, and, second, that bravura vocalization and impetuous speed are not possible or safe with large choruses. To this I reply, first, that the natural fault of the English when they are singing with genuine feeling is not slowness, but rowdiness, as the neighbors of the Salvation Army know; second, that it would undoubtedly be as risky to venture far in the bravura direction with a very small chorus as to attempt the Walküre fire-music or Liszt's Mazeppa in an ordinary theatre orchestra with its little handful of strings. But both these compositions are safe with sixteen first and sixteen second violins, because, though notes are dropped and mistakes made, they are not all made simultaneously, and the result is that at any given instant an overwhelming majority of the violins are right. For the same reason, I do not see why nine hundred basses, even if they were the stiffest and slowest in the world, could not be safely sent at full speed in the bravura style through Handel's easy diatonic semiquaver traits, as safely as our violinists are now sent through Wagner's demisemiquavers.

So much for the compatibility of speed with accuracy. As to safety, I need only appeal to the results achieved by Mr Manns on Friday, when he got away from The Messiah, which is too sentimental for him, to Israel, which is far more congenial to his temperament. The only choral number in this which was quite unsatisfactory was *I will exalt Him;* and here the shortcoming was made unavoidable by the peculiar style of the chorus, since it—like *And with His stripes* in The Messiah—requires a beauty of execution which would suffice for a mass by Palestrina, and which is out of the question under Handel Festival conditions. The other choruses were spirited and forcible—some of them magnificent. *He gave them hailstones, But the waters overwhelmed,* and *The horse and his rider* were tremendous: one felt after them that the festival had justified its existence beyond all cavil.

If these criticisms are to bear any fruit in raising the festival performances of The Messiah to a typical artistic perfection—a result which I believe to be quite possible, and certainly well worth striving for —they must be weighed, not by Mr Manns or the

Crystal Palace authorities, but by the local conductors throughout the country, who coach their contingents in the work, and send them up with preconceived ideas as to its execution which Mr Manns is powerless to change or even greatly to modify. Every contingent trained by a mere organist, to whom The Messiah is but a part of the drudgery of his professional routine, is simply a nuisance on the Handel orchestra. And every contingent trained by an artist who ranks the work among his treasures, and part of whose artistic ambition it is to hear at last in England a really adequate performance of it, is, as Judas Maccabæus says, "a thousand men."

1 July 1891

Music in Church

Professor Riseley, conferring with an assembly of professional musicians at Newcastle, complains of the absence of orchestras in England. I have often complained of this myself, without receiving any encouragement to believe that my grievance received the smallest attention. Mr Riseley, I see, appeals to Church and State for aid; and it is just possible that persistent hammering away in this direction might get something done in the course of half a century or so. At present every parish in England has a parish church in which instrumental and vocal music is performed at least once a week, and in which the congregation, however impatient of serious and elevated art on weekdays, resigns itself on Sunday to countenance the highest pretensions that music can make. Unfortunately, most of these churches are provided with nothing better in the way of instrumental music than a huge machine called an organ, which, though capable of great things in the hands of a first-rate player dealing with solo music specially written for it, is in many ways highly objectionable for accompanying choral music, and a quite atrocious substitute for orchestral accompaniments. The manipulator of this mechanical monster is generally selected by a sort of open competition, one applicant after another playing before a few gentlemen who bring a trained judgment of horses, crops, groceries, or dry goods to the assistance of the clergyman, who may perhaps know the difference between the Greek β and B flat, or perhaps may not. Every organist will tell you stories of the games he has had with these tribunals, and of the ingenious dodges, wholly irrelevant to his musical fitness, with which he has borne off appointments from less adroit competitors. Once accepted, an organist is underpaid; his authority in directing the services is jealously limited by the clergyman; and he is relegated to a social status intermediate between that of a gentleman and an organ-blower or gravedigger. Clearly, then, a church which has only an organ in the hands of an organist of no more than ordinary force of character will do little or nothing for music, and will presumably do less for The Church (as distinguished from the church) than it might if its services were musically decent. For my part, I have hardly ever heard a service at a country church without wondering at the extraordinary irreverence of the musical arrangements—the gabbling and bawling of the boys in the psalms, the half-hearted droning of the congregation in the hymns, and the trumpery string of modulations and tunes played by the organist, with perhaps a flight into comparative classicism with a number from Mozart's Twelfth Mass, the *Cujus Animam* from Rossini's Stabat, or the march from Le Prophète, to play the people out. When there is anything better than that, you always find, either that the incumbent (not the organist) is a musical enthusiast, or else that there are several churches in the neighbourhood which compete hotly with the

parish church for worshippers. Deplorable as this state
of things is, and deeply corrupted as the ears of most
English people become by their being trained from
youth up to listen patiently to bad music once a week,
it is not easy to see where the remedy is to come from
so long as no musical qualification is expected from
those who have the supreme control of a service that is
half music. This is hardly to be wondered at in view
of the fact that many bishops will ordain men who,
though they can satisfy the chaplain of their ability,
under stress of preparation, to blunder through the
Gospels in Greek, cannot read a chapter of the Bible
aloud in English intelligibly. And indeed I do not
pretend that The Church could fill its pulpits if its
ministry were to be made musical as well as spiritual.
The artistic part of the service should be placed under
the separate control of a capable artist, just as the
heating arrangements are placed in the hands of a
capable plumber. But since only those few clergymen
who are themselves artists can recognize or even understand this, present circumstances offer no chance
of the emancipation of the organist from the despotism
of the rector. The organist is, and will always be, a
slave. But if there were an orchestra in the church the
organist would have to be a conductor, capable of inspiring some degree of confidence in a whole band;
and the most inveterately obtuse incumbent could no
longer make him feel that he might be replaced by
any person who knew enough about the organ to strum
through a service, pending whose appointment one of
the young ladies from the rectory could keep things
going for a week or two. Besides, the artistic conscience of a band is a stronger resisting force than that
of an individual organist. It is always easier to say "We
object" than "I object." The parish church bands would
give the orchestral nuclei which Professor Riseley
wants. As a first step in reconciling public opinion to

them, let everyone of musical pretensions do his or her best to discredit the notion that the organ is a specially sacred kind of music machine. It is, as a matter of fact, quite the reverse; for I doubt if there is any instrument which so frequently and irresistibly provokes the player to profanity. Indeed, organists are far from being the majestic and self-contained men their office might lead outsiders to expect.

13 January 1892

Mendelssohn's Elijah

The performance of Elijah at the Albert Hall last Wednesday was one of remarkable excellence. The tone from the choir was clean and unadulterated: there was no screaming from the sopranos, nor bawling from the tenors, nor growling from the basses. In dispensing with these three staple ingredients of English choral singing Mr Barnby has achieved a triumph which can only be appreciated by those who remember as well as I do what the choir was like in its comparatively raw state some fifteen years ago. Nowadays he gets the high notes taken piano as easily as the middle ones; and the sharpness of attack and the willing vigor and consentaneousness of the singing when the music in hand is as familiar to the singers and as congenial to the conductor as Mendelssohn's, are all that could be desired.

I sat out the performance on Wednesday to the last note, an act of professional devotion which was by no means part of my plan for the evening; and I did not feel disposed to quarrel with Mr Barnby more than twice. The first time was over the chorus *Hear us, Baal,* which he quite spoiled by taking allegro molto. If he had taken it as Mendelssohn directed, allegro non troppo, with the quaver accompaniment excessively detached, and the theme struck out in pompous, stately strokes, the result would have convinced him that Mendelssohn knew quite well what he was about; and the chorus would not have discounted, by anticipation, the effect of the startled *Hear our cry, O Baal,* or of the frantic *Baal, hear and answer.* The second occasion was of the same kind. The chorus *Then did Elijah the prophet break forth like a fire* was taken almost twice too fast, in spite of Mendelssohn's instructions. For surely no difference of opinion as to the right tempo can extend to making a rattling allegro of a movement marked moderato maestoso. The consequence was that the unaccompanied phrase *And when the Lord would take him away to heaven* sounded ludicrously hasty; and there was no sensation at the end like that after *Thanks be to God: He laveth the thirsty land,* which, taken as Mendelssohn ordered it to be taken, roused the audience to enthusiasm. Madame Albani hardly needed the apology which was circulated for her on the ground of a "severe cold" which she simply had not got, though I have no doubt she was suffering, as we all were, from the abominable east wind. The selection of Mr Ben Davies and Madame Belle Cole for the tenor and contralto parts could not easily have been improved on; and though Mr Watkin Mills began badly, and did not at any time exactly break forth like a fire, he was not too far overparted.

The audience was a huge one, shewing, after all deductions for the numbers of the foolish people who only run after the reputations of the solo singers, that there is no falling off in the great popularity of Elijah. This need not be regretted so long as it is understood that our pet oratorio, as a work of religious art, stands together with the pictures of Scheffer and Paton, and the poems of Longfellow and Tennyson, sensuously beautiful in the most refined and fastidiously decorous way, but thoughtless. That is to say, it is not really

religious music at all. The best of it is seraphic music,
like the best of Gounod's; but you have only to think
of Parsifal, of the Ninth Symphony, of Die Zauberflöte,
of the inspired moments of Handel and Bach, to see
the great gulf that lies between the true religious
sentiment and our delight in Mendelssohn's exquisite
prettiness. The British public is convinced in its middle age that *Then shall the righteous shine forth as the
sun* is divine, on grounds no better and no worse than
those on which, in its callow youth, it adores beautiful
girls as angels. Far from desiring to belittle such innocent enthusiasm, I rather echo Mr Weller's plea that
"Arter all, gen'lmen, it's an amiable weakness."

At the same time, a vigorous protest should be en-
tered whenever an attempt is made to scrape a layer
off the praise due to the seraphs in order to spread it
over the prophet in evening dress, who, in feeble
rivalry with the Handelian prophet's song of the power
that is "like a refiner's fire," informs the audience, with
a vicious exultation worthy of Mrs Clennam, that "God
is angry with the wicked every day." That is the worst
of your thoughtlessly seraphic composer: he is a wonder whilst he is flying; but when his wings fail him, he
walks like a parrot.

11 May 1892

A Bad Oratorio

For some time past I have been carefully dodging Dr
Hubert Parry's Job. I had presentiments about it from
the first. I foresaw that all the other critics would
cleverly imply that they thought it the greatest oratorio
of ancient or modern times—that Handel is rebuked,
Mendelssohn eclipsed, and the rest nowhere. And I
was right: they did. The future historian of music,
studying the English papers of 1892–3, will learn that
these years produced two entire and perfect chryso-

lites, Job and Falstaff, especially Job. I was so afraid of being unable to concur unreservedly in the verdict that I lay low and stopped my ears. The first step was to avoid the Gloucester Festival. That gave me no trouble: nothing is easier than not to go to Gloucester. I am, to tell the truth, not very fond of Festivals. It is not that the oratorios bore me, or even the new works "composed expressly," the word "expressly" here indicating the extra-special dullness supposed to be proper to such solemn occasions. These things are the inevitable hardships of my profession: I face them as the soldier faces fire, feeling that it is the heroic endurance of them that raises criticism from a mere trade to a profession or calling. But a man is expected to have the courage of his own profession only. The soldier must face cold steel; but he may without derogation be afraid of ghosts. The doctor who braves fever may blench from shipwreck; and the clergyman who wars daily against the Prince of Darkness is permitted to quit a field in which he unexpectedly meets a mad bull. The musical critic is ready at duty's call to stand up fearlessly to oratorios, miscellaneous concerts, requiems, and comic operas; but it is no part of his bargain to put up with the stewards at a provincial festival. It is not that these gentlemen intend to be uncivil, or are by nature more evilly dispositioned than their fellow-creatures; but they have no manners, no *savoir vivre:* they are unsocially afraid of the public, snobbishly afraid of being mistaken for professional attendants, unaccustomed to their work (which requires either experience or tact and self-possession), and inflated with a sense of their importance instead of sobered by a sense of their responsibility.

Consequently they are fussy, suspicious, rude or nervous, as the case may be, constantly referring helplessly to the one or two of their number who have their wits about them, and not unfrequently blundering un-

intentionally to within a perilous distance of the point
at which the more choleric and muscular sort of visitor
will threaten violence and execute profanity, and the
more subtly malicious will patronizingly offer the blun-
derer a tip. By good luck, I have never myself been
outraged by a festival steward; but the mere flavor of
irresponsible and incompetent officialism poisons the
artistic atmosphere for me.

It brings before me the appalling centralization of
English intellectual and artistic life, and therefore of
social grace, with the consequent boorification of the
provinces. It will never be merrie England until every
man who goes down from London to a festival or other
provincial function will frankly say to his host, "My
friend: your house is uncommonly comfortable, and
your grub of the best. You are hospitable; and you
gratify my vanity by treating me, who am a Nobody
at home, as a Somebody from London. You are not
bad company when you go out into the fields to kill
something. But owing to the fact that you have been
brought up in a town where the theatre, the picture-
gallery, and the orchestra count for nothing, and the
exchanges count for everything, you are, saving your
presence, a hopelessly dull dog; and your son is growing up as dull a dog as you." Not a polite speech,
maybe; but you cannot make revolutions with rosewa-
ter; and what is wanted in English provincial life is
nothing short of a revolution.

Such being my sentiments, it will be understood that
I forewent Gloucester and Job last autumn without regret. I have explained the matter at some length, not
because I have not said all the above before, but solely
to put off for awhile the moment when I must at last
say what I think of Dr Parry's masterpiece. For I unluckily went last Wednesday to the concert of the Mid-
dlesex Choral Union, where the first thing that happened was the appearance of Dr Parry amid the burst

of affectionate applause which always greets him. That made me uneasy; and I was not reassured when he mounted the conductor's rostrum, and led the band into a prelude which struck me as being a serious set of footnotes to the bridal march from Lohengrin. Presently up got Mr Bantock Pierpoint, and sang, without a word of warning, *There was a man in the land of Uz whose name was Job.* Then I knew I was in for it; and now I must do my duty.

I take Job to be, on the whole, the most utter failure ever achieved by a thoroughly respectworthy musician. There is not one bar in it that comes within fifty thousand miles of the tamest line in the poem. This is the naked, unexaggerated truth. Is anybody surprised at it? Here, on the one hand, is an ancient poem which has lived from civilization to civilization, and has been translated into an English version of haunting beauty and nobility of style, offering to the musician a subject which would have taxed to the utmost the highest powers of Bach, Handel, Mozart, Beethoven, or Wagner. Here on the other is, not Bach nor Handel nor Mozart nor Beethoven nor Wagner, not even Mendelssohn or Schumann, but Dr Parry, an enthusiastic and popular professor, forty-five years old, and therefore of ascertained powers.

Now, will any reasonable person pretend that it lies within the limits of those powers to let us hear the morning stars singing together and the sons of God shouting for joy? True, it is impossible to say what a man can do until he tries. I may before the end of this year write a tragedy on the subject of King Lear that will efface Shakespear's; but if I do it will be a surprise, not perhaps to myself, but to the public. It is certain that if I took the work in hand I should be able to turn out five acts about King Lear that would be, at least, grammatical, superficially coherent, and arranged in lines that would scan. And I doubt not at all that some friendly and ingenious critic would say of it, "Lear is, from beginning to end, a remarkable work, and one which nobody but an English author could have written. Every page bears the stamp of G. B. S.'s genius; and no higher praise can be awarded to it than to say that it is fully worthy of his reputation." What critic would need to be so unfriendly as to face the plain question, "Has the author been able for his subject?"

I might easily shirk that question in the case of Job: there are no end of nice little things I could point out about the workmanship shewn in the score, its fine feeling, its scrupulous moderation, its entire freedom from any base element of art or character, and so on through a whole epitaph of pleasant and perfectly true irrelevancies. I might even say that Dr Parry's setting of Job placed him infinitely above the gentleman who set to music The Man that broke the Bank. But would that alter the fact that Dr Parry has left his subject practically untouched, whilst his music-hall rival has most exhaustively succeeded in covering his? It is the great glory of Job that he shamed the devil. Let me imitate him by telling the truth about the work as it appeared to me. Of course I may be wrong: even I am not infallible, at least not always.

And it must be remembered that I am violently prejudiced against the professorial school of which Dr Parry is a distinguished member. I always said, and say still, that his much-admired oratorio Judith has absolutely no merit whatever. I allowed a certain vigor and geniality in his L' Allegro ed il Pensieroso, and a certain youthful inspiration in his Prometheus. But even these admissions I regarded as concessions to the academic faction which he leans to; and I was so afraid of being further disarmed that I lived in fear of meeting him and making his acquaintance; for I had noticed that the critics to whom this happens become hopelessly corrupt, and say anything to please him without the least regard to public duty. Let Job then have the benefit of whatever suspicion may be cast on my verdict by my prepossessions against the composer's school.

The first conspicuous failure in the work is Satan, who, after a feeble attempt to give himself an infernal air by getting the bassoon to announce him with a few frog-like croaks, gives up the pretence, and, though a tenor and a fiend, models himself on Mendelssohn's St Paul. He has no tact as an orator. For example, when he says "Put forth thine hand now and touch all that he hath, and he will curse thee to thy face," there is not a shade of scepticism or irony in him; and he ineptly tries to drive his point home by a melodramatic shriek on the word "curse." When one thinks—I will not say of Loki or Klingsor, but of Verdi's Iago and Boito's Mefistofele, and even of Gounod's stage devil, it is impossible to accept this pale shadow of an excitable curate as one of the poles of the great world magnet.

As to Job, there is no sort of grit in him: he is abject from first to last, and is only genuinely touching when he longs to lie still and be quiet where the wicked cease from troubling and the weary are at rest. That is the one tolerable moment in the work; and Job passes from it to relapse into dullness, not to rise into greater strength of spirit. He is much distracted by fragments of themes from the best composers coming into his head from time to time, and sometimes cutting off the thread of his discourse altogether. When he talks of mountains being removed, he flourishes on the flute in an absurdly inadequate manner; and his challenge to God, *Shew me wherefore Thou contendest with me,* is too poor to be described.

Not until he has given in completely, and is saying his last word, does it suddenly occur to him to make a hit; and then, in announcing that he repents in dust and ashes, he explodes in the most unlooked-for way on the final word "ashes," which produces the effect of a sneeze. The expostulation of God with Job is given to the chorus: the voice that sometimes speaks through the mouths of babes and sucklings here speaks through the mouths of Brixton and Bayswater, and the effect is precisely what might have been expected. It is hard to come down thus from the "heil'gen Hallen" of Sarastro to the suburbs.

There is one stroke of humor in the work. When Job says, *The Lord gave, and the Lord taketh away: blessed be the name of the Lord,* a long and rueful interval after the words "taketh away" elapses before poor Job can resign himself to utter the last clause. That is the sole trace of real dramatic treatment in this dreary ramble of Dr Parry's through the wastes of artistic error. It is the old academic story—an attempt to bedizen a dramatic poem with scraps of sonata music.

Dr Parry reads, *The walls are broken down: destroyed are the pleasant places;* and it sounds beautifully to him. So it associates itself with something else that sounds beautifully—Mendelssohn's violin concerto, as it happens in this case—and straightway he rambles off into a rhythm suggested by the first movement of the concerto, and produces a tedious combination which has none of the charm or propriety of either poem or concerto. For the sake of relief he drags in by the ears a piece of martial tumult—*See! upon the distant plain, a white cloud of dust, the ravagers come*—compounded from the same academic prescription as the business of the dragon's teeth coming up armed men in Mackenzie's Jason; and the two pieces of music are consequently indistinguishable in my memory—in fact, I do not remember a note of either of them.

I have no wish to linger over a barbarous task. In time I may forgive Dr Parry, especially if he will write a few more essays on the great composers, and confine himself to the composition of "absolute music," with

not more than three pedal points to the page. But at
this moment I feel sore. He might have let Job alone,
and let me alone; for, patient as we both are, there are
limits to human endurance. I hope he will burn the
score, and throw Judith in when the blaze begins to
flag.

3 May 1893

MISCELLANY

Richard III as Music

A. B. Walkley has had the unspeakable audacity to
advise "the frolic Bassetto" to go to Richard III at the
Globe Theatre. This is a gibe at my earnestness, which
perhaps makes my column appear heavy to those who
are accustomed to the trivialities of dramatic criticism.
But I believe I have the support of those who are
weary of levity, of egotism, of senseless facetiousness,
of self-advertisement, and, I will add, of ignorance and
presumption. If, as Walkley implies, I have no sense of
humor—and I do not deny it nor regret it—at least my
readers are protected against misplaced jests and fleers
at men who feel their responsibility and do not trifle
with their mission.

As a matter of fact, I did go to the Globe, not because
Walkley wished me to hear "Mr Edward German's fine
music, with its Leitmotif after Wagner's plan" (ha! ha!
ha!), but because a musician only has the right to criticize works like Shakespear's earlier histories and tragedies. The two Richards, King John, and the last act
of Romeo and Juliet, depend wholly on the beauty of
their music. There is no deep significance, no great subtlety and variety in their numbers; but for splendor of
sound, magic of romantic illusion, majesty of emphasis,
ardor, elation, reverberation of haunting echoes, and

every poetic quality that can waken the heart-stir and the imaginative fire of early manhood, they stand above all recorded music. These things cannot be spectated (Walkley signs himself Spectator): they must be heard. It is not enough to see Richard III: you should be able to *whistle* it.

However, to the music! Mr Mansfield's execution of his opening scena was, I must say, deeply disappointing. When I heard his rendering of the mighty line—

In the deep bosom of the ocean buried,

which almost rivals "the multitudinous seas incarnadine" I perceived that Richard was not going to be a musical success. And when in that deliberate staccato—

I am determinéd to be a villain,

he actually missed half a bar by saying in modern prose fashion, "I am determin'd to be a villain," I gave him up as earless. Only in such lines as—

Framed in the prodigality of nature,

which simply cannot be put out of joint, was his delivery admirable. And yet his very worst achievement was—

Bound with triumphant garlands will I come,
And lead your daughter to a conqueror's bed.

Spectator, with reckless frivolity, has left his readers to infer that the magnificent duet with Miss Mary Rorke in which these lines occur, with the famous section beginning,

Send to her, by the man that slew her brothers,
A pair of bleeding hearts,

is by Cibber. "*Ecce iterum!* this scene is Cibber again" says Spectator. And this, mind, not that he does not know as well as I do that the lines are Shakespear's, but simply because, as Cibber was a sort of dramatic critic (he was an actor who wrote an apology, by no means uncalled for, for his own existence, though in justice I must add that it is still the best book on the English theatre in existence, just as Boswell's Journey to the Hebrides is still the best guidebook), Spectator wishes to prove him superior to Shakespear!

To return to Mr Mansfield. It is a positive sin for a man with such a voice to give the words without the setting, like a Covent Garden libretto. Several times he made fine music for a moment, only to shew in the next line that he had made it haphazard. His acting version of the play, though it is an enormous improvement on the traditional Cibberesque, notably in the third and fourth acts, yet contains some wanton substitutions of Cibber's halting, tinpot, clinking stuff for noble and beautiful lines by Shakespear, which would occupy no longer time in delivery. Why, for instance, is this passage avoided?

RICHARD'S MOTHER. . . . I prithee hear me speak;
 For I shall never speak to thee again.
RICHARD. So.
HIS MOTHER. Either thou wilt die, by God's just ordinance,
 Ere from this war thou turn a conqueror;
 Or I with grief and extreme age shall perish,
 And never more behold thy face again.

And so on. Is Mr Mansfield deaf, that he allows the dead hand of Cibber to filch this passage from Miss Leclercq and the audience? Or is a gentleman connected with this paper, who has shewn a suspicious familiarity with the Globe arrangements, the real author of the Mansfield version? If I were playing Richard I would sacrifice anything else in the play sooner than that monosyllable "So"; which tells more of Richard than a dozen stabbings and baby smotherings.

The last act also presents some unaccountable inconsistencies. Mr Mansfield valiantly gives every word of the striking solo following the nightmare scene; and he rejects "Richard's himself again" with the contempt it deserves. But instead of finishing the scene in mystery and terror by stealing off into the gloom to eavesdrop with Ratcliff, he introduces that vulgar Cibberian coda in the major key:—

Hark! the shrill trumpet sounds. To horse! Away!
My soul's in arms and eager for the fray.

Imagine a man at dead midnight, hours before the battle, with cold, fearful drops still on his trembling flesh, suddenly gasconading in this fashion. Shakespear waits until Richard is in the field, and the troops actually in motion. That is the magnetic moment when all the dreadful joy of the fighting man surges up in him, and he exclaims—

A thousand hearts are great within my bosom.

And now, as to Mr Edward German's music, "with its Leitmotif after Wagner's plan." Here is the principal theme of the overture:—

 etc.

And whenever Richard enters you hear the bassoons going: Pum-pum-pum, pum, pum, Paw! It is a Leitmotif certainly; but this very primitive employment of it is not "after Wagner's plan." Hang it all, gentlemen critics of the drama, have you never been to the opera? Surely you have heard at least Der Freischütz or Robert le Diable, or even Satanella, with their one or two comparatively undeveloped, unaltered, and uncombined Leitmotif labelling stage figures rather than representing ideas. Yet you can hardly have supposed that these were "after Wagner's plan."

What Mr Edward German has done is this: Having had about twenty-two players at his disposal, he has wisely written for the old Haydn-Mozart symphony orchestra: two flutes, two oboes, two clarinets, two bassoons, two horns, drums, and strings: no trumpets or trombones. He has also necessarily economized in the strings by doing without 'cellos. For these hardly Wagnerian forces he has written an overture and a series of intermezzos, all pretty and well put together, but none presenting a single point of novelty. The style is the style of—say Max Bruch: that is, everybody's style: Gounod's, Bizet's, Mendelssohn's, Verdi's, all styles *except Wagner's.*

The first *entr'acte* begins with a prolonged bassoon note and a slow triplet, which makes you rub your eyes and ask whether the curtain is not about to rise on the tower scene from Il Trovatore. The prelude to the last act is a reminiscence, and a very vivid one too, of the prelude and gipsy dance at the beginning of the tavern scene in Carmen. In short, Mr German knows his business, and has come off with credit; but his music is not specially dramatic in character, and would suit The Lady of Lyons just as well as Richard III. By the bye, why has he not taken the pastoral opportunity offered by the scene in which Richmond and his army scent the morning air on Bosworth Field? He should have divided the honors of this most effective bit of scene painting with Mr Telbin.

23 March 1889

The Marseillaise

This week seems to be devoted to celebrating the French Revolution of 1789 which produced such an effect on music that it has never been the same since. I can bring the connection down to this very week; for the first musical product of the Revolution was the Eroica Symphony, utterly unlike anything that had ever been heard in the world before. That very symphony, though nobody feels particularly excited about it now, was performed at the first Richter concert the other day. This would be an excellent opportunity to introduce a criticism of the concert; but unluckily I was not there—though that, of course, need not prevent me from writing a notice of it. I had gone down to Surrey to inspect the newest fashions in spring green; and when the concert began I was communing perplexedly with Nature as to the probability of catching the last train but one from Dorking.

Between ten and eleven, as I sat at Redhill Junction awaiting the arrival of the ten minutes to ten train, I meditated on the Revolution music—on its grandioseness, splendioseness, neuroseness, and sensationaloseness; on its effort, its hurry, its excitement, its aspiration without purpose, its forced and invariably diappointing climaxes, its exhaustion and decay, until in our own day everything that was most strenuously characteristic of it seems old-fashioned, platitudinous, puerile, forcible-feeble, anything but romantic and original. Just think of the mental condition of the enthusiastic musicians who believed that the operas of Meyerbeer were a higher development of those of Mozart, that Berlioz was the heir and successor of Beethoven, Schubert an immortal tone poet as yet only half come to light, Rossini such another as Handel, and Wagner a cacophonous idiot! It is not twenty years since this was quite an advanced program.

If, however, we are to have a Revolution, do not let us sing the Marseillaise. The incurable vulgarity of that air is a disgrace to the red flag. It corresponds so exactly in rhythmic structure with the Irish tune called The Red Fox, or, as Moore set it, Let Erin Remember the Days of Old, that the two airs can be harmonized, though not in what Cherubini would have considered strict two-part counterpoint. But compare the mechanical tramp and ignobly self-assertive accent of Rouget de Lisle's composition with the sensitiveness of the Irish melody and the passion that is in all its moods. My own

belief is that the men of Marseilles were horribly fright-
ened when they went to the front, as any sensible person would be; and Rouget de Lisle's tune enabled
them to face it out, exactly as "Ta-ran-ta-ra" encouraged the policemen in The Pirates of Penzance.

13 May 1889

In the West Country

I am, I suppose, in the west country, by which I mean
generally any place for which you start from Padding-
ton. To be precise, I am nowhere in particular, though
there are ascertained localities within easy reach of me.
For instance, if I were to lie down and let myself roll
over the dip at the foot of the lawn, I should go like
an avalanche into the valley of the Wye. I could walk
to Monmouth in half an hour or so. At the end of the
avenue there is a paper nailed to a tree with a sten-
cilled announcement that The Penalt Musical Society
will give a concert last Friday week (I was at it, as
shall presently appear); and it may be, therefore, that
I am in the parish of Penalt, if there is such a place.
But as I have definitely ascertained that I am not in
England either ecclesiastically or for the purposes of
the Sunday Closing Act; as, nevertheless, Wales is on
the other side of the Wye; and as I am clearly not in
Ireland or Scotland, it seems to follow that I am, as I
have honestly admitted, nowhere. And I assure you it
is a very desirable place—a land of quietly beautiful
hills, enchanting valleys, and an indescribable sober
richness of winter coloring. This being so, need I add
that the natives are flying from it as from the plague?
Its lonely lanes, where, after your day's work, you can
wander amid ghosts and shadows under the starry fir-
mament, stopping often to hush your footsteps and listen to a wonderful still music of night and nature, are
eagerly exchanged for sooty streets and gaslamps and

mechanical pianos playing the last comic song but two. The fact is, wages in the district do not reflect the sufficiency of the scenery: hence ambitious young men forsake their birthplace to begrime themselves in "the tinworks," symbolic of the great manufacturing industries of the nation, which have all, figuratively speaking, the production of tin as their final cause. I cannot walk far without coming upon the ruins of a deserted cottage or farmhouse. The frequency of these, and the prevalence of loosely piled stone walls instead of hedges, gives me a sensation of being in Ireland which is only dispelled by the appearance of children with whole garments and fresh faces acquainted with soap. But even children are scarce, the population being, as far as I can judge, about one-sixth of a human being per square mile. The only fit pleasures of the place are those of contemplation. Yet one day, as I was coasting a neighboring valley, the sylvan echoes were wakened by an abjectly monotonous Too Too too-too-too-too, Too Too too too-tooting on a poor sort of horn; and presently a huntsman appeared jogging along, followed by a pack of hounds full of eager excitement, which they had to waste, for want of anything else to do, in a restless wagging of their multitudinous tails which quite hid their bodies from me, exactly as the swordsman in the German tale kept himself dry in a shower of rain by waving his sword above his head. Then came some young gentlemen, their bored human instincts struggling with those which they shared with the pack. With them were many older men, of whom a few, if my observation is to be trusted, eke out their incomes by selling horses to the younger ones. Usually, when the hunt is up, my sympathies are with the fox, and I have nothing but contemptuous indignation for its pursuers; but on this occasion the foxless cortège, as it clattered slowly along, comforting itself with flasks and sandwiches, was such a hopeless failure that I pitied it, and would have even provided it with a quarry had I possessed a spirited young tiger or other carnivorous animal able to bring out the manly qualities which are the pride of the sportsman. Had these hunters been wise, they would have satiated their destructive instincts by criticizing musical performances in town, and devoted their country holidays to benevolence and poetry.

There is a band in this place. Two little cornets, four baritone saxhorns, and a euphonium, all rather wasted for want of a competent person to score a few airs specially for them; for the four saxhorns all play the same part in unison instead of spreading themselves polyphonically over the desert between the cornets and the tuba. When their strains burst unexpectedly on my ear on Christmas Day, I supposed, until I went cautiously to the window to reconnoitre, that there were only three instruments instead of seven. With a parish organist to set this matter right for them, and a parish bandmaster to teach them a few simple rules of thumb as to the manipulation of their tuning-slides, the seven musicians would have discoursed excellent music. I submit that, pending the creation of a Ministry of Music, the Local Government Board should appoint District Surveyors of Brass Bands to look after these things. There are also carol singers; but of them I have nothing to say except that the first set, consisting of a few children, sang with great spirit a capital tune which I shall certainly steal when I turn my attention seriously to composition. The second set came very late, and had been so hospitably entertained at their previous performances that they had lost that clearness of intention and crispness of execution which no doubt distinguished their earlier efforts.

But the great event of the Penalt season was the concert. It was taken for granted that I, as an eminent London critic, would hold it in ineffable scorn; and it was even suggested that I should have the condescension to stay away. But, as it happened, I enjoyed it more than any native did, and that, too, not at all derisively, but because the concert was not only refreshingly different from the ordinary London miscellaneous article, but much better. The difference began with the adventurousness of the attempt to get there. There were no cabs, no omnibuses, no lamps, no policemen, no pavement, and, as it happened, no moon or stars. Fortunately, I have a delicate sense of touch in my boot-soles, and this enabled me to discriminate between road and common in the intervals of dashing myself against the gates which I knew I had to pass. At last I saw a glow in the darkness, and an elderly countryman sitting in it with an air of being indoors. He turned out to be the bureau, so to speak; and I was presently in the concert-room, which was much more interesting than St James's Hall, where there is nothing to look at except the pictures of mountain and glacier accidentally made—like faces in the fire—by the soot and dust in the ventilating lunettes in the windows. Even these are only visible at afternoon concerts. Here there was much to occupy and elevate the mind pending the appearance of the musicians: for instance, there was St Paul preaching at Athens after Raphael, and the death of General Wolfe after West, with a masonic-looking document which turned out to be the school time-table, an extensive display of flags and paraffin lamps, and an ingenious machine on the window-blind principle for teaching the children to add up sums of money of which the very least represented about eleven centuries of work and wages at current local rates. It presently appeared that the Penalt Musical Society had adopted one of the most advanced suggestions in Wagner's famous Dresden plan for the reformation of the theatre: to wit, the constitution of a Concert and Theatre department under the Minister

of Public Worship. In Penalt, accordingly, the music
was under the supreme control of the clergyman. He
was conductor, he was accompanist, he was *entrepre-
neur,* he was (in emergencies) leader of the choir, he
was chairman, he was master of the ceremonies, and
he had written and composed all the comic songs and
trios on local topics. He even mingled the politician
and sociologist with the composer—again reminding
one of Wagner in Dresden; for one of his compositions
dealt with the Parish Councils Bill, and another with
the recent coal difficulties. Furthermore, he had rehearsed the concert thoroughly; and this is the beginning and the end of true righteousness.

The program shewed how varied are the resources
of a country parish compared to the helplessness of a
town choked by the density and squalor of its own
population. We had glees—Hail, Smiling Morn, The
Belfry Tower, etc.—by no means ill sung. We had feats
of transcendent execution on the pianoforte, in the
course of which the Men of Harlech took arms against
a sea of variations, and, by opposing, ended them to
the general satisfaction. But it was from the performances of the individual vocalists that I received the
strongest sense that here, on the Welsh border, we were
among a naturally musical and artistic folk. From the
young lady of ten who sang When you and I were
young, to the robust farmer-comedians who gave the
facetious and topical interludes with frank enjoyment
and humor, and without a trace of the vulgarity which
is the heavy price we have to pay for professionalism
in music, the entertainment was a genuine and spon-
taneous outcome of the natural talent of the people.
The artists cost nothing: the pianoforte-tuner, the
printer, and the carpenter who fixed the platform can
have cost only a few shillings. Comparing the result
with certain "grand concerts" at St James's Hall, which
have cost hundreds of pounds, and left me in a con-

dition of the blankest pessimism as to the present and
future of music in England, I am bound to pronounce
the Penalt concert one of the most successful and encouraging of the year.

If I dared, I should proceed to criticize the singers
in detail. But only an experienced critic knows the
frightful danger of doing this. Everywhere alike, in the
most outlandish village and the greatest capital, amateur singers are the same—one incautious word of appreciation and they are off to study for the operatic
stage, abandoning all their real opportunities in life for
a doubtful chance of reaching that mirage which looks
like the Albert Hall and the Opera, but which is really
a huge casual ward of vagabonds and humbugs, whose
punishment for having attempted to make Art their
catspaw in snatching at riches and fame is perpetual
envy and disappointment. Let me, therefore, explicitly
forewarn all concerned that when I confess to having
been touched and charmed by some of the songs—nay,
to having caught a gleam of that "sacred fire" of which
we used to talk long ago in the performance of He
thinks I do not love him, and of Mr Blockley's old-fashioned setting of Tennyson's O swallow, swallow, I do
not mean that if the singers had been transferred from
the little schoolroom and the mild cottage-piano to the
stage of Covent Garden or the platform of St James's
Hall, with a full orchestra thundering round them, they
could have produced the same effect. Suffice it that
they did produce it in Penalt, and gave me thereby
greater pleasure than I often get from singers with far
greater pretensions. And in one respect their superiority was absolute as well as relative. All their voices
were unspoiled. They sang in low keys and used their
chest registers a good deal; but the moment the music
went above the natural range of that register they unaffectedly quitted it for the comparatively light and
unassertive, but sweet and pure falsetto. Need I add

that they were untaught, though they probably do not know how heartily they are to be congratulated on that fact. One lady, who sang modern drawing room ballads by Stephen Adams and Weatherly, rather alarmed me at first by a very effective use of her lower notes, as if she were determined to rival Miss Mackenzie. Not that I objected to her using them effectively, but I feared that she would presently try to force that rich quality of tone all over her voice. But no: she also was content to have that quality only where Nature gave it to her; and when the concert was over and we all plunged again into the black void without, where we jostled one another absurdly in our efforts to find the way home, I had quite made up my mind to advise all our fashionable teachers of singing to go to the singers of Penalt, consider their ways, and be wise.

10 January 1894

As Far as Greenwich

Last Saturday evening, feeling the worse for want of change and country air, I happened to voyage in the company of Mr William Archer as far as Greenwich. Hardly had we inhaled the refreshing ozone of that place for ninety seconds when, suddenly finding ourselves opposite a palatial theatre, gorgeous with a million gaslights, we felt that it was idiotic to have been to Wagner's Theatre at Bayreuth and yet be utterly ignorant concerning Morton's Theatre at Greenwich. So we rushed into the struggling crowd at the doors, only to be informed that the theatre was full. Stalls full; dress circle full; pit, standing room only. As Archer, in self-defence, habitually sleeps during performances, and is subject to nightmare when he sleeps standing, the pit was out of the question. Was there room anywhere, we asked. Yes, in a private box or in the gallery. Which was the cheaper? The gallery, decidedly. So up we went to the gallery, where we found two precarious perches vacant at the side. It was rather like trying to see Trafalgar Square from the knifeboard of an omnibus half-way up St Martin's Lane; but by hanging on to a stanchion, and occasionally standing with one foot on the seat and the other on the backs of the people in the front row, we succeeded in seeing as much of the entertainment as we could stand.

The first thing we did was to purchase a bill, which informed us that we were in for "the entirely original pastoral comedy-opera in three acts, by B. C. Stephenson and Alfred Cellier, entitled Dorothy, which has been played to crowded houses at the Lyric Theatre, London, 950 and (still playing) in the provinces 788 times." This playbill, I should add, was thoughtfully decorated with a view of the theatre showing all the exits, for use in the event of the performance proving unbearable. From it we further learnt that we should be regaled by an augmented and powerful orchestra; that the company was "Leslie's No. 1"; that C. J. Francis believes he is now the only HATTER in the county of Kent who exists on the profits arising solely from the sale of HATS and CAPS; and so on. Need I add that Archer and I sat bursting with expectation until the overture began.

I cannot truthfully say that the augmented and powerful orchestra proved quite so augmented or so powerful as the composer could have wished; but let that pass: I disdain the cheap sport of breaking a daddy-long-legs on a wheel (butterfly is out of the question, it was such a dingy band). My object is rather to call attention to the condition to which 788 nights of Dorothying have reduced the unfortunate wanderers known as "Leslie's No. 1." I submit to Mr Leslie that in his own interest he should take better care of No. 1. Here are several young persons doomed to spend the flower of their years in mechanically

repeating the silliest libretto in modern theatrical literature, set to music which, pretty as it is, must pall somewhat on the seven hundred and eighty-eighth performance.

As might have been expected, a settled weariness of
life, an utter perfunctoriness, an unfathomable inanity
pervaded the very souls of "No. 1." The tenor, originally, I have no doubt, a fine young man, but now
cherubically adipose, was evidently counting the days
until death should release him from the part of Wilder.
He had a pleasant speaking voice; and his affability
and forbearance were highly creditable to him under
the circumstances; but Nature rebelled in him against
the loathed strains of a seven-hundred-times-repeated
rôle. He omitted the song in the first act, and sang
Though Born a Man of High Degree as if with the
last rally of an energy decayed and a willing spirit
crushed. The G at the end was a vocal earthquake.
And yet methought he was not displeased when the
inhabitants of Greenwich, coming fresh to the slaugh-
ter, encored him.

The baritone had been affected the other way: he
was thin and worn; and his clothes had lost their lustre.
He sang *Queen of My Heart* twice in a hardened manner, as one who was prepared to sing it a thousand
times in a thousand quarter hours for a sufficient wa-
ger. The comic part, being simply that of a circus clown
transferred to the lyric stage, is better suited for infinite repetition; and the gentleman who undertook it
addressed a comic lady called Priscilla as Sarsaparilla
during his interludes between the *haute-école* acts of
the prima donna and tenor, with a delight in the rare
aroma of the joke, and in the roars of laughter it
elicited, which will probably never pall. But anything
that he himself escaped in the way of tedium was
added tenfold to his unlucky colleagues, who sat out
his buffooneries with an expression of deadly malig-

nity. I trust the gentleman may die in his bed; but he would be unwise to build too much on doing so. There is a point at which tedium becomes homicidal mania. The ladies fared best. The female of the human species has not yet developed a conscience: she will apparently spend her life in artistic self-murder by induced Dorothitis without a pang of remorse, provided she be praised and paid regularly. Dorothy herself, a beauteous young lady of distinguished mien, with an immense variety of accents ranging from the finest Tunbridge Wells English (for genteel comedy) to the broadest Irish (for repartee and low comedy), sang without the slightest effort and without the slightest point, and was all the more desperately vapid because she suggested artistic gifts wasting in complacent abeyance. Lydia's voice, a hollow and spectral contralto, alone betrayed the desolating effect of perpetual Dorothy: her figure retains a pleasing plumpness akin to that of the tenor; and her spirits were wonderful, all things considered. The chorus, too, seemed happy; but that was obviously because they did not know any better. The pack of hounds darted in at the end of the second act evidently full of the mad hope of finding something new going on; and their depression, when they discovered it was Dorothy again, was pitiable. The S.P.C.A. should interfere. If there is no law to protect men and women from Dorothy, there is at least one that can be strained to protect dogs.

I did not wait for the third act. My companion had several times all but fallen into the pit from sleep and heaviness of spirit combined; and I felt as if I were playing Geoffrey Wilder for the millionth night. As we moped homeward in the moonlight we brooded over what we had seen. Even now I cannot think with composure of the fact that they are playing Dorothy tonight again—will play it tomorrow—next year—next decade—next century. I do not know what the average lifetime of a member of "No. 1" may be; but I do not think it can exceed five years from the date of joining; so there is no question here of old men and old women playing it with white hair beneath their wigs and deep furrows underlying their make-up. Doubtless they do not die on the stage: they first become mad and are removed to an asylum, where they incessantly sing, One, two, three: one, two, three: one, two, three: one, two, be wi-eyes in, ti-I'm oh, Ph-ill is, mine, etc., until the King of Terrors (who ought to marry Dorothy) mercifully seals their tortured ears for ever.

I have always denounced the old-fashioned stock company, and laughed to scorn the theorists who fancy that they saw in them a training school for actors; but I never bargained for such a thing as this 789th performance of Dorothy. No: it is a criminal waste of young lives and young talents; and though it may for a time make more money for Mr Leslie, yet in the end it leaves him with a worn-out opera and a parcel of untrained novices on his hands when he might have a repertory of at least half a dozen works and a company of fairly-skilled artists able to play them at a day's notice. We exclaim at the dock directors' disregard of laborers' bodies; but what shall we say of the managers' disregard of artists' souls. Ti, rum ti ty, rum ti ty, rum ti ty, rum m m: tiddy tum tiddy tum tiddity, tum! Heavens! what hum I? Be wi-eyes in—Malediction!

13 September 1889

Diction

One day when I was expatiating to a friend on the importance of teaching people to speak well, he asked me dubiously whether I did not find that most men became humbugs when they learnt elocution. I could not deny it. The elocutionary man is the most insufferable of human beings. But I do not want anybody to become elocutionary. If your face is not clean, wash it: don't cut your head off. If your diction is slipshod and impure, correct and purify it: don't throw it away and make shift for the rest of your life with a hideous affectation of platformy accent, false emphases, unmeaning pauses, aggravating slowness, ill-conditioned gravity, and perverse resolution to "get it from the chest" and make it sound as if you got it from the cellar. Of course, if you are a professional humbug—a bishop or a judge, for instance—then the case is different; for the salary makes it seem worth your while to dehumanize yourself and pretend to belong to a different species. But under ordinary circumstances you had better simply educate your ear until you are fairly skilful at phonetics, and leave the rest to your good sense.

The above remarks express indirectly but unmistakably that I have just been to a students' concert at the Guildhall School of Music. I claim the right to measure the Guildhall School by a high standard. Your "Royal" Academies and Colleges do not appeal to me: I am a Republican, and cannot understand how any person with an adequate sense of humor can consent to have a crown stuck on his head at this time of day. But the Guildhall School is our civic school; and the time is coming when that term will have some real significance in London. Already the young savages and Philistines of the commercial classes crowd thither, and leave the private teacher lamenting and penniless. Now, the first thing that the savages and Philistines need to be taught is the art of speech. A finely skilled professor of diction would be cheap at a thousand a year at the Guildhall School. Fancy my feelings when I found that there is no such functionary in the place.

Doubtless this will strike the teaching staff as unfair. But I did not fail to perceive that the unfortunate pupils had been drilled and drummed into articulating their consonants clearly. When they came to an Italian

T or D, in forming which the tongue makes an air-tight junction with the teeth until the consonant explodes, they conscientiously tucked up their tongues against their palates in true British fashion and brought out their native T or D much as a Sheffield hydraulic piston would, with plenty of hissing. Such a sound as this, followed by a racy Brixton or Bradford diphthong, produces an effect in an Italian song of the old school that would make a vivisector's mouth water. Imagine a young lady sent out by her master to sing Handel's *Lascia ch'io pianga* without a word to warn her that the reiterated "e che sospire" is not pronounced "Ayee Kayee Soaspearayee." I forbear further illustration. The subject is too painful. Suffice it to say, that if Mr Tito Pagliardini were to hear an air by Stradella or Pergolesi uttered by a Guildhall pupil, he would rush from the building across the Embankment, and bury the horrid memory in the Lethean Thames.

Yet diction is not one of the lost arts. Coquelin does not speak in the Guildhall manner; nor Salvini, nor Joseph Jefferson, nor Henry Irving, nor Ada Rehan, nor Antoinette Sterling, nor Mrs Weldon, nor dozens of other speakers and singers. And remember that, though the public is not an expert, and cannot place its finger on the exact details in which the Guildhall novices differ from these finished artists, yet it hears a difference, though it mercilessly ascribes it to native vulgarity on the one hand and native distinction on the other. But it is absurd to brand young singers as vulgar because they, having spent their lives between the City and Holloway, know no other mode of speech than that which is vernacular in those regions. Half a dozen early lessons in phonetics from someone who knew at least a little about them—not necessarily a Mus. Bac. or Mus. Doc.—would set them in the right way.

Such teachers are to be found, if the Guildhall authorities care to find them. On Saturday last I received an invitation to the Albert Hall from a Mr P. J. Kirwan, who is doubtless a well-known reciter, but of whom I had never heard until that day. I found him to be an artistic speaker with a cultivated voice and a tact in comedy that enabled him to pass off all his humorous selections at about six times their literary value. His delivery of Drayton's Agincourt was most musical, though here and there the legitimate mark of the school of Mr Irving intensified into illegitimate Irvingism. One of Mr Irving's objectionable peculiarities is a trick of spoiling a vowel occurring between m and n, by continuing the humming sound of these letters through it instead of letting it flash out clearly between them. Thus his "man" or "men" becomes a monstrosity, which Mr Kirwan has picked up. Again, Mr Irving's "oo" varies from French "eu" to English "aw"; and Mr Kirwan, in pronouncing "fury" as "fieurie" or "fyawry" clearly slips into a mere imitation. Nor is he wholly guiltless of unmeaning pauses. "Along that wild and weatherbeaten coast" cannot reasonably be read as "Along that wild and weatherbeaten. Coast." Similarly, the difference between "And did the deed for ever to be sung" and "And did the deed for ever to be. Sung" is the difference between sense and nonsense.

Whilst I am in the way of faultfinding, I may as well say that I protest altogether against the Reciter's theory that verse should be disguised as prose in its oral delivery. All poets read their verses sing-song, which is the right way: else why the deuce should they be at the trouble of writing in verse at all?

7 February 1890

La Vie Parisienne

I am strongly of opinion that the Channel Tunnel should be proceeded with at once. There are worse things than foreign invasions, worse things even than

foreign conquest, worse things than the extinction of
England as a nation, if you come to that. I came over
yesterday morning from Calais; and—but enough! The
subject is not dignified; and it is hackneyed. All I will
say is, that never again whilst I live—and yet I have
made the same vow before, and broken it. Still, do not
suppose that that silver streak of which you are so
proud does not cost you something in the way of Continental musical news in the course of the year. But
for it, The Star would be as great a musical power in
Europe as it is in England.

Paris is, as usual, imposing on American greenhorns
and British Philistines as a city artistic before everything, with specialities in cookery and well-dressed
women. I am not an artistic novice, English or American; and I am not to be taken in. Paris is what it has
always been: a pedant-ridden failure in everything
that it pretends to lead. Mozart found it so more than
a hundred years ago: Wagner found it so half a century ago: Corno di Bassetto regrets to say that he finds
it so today. In music, it prides itself on its Opera, which
is about twenty years behind Covent Garden; and
Covent Garden, as everybody knows, is thirty years behind time: even New York leaving it nowhere. I went
to the Paris Opera on Monday to fulfil my mission of
hearing Saint-Saëns' new opera Ascanio. I need not
waste many words on the music of it. There is not an
original phrase in it from beginning to end. The tragic
scenes are secondhand Verdi; the love scenes are secondhand Gounod; the "historic" scenes are secondhand
Meyerbeer. A duller potboiler I would not desire to
hear anywhere. The orchestra is hardly better than the
Covent Garden orchestra was in the seventies, before
we got tired of the Gye-Mapleson managements that
learned nothing and forgot nothing, and passed
Vianesi, the conductor, on to Paris, where his immense
industry, his cleverness, his ostentation, and his thor-

ough superficiality enabled him to take root at once.
Vianesi looks younger than ever, and is still on the alert
for opportunities of turning conspicuously to the wood
wind and brass, and offering them superfluous leads to
shew how completely he has the score at his finger-
ends; whilst the men have cultivated his slapdash,
noisy style—or want of style—to the highest imperfection.

As to the singers, there is Lassalle, who brings down
the house in a roaring duet with the tenor in the second
act, and moves it to sentimental admiration in a mock
pathetic passage in the fourth, beginning, *"Enfants: je
ne vous en veux pas."* Lassalle can hardly believe in the
part of Benvenuto Cellini; but he believes immensely
in Lassalle, and so manages to make things go with an
effective air of conviction. Madame Adiny is undeniably what we call a fine figure of a woman; but her
tremolo and her superb screaming power leave in the
shade even the lady who played Desdemona here in
Verdi's Otello at the Lyceum last year. Plançon, as
Francis I, and Madame Eames, as Colombe, sang
pleasantly enough; and I have no right to find fault
with Madame Bosman as a capable if not highly distinguished representative of the old-fashioned type of
"dramatic" singer, merely because I object to the entire species. The acting was the old impossible Rich-
ardson's Show strutting and swaggering, pitiful to see;
and the libretto, like the music, was a string of commonplaces, culminating in Madame Adiny keeping
Madame Bosman in a golden shrine in a public room
for three days, at the expiry of which Madame Bosman
was found dead "for Benvenuto's sake," which was the
more affecting inasmuch as there was not the smallest reason why she should have got into the shrine in
the first place or forborne to call on somebody to let
her out in the second.

On the whole, I am afraid I must dismiss Ascanio

as an elaborate and expensive tomfoolery, and applaud the wisdom of those frequenters who came only for the ballet, which, though artificial as it well could be— classical, in short—was good of its kind. Yet Ascanio bored me less than Barbier's Joan of Arc at the Porte St Martin, with Gounod's music, and Sarah Bernhardt in the title part. Barbier, as everybody knows, is the man to go to if you want a great subject debased for operatic purposes. He can turn a masterpiece by Shakespear or Goethe into a trashy melodrama in the twinkling of an eye. He fell on Joan of Arc years ago and fixed her up (no other expression conveys the process) for the Gaieté. Now she is dragged to light again with considerable excisions—all heartily welcome—for Madame Bernhardt. In the music, Gounod imitates himself almost as mechanically as Saint-Saëns, and more exclusively. The best number is the vision of St Margaret and St Catherine. Even now, when his fount runs yet drier than in the last decade, Gounod can always write heavenly music. But Sarah is really too bad. We all know her way of pretending to act when there is no part for her—how sweetly she intones her lines and poses like a saint. This is what she does in Joan. There is no acting because there is no play; but she sends the lines out in a plaintive stream of melody throughout which only a fine ear can catch the false ring. You would almost swear that they meant something and that she was in earnest. Not until the final scene at the stake does the affair become thin enough for even the American and British tripper to see through it. Sarah did not wink once: perhaps because she did not catch my eye, perhaps because she was in no humor for making fun of herself. It must be wearisome to keep up that make-believe night after night, knowing all the time that her serious work is going on without her at the Français.

Of course, I went to the Français for the sake of the

traditions of the house of Molière, and found them to consist of equal parts of gag and horseplay, in no way superior—distinctly the contrary, in fact—to those established only the other day in Mr Benson's company for Hamlet and The Taming of the Shrew. But if the traditions are feeble, the acting is not; and not many things are more enjoyable than an Easter Monday afternoon performance of Le Bourgeois Gentilhomme by the Comédie Française. Monsieur Jourdain can only be enjoyed in Paris, because he is himself bourgeois Paris incarnate. When the play is over you can continue your study of his flunkeyism in his petrified Lord-Mayor's-coach of an opera house; his helpless incapacity for art, and consequent subjection to any pedant who will talk to him about something that he can understand (something quite beside the purpose of art, necessarily) in the Louvre; and his petty rationalism and delight in unreasonable scraps of logic anywhere you please. If I ever take to playwriting (one never knows how low one may fall) I shall do a London Bourgeois Gentilhomme—quite as curious a creature in his way.

However, my main business here is not with the Comédie Française, but with a certain "Soirée Musicale et Littéraire du Vendredi Saint" at the Winter Circus. The sensation here was the appearance of the divine Sarah in a divine character—that of the Virgin Mary, no less. She did more than this, however: she doubled her part with that of Mary Magdalen. Philippe Garnier confined himself to the leading character of Jesus; and Brémont compendiously undertook Pilate, Annas, Caiaphas, Peter, and Judas Iscariot. The work was described as "a mystery in five parts" by Edmond Haraucourt, and was entitled The Passion. A large dose of Berlioz, Beethoven, and Wagner was administered first to get us into the proper frame of mind; and then the mystery began. Sarah, in a dress of the purest, softest white, and with her complexion made up with really exquisite delicacy into a faint blush that could hardly have been more virginal, was well received. The Passion began amid a hush of expectation, and soon proved to be fully equal in depth of thought and novelty of illustration to our finest specimens of modern oratorio libretti. Sarah sang—sung as usual, holding the book in her right hand and waving her left in the air with a rhythmic persuasiveness that did wonders in soothing the distressing cough that soon became epidemic. On the whole the audience bore up bravely until Garnier rose to deliver a sort of Sermon on the Mount some forty minutes long. In quarter of an hour or so the coughing took a new tone: it became evident that the more impatient spirits were beginning to cough on purpose, though their lungs were as sound as Garnier's own. Then came a voice crying "Music, music," followed by applause, laughter, and some faint protest. Garnier went on, as if deaf. Presently another voice, in heartfelt appeal, cried, "Enough, enough." The reception of this was unmistakably sympathetic; and Sarah's shoulders gathered themselves expressively; but Garnier held on like grim death; and again the audience held their hand for a moment on the chance of his presently stopping; for it seemed impossible that he could go on much longer. But he did; and the storm broke at last all the more furiously because it had been so long pent up. In the midst of it a gentleman rushed down the grades of the amphitheatre; crossed the arena; and shook hands demonstratively with Sarah, then Garnier, then with Brémont. This was Haraucourt himself; and he capped his protest by shaking his fist at the audience, who reiterated their fundamental disagreement with him on the merits of his poem by yells of disapproval. Hereupon, exasperated beyond endurance, he took the extreme step of informing them that if they persisted in their behavior he would there and then leave the room. The threat prevailed. An awe-struck silence fell upon the multitude: and the poet was moving loftily towards his seat when a lady, presumably his wife, threw herself on his neck and rained kisses on him. This affecting spectacle moved the gentlemen in the neighborhood to offer him their hands, which he took in an impressive attitude. Then he sat down; and the imperturbable Garnier started again. But soon the conviction spread that even at the risk of Haraucourt fulfilling his terrible threat, the speech must be stopped. Garnier, whose demeanor throughout was a model of perfect taste, at last exchanged glances with his colleagues, and then with the politest deprecation began: "Ladies and gentlemen: if you don't wish it"—whereupon the people in the arena expressed their opinion that the conduct of the five franc snobs was disgraceful, and the snobs in question vehemently gave Garnier to understand that there was no "if" at all in the question—that they didn't wish it and wouldn't have it. Sarah, in lively pantomime, conveyed her thanks to the arena; but I could not help suspecting that she was privately of the gallery's opinion. At last the three artists held a consultation, at the end of which Garnier sat down, and Sarah started at a scene only a few pages from the end. The audience accepted the compromise; Haraucourt made no further protest except by applauding occasionally; and the remainder of The Passion was dispatched without further interruption.

The anti-Wagner party was present in full force. It consists of six old gentlemen, more or less like the Duke of Cambridge in personal appearance, who make faces and stop their ears whenever an unprepared major ninth occurs in the harmony. As the audience was some thousands strong, and enthusiastically opposed to the veterans, they did not make much headway. Wagner always maintained that the great Tannhäuser fiasco

was a success with the gallery; and there is no serious
reason to doubt that he was right. Lamoureux's orchestra played with refinement and precision; but the first
movement of the C minor symphony was taken in the
old empty, hurried, vapidly elegant way; and in the
overture to Tannhäuser the brass, reinforced by two extra cornets and a fourth trombone (a monstrous li-
cense), played like a coarse cavalry band, and blared
out the Pilgrims' March in a most detestable manner,
making the famous violin figure quite inaudible. One
moral of which is that London, which declined to accept Lamoureux as a great conductor, and took Richter
to its bosom, is as far ahead of Paris in musical judgment as in most other things.

11 April 1890

The Popular Dramatist

I can only describe L'Enfant Prodigue, at the Prince
of Wales's, as touching. I was touched when I laughed
no less than when I retired in tears at the end of the
third act. But my emotion was not caused by the music.
That is simply conventional French ballet music and
mélodrame, elegantly fitted with all the latest harmonic
refinements. And I must add that if the piece is going
to have anything like the vogue here which it enjoyed
at the Bouffes Parisiens, M. André Wormser had better
lose no time in rescoring it for a full band. Accompaniments played by a pianist and eked out by a handful
of wind-players and a string quartet are tolerated in
Paris, where you will see Offenbach's operas treated
in this way even at the Eden Theatre; but here such
makeshifts stamp a performance as cheap and provincial, and that, too, on good artistic grounds.

For the rest of this most entertaining dumb show I
have nothing but praise. The service rendered by the
music in making the drama intelligible is not great:

there is only one point which would not be as intelligible to a deaf man as it was to me. That was the stipulation made by Phrynette that the Baron must marry her, a point which could easily be conveyed by pantomime, but which was more concisely and amusingly intimated by the introduction of the opening strain of Mendelssohn's wedding march in the orchestra. And nothing could be funnier or more felicitous than the humorous allusion to the same theme when the Baron is left alone. His shake of the head, accompanied by that mocking little scherzando, tells, better than the most elaborate pantomime could without music, that he has not the smallest intention of keeping his promise.

In estimating the value of these eulogies, it must be remembered that although the satisfaction of seeing a simple thing consummately well done is most joyful and soothing after a long and worrying course of complex things imperfectly done, the simple success must not therefore be placed above the complex half success. A drama consisting of a series of emotions, so obvious in their provocation and so conventional in their sequence that they can be made intelligible to a general audience by pure phenomena is child's play compared to ordinary drama, or opera, although no actor can venture upon it without a degree of skill in pantomime which most speakers and singers think (erroneously) that they can afford to do without. This much being admitted, I may safely proceed to say that on the chance occasions when I descend from the opera house to the theatre I am often made to feel acutely that the play would be much more enjoyable if the dialogue were omitted. To me the popular dramatist always appears as a sympathetic, kindly, emotional creature, able to feel and to imagine in a pleasantly simple and familiar groove, but almost destitute of intellect, and therefore unable to think or to write. Whilst he is merely emotioning he is the best of good company for an easygoing hour of sentimental relaxation; but the moment he opens his mouth he becomes insufferable; you feel like the policeman in one of Wilkie Collins's novels, who, when the butler collared him, could only say patiently, "You don't know how to do it in the least." If the *dramatis personæ* would only love and languish and storm and despair in dumb show and "do it beautifully," as Hedda Gabler enjoined upon her lover when he consented to shoot himself, then all the valuable parts of the play would be brought into full prominence, and all the rubbish eliminated. L'Enfant Prodigue proves triumphantly that this is quite practicable. Therefore, to those well-known dramatists of ours who have immense hearts but no brains worth mentioning—I cannot give names, as I never know one from the other, the drama not being my regular department—I most earnestly recommend the adoption of the dumb show form in future. Let them, as Hegel would have said, remain in the stage of consciousness without attempting to advance to that of scientific understanding. Or, as someone else actually has said—I forget who; but it was not Hegel—let them "cut the cackle, and come to the 'osses."

8 *April 1891*

Incidental Music

I have seldom been more astonished than I was last week, when the manager of the Haymarket Theatre offered me an opportunity of hearing the music which Mr Henschel has just composed for Hamlet. Not only had I never heard of a tragedian regarding incidental music as having any interest separable in the remotest degree from his own performance, or as being a less mechanical part of that than the last touch of paint or limelight, but I had been brought up to believe that

Hamlet in its natural state consisted musically of the march from Judas Maccabæus for the entry of the Court, and the Dead March in Saul for Hamlet's death, the *entr'actes* being selected from no longer popular overtures such as La Sirène, etc. My opinion of Mr Tree consequently rose to such a pitch as to all but defeat the object of my visit to the last rehearsal; for instead of listening to Mr Henschel's interludes, I spent the intervals in explaining to Mr Tree exactly how his part ought to be played, he listening with the patience and attention which might be expected from so accomplished an actor. However, I heard enough with one ear to serve my purpose.

What Mr Henschel has done with his opportunity cannot be described off-hand to those who have never thought over the position of the composer in the theatre. For him there are two extremes. One is to assume the full dignity of the creative musician, and compose an independent overture which, however sympathetic it may be with the impending drama, nevertheless takes the forms proper to pure music, and is balanced and finished as a beautiful and symmetrical fabric of sounds, performable as plain Opus 1000 apart from the drama, as satisfactorily as the drama is performable apart from it. Example: Egmont, in which Beethoven and Goethe associate as peers in their diverse arts, Beethoven not merely illustrating Goethe's masterpiece, but adding a masterpiece of his own on the same subject. The other extreme is to supply bare *mélodrame*, familiar samples of which may be found in the ethereal strains from muted violins which accompany the unfolding of transformation scenes in pantomimes, the animated measures which enliven the rallies in the harlequinade, or the weird throbbings of the ghost melody in The Corsican Brothers.

The production of these is not musical composition:

it is mere musical tailoring, in the course of which the *mélodrame* is cut and made to the measure of the stage business, and altered by snipping or patching when it comes to be tried on at rehearsal. The old-fashioned actor got his practical musical education in this way; and he will tell you that certain speeches are easy to speak "through music" and frightfully hard without it; or, as Richard III, he will work himself up to the requisite pitch of truculence in the "Who intercepts me in my expedition?" scene, partly by listening to the trumpets, and partly by swearing at them for not playing louder.

Beyond this he is so untutored that he will unhesitatingly call upon the *chef d'orchestra* to "stop that music" in the very middle of a suspension, or with a promising first inversion of the common chord, or on a dominant seventh or the like, quite unconscious of the risk of some musician rising in the theatre on the first night and saying, "I beg your pardon for interrupting you, sir; but will you kindly ask the band to resolve that four-to-three before you proceed with your soliloquy?" The idea that music is written in sentences with full stops at the end of them, just as much as dramatic poetry is, does not occur to him: all he knows is that he cannot make the audience shudder or feel sentimental without music, exactly as the comedian knows that he cannot make the audience laugh unless the lights are full on. And the music man at the theatre seldom counts for more than a useful colleague of the gas man.

This state of things at last gives way to evolutionary forces like other states of things. The rage for culture opens a career for cultivated men (not merely cultivated players) as theatrical managers and actors; and the old-fashioned actors and managers find themselves compelled by stress of competition to pose as con-

noisseurs in all the arts, and to set up Medicean reti-
nues of literary advisers, poets, composers, artists,
archæologists, and even critics. And whenever a masterpiece of dramatic literature is revived, the whole
retinue is paraded. Now the very publicity of the parade makes it impossible for the retinue to be too ser-
vile: indeed, to the full extent to which it reflects lustre
on the manager can it also insist on having a voice in
the artistic conduct of his enterprises.

Take the composer, for instance. No actor-manager
could tell Sir Arthur Sullivan to "stop that music," or
refuse to allow Mr Henschel to resolve his discords.
On the other hand, no manager will engage an orchestra of from eighty to a hundred performers for an overture and *entr'actes;* and no actor will sacrifice any of
the effectiveness of his business in order to fit it to the
music; whilst at the same time the actor-manager ex-
pects all the most modern improvements in the way
of "leading motives," which make excellent material
for press-cuttings. The situation being thus limited, the
composer submits to become a musical tailor as far as
the *mélodrame* is concerned, but throws over the
manager completely in the overture and *entr'actes* by
composing them with a view to performance as "an
orchestral suite" at the Crystal Palace or London
Symphony concerts, laying himself out frankly for a
numerous orchestra and a silent audience, instead of
for a theatre band contending feebly with the chatter
of the dramatic critics. Clearly he might venture
upon a great overture like Egmont or Coriolan but
for the modern improvements—the leading motives
—which are an implied part of his contract. The tragedian must have his motive; and the leading lady, even
when she is not the most influential person in the
theatre, is allowed to have one also as a foil to the
tragedian's. Macduff, Richmond, and Laertes will soon

advance their claims, which are obviously no more valid than those of high-reaching Buckingham, Duncan, Polonius, and Claudius.

Mark my words: as actors come to understand these things better, we shall have such scenes at rehearsal as have never before been witnessed in a theatre— Rosencrantz threatening to throw up his part because his motive is half a bar shorter than Guildenstern's; the Ghost claiming, on Mozart's authority, an absolute monopoly of the trombones; Hamlet asking the composer, with magnificent politeness, whether he would mind doubling the basses with a contrafagotto in order to bring out the Inky Cloak theme a little better; Othello insisting on being in the bass and Olivia on being in the treble when their themes are worked simultaneously with those of Iago and Viola, and the wretched composer finally writing them all in double counterpoint in order that each may come uppermost or undermost by turns.

Pending these developments our composers lean towards compromise between the leading motive system and the old symphonic form. At first sight a double deal seems easy enough. Use your bold Richard motive or your tragic Hamlet motive as the first subject in your overture, with the feminine Ophelia theme as the second subject ("happily contrasted," as the analytic programist is sure to say if he is a friend of yours), and then proceed in orthodox form. Unfortunately, when this formula comes to the proof, you find that a leading motive is one thing and a symphonic subject another, and that they can no more replace one another than drawings of human figures in dramatic action can replace arabesques. It is true that human figures can be expressed by curved lines, as arabesques are; and there are arabesques composed of human figures, just as there are pictures in which the figures are decorations. In the hands of the greatest

masters the success of the combination of decorative
and dramatic seems complete, because every departure from perfect grace and symmetry produces a
dramatic interest so absorbing that the spectator feels
a heightened satisfaction instead of a deficiency.

But take a picture in which the epic and dramatic
elements have been wrought to the highest pitch—say
Ford Madox Brown's Lear and Cordelia—and contrast
it with a shutter decorated by Giovanni da Udine.
Imagine Giovanni trying to tell the story of Lear in his
own way as convincingly as Madox Brown has told it,
or Madox Brown attempting to give his picture the
symmetry of Giovanni's shutter. The contrast at once
reveals the hollowness of the stock professorial precept
about uniting the highest qualities of both schools,
which is seen to mean no more than that a man may
reasonably prefer Tintoretto's Annunciation in the
Scuola di San Rocco because the flight of angels shoot-
ing in through the window is more graceful than
Giovanni's designs, whilst the story of the virgin is as
well told as that of Cordelia. But in subjects where
flights of angels are unworkable, Tintoretto had, like
Brown, to fall back on qualities of beauty not in the
least arabesque.

Bring up a critic exclusively on such qualities, and
he will find Giovanni vapidly elegant, empty, and
artificial; whereas if you nurse him exclusively on
arabesque he will recoil from Madox Brown as being
absolutely ugly and uncouth. In fact, though Madox
Brown is no less obviously the greatest living English
epic painter than Mr Burne-Jones is the greatest decorative painter, his friends are at present collecting a
thousand pounds to get him out of pecuniary difficulties which are no fault of his own, but a consequence
of the nation being still too exclusively addicted to
arabesques and pretty sentimentalities. Just as pictorial story-telling, having a different purpose from ara-

besque, has necessarily a different constructive logic,
and consequently must seek a different beauty; so the
dramatic composer must proceed differently from the
composer of absolute music. If he tries to walk with
one foot in each way, he may be as fine a musician as
Sterndale Bennett was, and yet not be safe from producing futilities like Paradise and the Peri.

Take, for example, the overture to Richard III,
which Mr Edward German, a musician of considerable
talent, composed for Mr Mansfield. In this work the
first subject begins as a genuine Richard motive; but
in order to adapt it to sonata treatment it is furnished
with an arabesque tail, like a crookbacked mermaid,
with the result that the piece is too clumsy to be a
good overture, and yet too trivially shapely to be a
fitting tone symbol of Richard III. It is far surpassed
by Grieg's Peer Gynt music, which consists of two or
three catchpenny phrases served up with plenty of
orchestral sugar, at a cost in technical workmanship
much smaller than that lavished on Mr German's overture. But the catchpenny phrases are sufficiently to the
point of the scenes they introduce, and develop—if
Grieg's repetitions can be called development—according to the logic of those scenes and not according
to that of Haydn's symphonies. In fact, Grieg proceeded as Wagner proceeded in his great preludes,
except that, being only a musical grasshopper in comparison with the musical giant of Bayreuth, he could
only catch a few superficial points in the play instead
of getting to the very heart and brain of it.

Mr Henschel has wisely taken the same course,
avoiding arabesques, and sticking to the play and
nothing but the play throughout, except in one passage where he casts the oboe for the part of "the cock
that is the trumpet [not the oboe] to the morn." This
bird is usually *persona muta;* and Mr Henschel had
better have left him so. Save in this one bar, the *mélo-*

drame is the simplest and most effective I can remember. Then there are preludes—Hamlet tragic but irresolute for Act I, Ophelia a trifle gushing for Act II, Hamlet ferocious and deaf to Ophelia's blandishments for Act III, Dirge for the Drowning for Act IV, and Pastorale (with real birds) for Act V. Of all which I shall have more to say when I hear them in full orchestral panoply at the postponed London Symphony concert. For the present, suffice it to say that they go deeper than Grieg, besides confining themselves, as aforesaid, strictly to their own business, without any digressions into arabesque.

27 January 1892

Paderewski

By the time I reached Paderewski's concert on Tuesday last week, his concerto was over, the audience in wild enthusiasm, and the pianoforte a wreck. Regarded as an immensely spirited young harmonious blacksmith, who puts a concerto on the piano as upon an anvil, and hammers it out with an exuberant enjoyment of the swing and strength of the proceeding, Paderewski is at least exhilarating; and his hammer-play is not without variety, some of it being feathery, if not delicate. But his touch, light or heavy, is the touch that hurts; and the glory of his playing is the glory that attends murder on a large scale when impetuously done. Besides, the piano is not an instrument upon which you can safely let yourself go in this fashion.

18 June 1890

It is greatly to be desired, however, that some skilful surgeon should dexterously split Paderewski into two separate persons—Paderewski the composer and Pade-

rewski the pianist. At present they interfere with one
another constantly. The pianist no sooner gets excited
by the orchestra than he says to the composer, "I understand, I'll do it for you. Leave it all to me," and
takes the matter into his own itching fingers. At such
moments the composer, if he were split off as I suggest, could say, "Do hold your noise. Do you suppose
I am going to reduce my grand passages to a mere
paroxysm of banging and clattering on your box
of wires merely because you cant keep your hands
quiet?"

The fact is, Paderewski, though he writes for the orchestra with excellent judgment, shews the deafest
partiality when he comes to write for the pianoforte.
He cannot deny it a lion's share in all the good things,
whether they suit it or not; and the result is that in
most of the big climaxes he is making such a thundering noise that he cannot hear the orchestra, whilst the
orchestra is making such a thundering noise that the
audience cannot hear him, and can only gaze raptly
at the inspiring spectacle of his fists flying in the air
as he trounces the keyboard. He had much better use
a big drum for such emergencies: the sensation of
playing it would be equally exhilarating; the fingering
would be easier; and everybody would hear it. There
is another technical consideration which I must urge if
I am to concede the desirability of developing the
capacity of the pianoforte as an orchestral instrument
to the utmost.

In that case, I submit that one pianoforte is not
enough to cover the ground. When Paderewski writes
horn parts in his scores he not only employs four instruments, so as to be able to sound four horn-notes
simultaneously if necessary: he also divides the four
into two pairs, each of diverse range and quality of
tone, so that his first horn-player can produce one set
of notes and effects, and his fourth another. Now the

pianoforte, as used by Paderewski, is an instrument highly specialized for his use so as to produce the utmost lightness, swiftness, and precision of action; and it so happens that an excess of these qualities can only be gained at the cost of richness and softness of tonecolor. Paderewski's pianos are made by Erard; but the ordinary Erard grands used by people who are not Paderewskis are much more delightful instruments, though the mechanical difference is probably only a matter of a layer of felt on the hammer.

I suggest, then, that if Paderewski wishes to combine the orchestral effect of the piano as a very brilliant, steel-hard, and transcendently facile and florid instrument of percussion, with that of its richer and more majestic qualities, he should write his fantasias for two pianofortes, a virtuoso's hair-trigger Erard and a normal Erard. If the difference in tone-color between a clarinet in C and one in A, or between a horn in D and one in B flat basso, is worth considering in composition, I do not see why the equally remarkable difference between a Pleyel and a Steinway piano should be ignored. It would add a new sensation to the performance of that Polish Fantasia if there were two pianos on the platform, with the pianist rushing from one to the other according to the character of the passage he was about to play. I do not say that the effect of the multiplication of pianos would be worth what it would cost: what I do say is, that in Paderewski's fantasia not all his power of modifying the tone of the instrument by his touch conceals the fact that the supreme qualifications of the instrument for certain passages act as disqualifications for certain others, and that this could be got over by using two pianos.

At the same time, I had rather see Paderewski, in his next composition for orchestra, drop the piano altogether. It is the one instrument that he does not understand as a composer, exactly because he under-

stands it so well as an executant. The fantasia was
very well received, though the audience most certainly did not mean to encore the finale. What they
were after was a solo; and Paderewski, in accepting
their persistent acclamations as an encore of a full
third of his fantasia, took a diabolical revenge on
them, consciously or unconsciously, for their shameless
mendicity. His performance of Schumann's concerto
was enormously satisfactory. If the band had only been
able to follow his gradations of tone and to make the
little orchestral rejoinders to the pianoforte a little less
stolidly, as much might be said for the whole performance. It was impossible not to rejoice in his complete
comprehension of the work, and the certainty with
which he found the right tempo, handling, and expression for every phrase, so that it came out as a
living utterance and not as a mere finger trait committed to memory.

29 November 1893

A Recital Lecture

Everybody knows the story of "Have a piano, Thack";
although I believe "Atlas" alone ever tells it correctly. I
prophesy that it will presently be grafted on to the
biography of Paderewski, in the form of "Have a lecture, Paddy." For it is actually coming to this, that
people are demanding lecturers at recitals, to save
them the trouble of reading analytic programs, and to
relieve the tedium of the music. The plan, after all,
has its advantages. In St James's Hall, where you get
not only a trained pianist, but—what is quite as necessary to a first-class recital—a trained audience, I
doubt whether the lecturer would be tolerated; but
for smaller semi-private recitals, where the little audience is not trained, but is quite willing to be if only
someone will take it in hand, the musical lecture can

be made a useful institution enough. I came to this
conclusion at a "recital-lecture" given by Mrs Liebich,
the subject being Chopin. It was clearly better for the
audience, assuming them to have come in a quite un-
instructed condition, to be told something about Chopin than to hear a string of his compositions played
straight off without a notion of their bearings. At the
same time, the arrangement created certain difficulties. For instance, Mrs Liebich delivered the lecture;
and Mr Liebich played the "illustrations." Now Mr
Liebich, though a perfectly presentable player, is not
a Paderewski or a Rubinstein; therefore he was entitled to a certain forbearance on the lecturer's part in
the matter of raising expectations. I regret to say that
his claims in this direction were not deferred to by
Mrs Liebich. She seemed to revel in prefacing each
performance with a description which might conceivably have been realized by Paderewski, Rubinstein,
Liszt, and Chopin himself all rolled into one, especially if powerfully aided by the electric atmosphere
of a vast hall crowded with imaginative enthusiasts,
but which was out of the question for the unaided skill
of Mr Liebich in the select afternoon quietude of Mrs
Richards's drawing room in Stanley Crescent. One
passage struck me as particularly inconsiderate. A man
may be a very solid musician and skilful pianist, and
yet not be able to play a mazurka. That, as it happened, was Mr Liebich's predicament. In the heroic
measure of the polonaise he was at his ease; but the
mazurka eluded him: he could not make it dance a
step. Yet Mrs Liebich, who must have known this,
positively expatiated on the rarity of successful ma-
zurka-playing among pianists, and the necessity of
judging Chopin's mazurkas in particular only by the
performances of those who catch the true genius of the
dance. Then, instead of frankly adding, "As my husband is one of those players who cannot manage a
mazurka, we had better pass on to those broader,
stronger rhythms which appeal to his robust Germanic

temperament," she sat down, leaving the audience under the impression that he was about to give an exhibition of the most highly specialized aptitude for the
mazurka. What made it more cruel was that Mr
Liebich seemed a perfectly quiet, well-bred, unos-
tentatious musician—one who would never by himself
dream of making such pretensions. But of course Mrs
Liebich did not intend this: it arose out of her conscientious endeavor to say the correct thing about
Chopin. What she does not see is, that this correct
thing is an uninteresting abstraction, only to be re-
sorted to on occasions when it happens to be convenient to say nothing at all in a few well-chosen
words. Her lecture was carefully prepared and carefully delivered; but the care was the effect of a modesty as to the value of her own opinion which made
her shrink from the audacity of sincerity. She did not
presume to give us her personal view of Chopin, or to
express the conventional view in the language she
habitually uses herself in social intercourse. She has
not yet discovered that in literature the ambition of
the novice is to acquire the literary language: the
struggle of the adept is to get rid of it. Though I would
not dissuade her from cultivating the literary language
until she has brought its logic and its economy to the
utmost attainable perfection, she may take my word
for it that her meaning will never be seized instantly
in all its fullness by the instinct and feeling of her
audience, unless she expresses it in vernacular language. In several passages her lecture was quite artificial: it did not rise above a carefully compiled bio-
graphical statement, interlined with an auctioneer's
catalogue of Chopin's works, her own individuality being suppressed throughout in a thoroughly ladylike
way. Now it is one thing to be a lady and quite another
thing to be a lecturer. Lecturing is in its own nature
a hopelessly unladylike pursuit. It is not ladylike to
monopolize the whole conversation for an hour. I
greatly doubt whether it is strictly ladylike to appear
even remotely conscious of the existence of such a per-

son as Madame Sand, much less of her relations with Chopin. Now, since it is impossible to lecture at all without committing such crimes as these, and since you may as well be hung for a sheep as a lamb, why hesitate to perpetrate the final outrage of letting loose your individuality, and saying just what you think in your own way as agreeably and frankly as you can? Of course you may have no opinion; but in that case, how much easier it would be to simply read aloud the article on Chopin from Grove's Dictionary, or some other standard work, instead of taking weary pains to produce a bad paraphrase of it?

I must apologize to Mrs Liebich for making her lecture the text of so ponderous a discourse on lecturing, for her discourse was far more entertaining than the ordinary private concert; but if the musical lecture is going to become an institution, it is my business to pounce on its weak points, with a view to its improvement, and, finally, to such perfection as it is capable of.

6 December 1893

The Public

Elsewhere you will find a letter on The Music of the People, by Mr Marshall-Hall, a young composer who is much spoken of among the young lions of Mr Hamish McCunn's generation. At one of Mr Henschel's concerts Mr Santley sang some portions of an opera, the poem and music of which were by Mr Marshall-Hall. I was not at that concert, so I am quite out of it as far as Mr Marshall-Hall's music is concerned; but I am delighted to find him, as a representative of young genius, denouncing the stalls, trusting to the gallery, waving the democratic flag, and tearing round generally. Young genius has rather a habit, by the way, of writing to my editor to denounce me as flippant and unenlightened, and to demand that I also shall tear round and proclaim the working man as the true knower and seer in Art. If I did, the working man would not think any the better of me; for he knows well enough that

society is not divided into "animated clothes-pegs" on
the one hand and lovers of Beethoven in ligatured
corduroys on the other. For Beethoven purposes society
is divided into people who can afford to keep a piano
and go to operas and concerts, and people who cannot.
Mr Marshall-Hall's idea that the people who cannot
are nevertheless screwed up to concert pitch by honest,
thorough, manly toil, shews that, though he be an expert in the music question, in the labor question he is
a greenhorn.

Take a laborer's son; let him do his board-schooling
mostly on an empty stomach; bring him up in a rookery
tenement; take him away from school at thirteen; offer
him the alternative of starvation or 12 to 16 hours work
a day at jerry building, adulterated manufactures, cou-
pling railway waggons, collecting tramway fares, field
labor, or what not, in return for food and lodging which
no "animated clothes-peg" would offer to his hunter;
bully him; slave-drive him; teach him by every word
and look that he is not wanted among respectable people, and that his children are not fit to be spoken to
by their children. This is a pretty receipt for making an
appreciator of Beethoven.

The truth is, that in the innumerable grades of culture and comfort between the millionaire on the one
hand, and the casual laborer on the other, there is a
maximum of relish for art somewhere. That somewhere
is certainly not among the idle rich, whose appetites
for enjoyment are not sharpened by work, nor is it
among those who, worn out by heavy muscular toil,
fall asleep if they sit quiet and silent for five minutes
of an evening. Professional and business men of musical tastes who work hard, and whose brains are of such
a quality that a Beethoven symphony is a recreation
to them instead of an increased strain on their mental
powers, are keen patrons of music, though, in outward
seeming, they belong to the animated clothes-peg
section. Middle-class young ladies, to whom there is
no path to glory except that of the pianist or prima
donna, frequent St James's Hall with astonishing per-

sistence, and eventually form musical habits which out-
last their musical hopes.

The musical public is the shilling public, by which
I mean the people who can afford to pay not more than
a shilling once a week or so for a concert without going
short of more immediately necessary things. Music can
be better nourished on shilling, sixpenny, and three-
penny seats than on the St James's Hall scale. The laborers are so enormously numerous that the absolute
number of their exceptional men—men who will buy
books out of 13s. a week in the country and 18s. in a
town, and find time to read them while working 12
hours a day—is considerable. The more comfortable
members of the artisan class can often afford a shilling
much better than the poorer middle-class families; but
it has a certain customary and traditional scale of expenditure, in which concerts stand at threepence or
sixpence, shillings being reserved for the gallery of a
West-end theatre, and half-crowns for Sunday trips to
Epping Forest and for extra refreshments.

After these come the innumerable "poor devils" of
the middle class, always craving in an unaccountable
way for music, and crowding the Promenade Concerts
on classical nights, the Albert Hall gallery, and wherever else decent music is to be heard cheaply. To these
three classes Mr Marshall-Hall must look for the little
that is now possible in the way of a musical public.
Even when we have supplied all three with as much
music as they can stomach, the laborer in ligatured
corduroys will still open his eyes to darkness, and the
vapid snob grub like a blind puppy in the light. What
we want is not music for the people, but bread for the
people, rest for the people, immunity from robbery and
scorn for the people, hope for them, enjoyment, equal
respect and consideration, life and aspiration, instead
of drudgery and despair. When we get that I imagine
the people will make tolerable music for themselves,
even if all Beethoven's scores perish in the interim.

31 May 1889

THE COLLECTED WORKS OF HAROLD CLURMAN

Six Decades of Commentary on Theatre, Dance, Music, Film, Arts, Letters and Politics

edited by Marjorie Loggia and Glenn Young

"...RUSH OUT AND BUY *THE COLLECTED WORKS OF HAROLD CLURMAN*... Editors Marjorie Loggia and Glenn Young have assembled a monumental helping of his work ...THIS IS A BOOK TO LIVE WITH; picking it up at random is like going to the theater with Clurman and then sitting down with him in a good bistro for some exhilarating talk. This is a very big book, but Clurman was a very big figure."

JACK KROLL, Newsweek

"THE BOOK SWEEPS ACROSS THE 20TH CENTURY, offering a panoply of theater in Clurman's time... IT RESONATES WITH PASSION."

MEL GUSSOW, The New York Times

CLOTH•$49.95
ISBN 1-55783-132-7

APPLAUSE

NEW YORK • LONDON

THE LIFE OF THE DRAMA

by ERIC BENTLEY

"The most adventurous critic in America."

—Kenneth Tynan

"Eric Bentley's radical new look at the grammar of theatre...is a work of exceptional virtue, and readers who find more in it to disagree with than I do will still, I think, want to call it CENTRAL, IN-DISPENSABLE...If you see any crucial interest in such topics as the death of Cordelia, Godot's non-arrival...THIS IS A BOOK TO BE READ AGAIN AND AGAIN."

—Frank Kermode, *The New York Review of Books*

"*The Life Of The Drama*...is a remarkable exploration of the roots and bases of dramatic art, THE MOST FAR REACHING AND REVELATORY WE HAVE HAD."

—Richard Gilman, *Book Week*

ISBN: 1-55783-110-6

APPLAUSE

THE GRAHAM GREENE FILM READER

edited by David Parkinson

"MAGNIFICENT ... THE BEST COLLECTION OF FILM CRITICISM ... A SUPERB BOOK! THERE IS RELISH IN HIS PRAISE AND PUNISHMENT IN HIS HOPES AND IN HIS DESPAIR, AND IN HIS LOVE OF THE TECHNICAL LANGUAGE OF THE MOVIES"
–**PHILIP FRENCH**, TIMES LITERARY SUPPLEMENT

"ONE OF HIS BEST BOOKS...GREENE'S PROSE IS MORE GRACEFUL THAN ANY STAR."
–**CHRISTOPHER HAWTREE**, EVENING STANDARD

"HIS CRITICAL WRITING ABOUT THE CINEMA IS ALMOST AS IMPORTANT AS HIS CONTRIBUTION TO THE ART OF CINEMA ITSELF."
–**DILYS POWELL**, THE DAILY TELEGRAPH

"A SUPERB VOLUME! AMONG THE MOST TRENCHANT, WITTY AND MEMORABLE COLLECTIONS OF FILM REVIEWS ONE IS EVER LIKELY TO READ!"
–**ANTHONY QUINN**, THE SUNDAY TIMES

ISBN: 1-55783-188-2 • cloth • $35.00

APPLAUSE